# The Dynamics of Decentralization

# The Canada-United Kingdom Colloquia Series

# The Dynamics of Decentralization

## Canadian Federalism and British Devolution

**Trevor C. Salmon and Michael Keating, Editors**

Published for the School of Policy Studies, Queen's University
by McGill-Queen's University Press
Montreal & Kingston • London • Ithaca

**Canadian Cataloguing in Publication Data**

Main entry under title:

The dynamics of decentralization : Canadian federalism and British devolution

(The Canada-United Kingdom colloquia series ; 3)
Proceedings of a conference entitled Decentralisation and regionalisation :
more power to the people?, held in Newcastle, Northern Ireland, Nov. 18-21,
1999.
Includes bibliographical references.
ISBN 0-88911-895-7

1. Decentralization in government – Canada – Congresses.
2. Decentralization in government – Great Britain – Congresses.
3. Federal government – Canada – Congresses. 4. Regionalism – Great Britain
– Congresses. 5. Canada – Politics and government – 1993-    – Congresses.*
6. Great Britain – Politics and government – 1997-    – Congresses.
I. Salmon, Trevor C. II. Keating, Michael, 1950-    . III. Queen's University
(Kingston, Ont.). School of Policy Studies. IV. Series.

JL75.D96 2001        320.971'09'049        C00-933012-7

# Contents

# Acknowledgements

Powerful decentralizing trends are reshaping governance in many countries. Once highly centralized systems are creating new forms of regional government, and long-standing federations are transferring greater authority to state and provincial governments. One striking consequence of this process is that the traditional dichotomy between unitary and federal states is being swept away, to be replaced by increasingly common dynamics of decentralized politics and government. British devolution and Canadian federalism illustrate this institutional convergence well, and this book explores the similarities and differences in these two forms of decentralization.

*The Dynamics of Decentralization: Canadian Federalism and British Devolution* represents a contribution to policy debates from the Canada-United Kingdom Colloquia. Each year, the Colloquia bring together parliamentarians, policymakers, academics, representatives from the private sector, members of the media and other social commentators from both countries to discuss important policy issues. Inaugurated in 1984, the Colloquia constitute an integral part of the relationship between the two countries, confirming the contemporary relevance of a link deeply embedded in history. The role of the Colloquia was highlighted by Prime Ministers Blair and Chrétien in a joint declaration issued during the Denver summit of the G7 countries in 1997, and again in 1998 when Prime Minister Chrétien paid an official visit to London.

The Colloquia are sustained by a unique four-way partnership. They are supported by the Department of Foreign Affairs and International Trade in Canada and the Foreign and Commonwealth Office in the UK. They are organized by the School of Policy Studies of Queen's University on the Canadian side, and the British Committee of the Canada-United Kingdom Colloquia in the UK.

This book flows from a colloquium held in County Down, Northern Ireland in November 1999, a period in which the future of devolved government in that region was very much in the balance. We would like to thank Trevor Salmon and

Michael Keating for serving as editors of the book, and the contributors from both sides of the Atlantic whose thoughts are captured between its covers.

*The Dynamics of Decentralization: Canadian Federalism and British Devolution* is the third title in a new series published for the Colloquia by McGill-Queen's University Press. We would like to thank the Publications Unit of the School of Policy Studies and McGill-Queen's University Press. The happy partnership between these two organizations has made the series a reality, and we extend our appreciation to the two teams for their support.

*Baroness Fookes of Plymouth*  
*Chairman, British Committee*  
*Canada-United Kingdom Colloquia*

*Keith G. Banting*  
*Director*  
*School of Policy Studies*

# 1

# Introduction

*Trevor C. Salmon and Michael Keating*

It has become part of received wisdom that the state in advanced industrial societies is undergoing a profound transformation. There is much less agreement on the nature of this transformation or its significance. Some see a rolling back, or hollowing out of the state; others insist that it is merely reconfiguring the better to discharge its functions. The question is a complex one and is too often approached at a general, abstract level rather than through detailed examination of what is happening in particular places. It is clear that the state is faced with new challenges from three directions: from above, from below, and laterally. From above, it confronts a panoply of effects summarized by the term "globalization." These include the need to compete in a free trading world, the rapid mobility of capital, the global reach of new technologies, and the rise of transnational corporations whose annual turnover sometimes rivals those of the smaller states themselves. At the same time, regional free trade regimes such as the North American Free Trade Agreement (NAFTA) and the European Union (EU) affect, in their different ways, the ability of states to exercise their sovereign powers.

From below, the state is challenged by the new regionalism, in which local and regional economies are recognized as the critical nexus of economic change and dynamism and in which regions and cities increasingly compete directly within global markets, rather than as integral parts of managed national economies. Regions, stateless nations, and cultural groups are also making themselves heard, with demands for greater recognition and autonomy and in many cases have seen the evolving transnational order as an opportunity to stake their own claims. It may be, as nationalists in Scotland and Quebec claim, that in a free trading world national independence is a more practical and less costly proposition, but even those pressing for lesser degrees of recognition and home rule now incorporate the transnational dimension into their arguments. So the old boundaries between foreign affairs, the prerogative of central governments, and domestic affairs, in which powers can be shared, is breaking down, most notably in the European Union in which large swathes of domestic policy have been taken over by the continental regime.

Laterally, the state is challenged by the advance of markets and the general acceptance, even by social democratic parties, of the limitations of the state in economic and social regulation; whether this is an inescapable effect of globalization or an ideological paradigm shift is still an open question. Civil society, that realm of public action not directly dependent on the state, has also become important, especially as a way of recognizing pluralism, difference, and group rights.

Canada and the United Kingdom are particularly appropriate cases for examining the meaning and effects of these changes. Both are multinational societies with a high degree of diversity and pluralism. Historically Canada has struggled over how to recognize the distinct needs and rights of Quebec and of its native peoples, while regionalism, especially in the west and the Maritime provinces, has been a potent force. The United Kingdom has long faced the challenge of accommodating its four nationalities and has dealt with each in a very different way. Both countries are now facing the new challenge of multiculturalism as groups other than the "founding nations" look for recognition of their own traditions. Canada and the UK are both welfare states, in which social provision is supported both by a sense of national solidarity as well as by more abstract conceptions of justice. Both are highly dependent on world trade and have in recent years been committed to trade liberalization and the embrace of global markets.

Global change and state transformation have posed multiple challenges to Canada and the UK but the focus of the 1999 Colloquium was on the territorial dimension. The first challenge is to the constitutional structure of the state. Both constitutions are the product of the eighteenth and nineteenth centuries. Canada's founding document is the *British North America Act* of 1867, repatriated and modified in 1982 with the addition of a Charter of Rights and Freedoms. The United Kingdom dates from the union of 1707 with Scotland and of 1801 with Ireland, modified by the secession of most of Ireland in 1922. Both have been going through a period of turmoil as their constitutional arrangements are adapted to fit the changing demands of modern governing as well as the challenge of minority nations. Kenneth Morgan traces the history of nationalism in the UK and shows how a British identity was made and unmade, and how governments have responded with partial and ad hoc solutions, potentially transforming the state but leaving many issues, notably the future of England, in suspense. Michael Keating explains the constitutional settlement of 1997-2000, with its strongly asymmetrical features and, like Morgan, sees this as an unfinished process. Trevor Salmon picks up the issue of Scotland's role in a Europe and a wider world in which the distinction between domestic and foreign policy is ever less clear; again the future appears to be open.

Canada's experience of multinationalism and pluralism may resemble that of the United Kingdom, but its federal system and written constitution have demanded a very different way of addressing these questions. Richard Simeon summarizes the experiences of constitutional reform in Canada and draws some lessons for the United Kingdom. Because of the need to gain approval of both the federal parliament and the provinces for constitutional amendments, every group has an opportunity to hold the resolution of others' grievances hostage to its own demands. Constitutional reforms have therefore expanded into complex package deals which themselves have then provoked more oppositions, the most obvious example being the Charlottetown Accord of 1992 in Canada. In the UK, on the other hand, a government with a parliamentary majority can proceed in an incremental and asymmetrical manner. While Simeon is certainly right to emphasize this crucial institutional difference, it should also be noted that the UK took over a hundred years, from 1886 to 1998, to realize Gladstone's Home Rule program in spite of manifest demands in Ireland and Scotland; and that, when Canada was able to use parliamentary majorities to push through the *Constitution Act, 1982* Quebec refused to recognize this and continues to regard the change as illegitimate. Simeon also notes the refusal in Canada to contemplate asymmetrical government, while in the UK it is regarded with equanimity. Finally, he considers the relevance of Canadian experience for the evolving federal arrangement in the UK.

A second set of issues concerns economic and social policy. Globalization and state restructuring have brought into question the traditional mechanisms of regional policy practised in both Canada and the UK. States can no longer manage their spatial economies using the old instruments of incentives and controls, while regions are increasingly looking to their own potential to improve their competitive position. A new geography of economic disparities is emerging, both between and within regions. George Quigley summarizes these issues and, looking at the experience of the United Kingdom, concludes that there is a role for regions in positioning themselves as nodes within a global economic framework.

Economic restructuring has had massive effects on social welfare, altering the old roles and reward structures by region, by class, by age, and by gender. This has posed a serious challenge for the welfare state. Governments have responded to this in a variety of ways. There has been a general move from universal programs to targeted ones, and to new definitions of the target groups. Governments have decentralized some programs, either seeking to offload the financial and political burden of adjustment or, more positively, to ensure that programs are better designed for specific groups and places. There has been a certain tendency to privatization, though this has varied considerably from one country to another.

The emphasis has been placed on self-help rather than on social solidarity as a mark of national unity, although central governments have sought to retain some programs to preserve their profile. Finally, governments have sought to link social welfare policy to labour market policy and to the needs of economic growth.

Several of our contributors address these issues. Nicola McEwen looks at the role of the welfare state and "social citizenship" in Canada and the UK and sees a conflict between this and neo-liberalism and deregulation. As the state framework weakens, Quebec and Scotland may be seen by their citizens as the principal arena for sustaining social solidarity although, with the budget deficit eliminated, the Canadian federal government is seeking to get back into making payments directly to citizens. The conflicts among objectives, particularly between functional effectiveness and the need for political visibility, is compounded in Canada by the complexities of federalism. Claude Forget argues that this has sometimes produced sub-optimal outcomes and recommends instead that the courts be given the responsibility for upholding social rights on a pan-Canadian basis. Other contributors, more sceptical about the spread of judicial activism in Canada, might demur. Harvey Lazar and Peter Stoyko give a detailed account of the evolution of labour market policies in Canada, bringing out the complexities and the effects of federal institutions on program design and delivery. The general trend is to a reduction in social support, a certain decentralization and a continuing intergovernmental cooperation. Jane Jenson also looks at Canada's "citizenship regime" as evidenced through social and labour market policy. As elsewhere the state has retrenched and recast social support in the language of markets and investment. After a period of severe downsizing, federal and provincial governments have begun to spend again but have redefined the citizenship regime and shifted their focus from adults, who are all seen as actual or potential workers, to children.

Another critical dimension to state restructuring concerns democracy and the role of the citizen. Both countries have seen a move to entrench individual citizen rights against governments through the Canadian Charter of Rights and Freedoms and the incorporation of the European Convention on Human Rights into UK law. Such constitutionally entrenched rights are clearly at odds with the common Westminster tradition of parliamentary sovereignty and both states have left themselves with an escape clause. In Canada governments can use the "notwithstanding clause" to overturn court rulings on certain parts of the Charter; the opt-out provision has to be renewed or allowed to lapse after five years. In the UK, the *Human Rights Act* allows the courts to declare Westminster statutes contrary to the Convention, but it is up to Parliament to provide the remedy under an expedited procedure. For the devolved assemblies, however, the Convention is directly applicable and the effects in Scotland have already been dramatic and unanticipated. Canadian experience with the Charter has a lot to show here, as Simeon notes. Hugh Segal concludes the collection with a wide-ranging review of citizenship in the new era. He argues that the relationship of the citizen to the state will need to change to take into account cultural and national pluralism, the emergence of new social and economic spheres, and the new global order.

# 2

# Regional and National Identities in the United Kingdom

*Kenneth O. Morgan*

As I write this chapter, there hangs on the wall behind me a souvenir from my only interesting ancestor. It is a large, unwieldy Napoleonic musket which he apparently used at the Battle of Trafalgar, where he served as a press-ganged sailor on one of Nelson's men-o'war. It is a relic of a tense, violent era in British history, when, apart perhaps from 1940, fear of foreign invasion was stronger than at any period since the coming of the Spanish Armada. But, partly for that very reason, it reminds us that during the Napoleonic Wars, the problems of national identity and of the essence of Britishness, including "ruling the waves," appeared more clear-cut than at any other period of our history. In 1805 British national consciousness seemed quite unambiguous. It was insular and it was Protestant, founded on trade and enterprise, insular sovereignty, and naval power. The national anthem and the Union Jack, recently amplified by the union with Ireland in 1800, were its symbols, and the omnipresent sailor, "jolly Jack Tar," complete with pigtail, its popular embodiment.

Yet the problems of British national identity were only just beginning. For one thing, it was clear that the idea of Britain was very hard to disentangle from the notion of "England"; indeed the majority of the inhabitants of these islands made no attempt to do so. Further, the years after the Napoleonic Wars, a time of surging imperial power, were marked also by growing ethnic pluralism and political schizophrenia. The problems of defining the national identity, apparently ended with the defeat of the Jacobites in 1745 and a series of successful wars against the French, were to become ever more complex, as did the whole gamut of issues relating to national and regional identity within the so-called United Kingdom. A major reason was the coming of industrialization. The growth of industry is commonly thought to have encouraged a great mood of national integration in Britain, with the spread of railways, nationwide industries, and a new national capital market and financial structure.

So, in many ways, it did, and social and cultural forces such as the movement of population from rural communities and the rapid spread of literacy brought British people together as never before. But it also served to divide them anew. It gave a new local and national focus to the different parts of Britain. Through newspapers and chambers of commerce and a spread of local cultural, religious, and social institutions, it encouraged a new sense of region. This was most obviously exemplified by the emergence of major cities like Manchester and Leeds as regional metropolises, but was also shown in the varying authority of a hierarchy of country and market towns over the surrounding countryside. The growth of suburbs, even in due time of Betjeman's "Metroland," complicated the picture still further.

The rise of industry and commerce had an even more powerful impact on the Celtic nations. In a variety of ways, it stung their sense of national identity awake. Glasgow, Cardiff, and Belfast became both great imperial cities and ports, pivots of the Atlantic economy, but also, not least through their growing service sectors, focuses of the growing self-assertive identity of Scotland, Wales and, to some degree, the province of Protestant Ulster. The more emphatic the growth of the industrial and trading economy in the mid- and late-Victorian years, the more identifiable and assertive the national identity of the Celtic nations became.

Ireland was always seen as a separate country. Its role in the British Empire was ambiguous. Since the Stuart Plantations, it had been in part a colonized territory but also an integral part of the colonizing process in the British territories overseas, notably in North America. It was merged with Great Britain only in 1800 and a variety of domestic movements from the Catholic Association under O'Connell to the Irish Nationalist Party under Parnell at the end of the century and the rise of Sinn Fein thereafter under Arthur Griffith, testified to the emphatic national awareness of the Irish people, for all the religious complications emergent in Protestant Ulster.

In Scotland and in Wales, the sense of identity took markedly different forms. The growth of political democracy from 1867 onward emphasized the difference. Modern Scotland had emerged from a sovereign state, joined to England in 1707 in a formal Act of Union. Thereafter, it retained its own distinctive institutions, its Presbyterian Church, its educational system, and very importantly its own legal system, even its own banknotes. It also had something of much social import — its own historic ruling class, the aristocratic lairds who retained their estates and their mystique after the rout of the Jacobites. Through the influential novels of Sir

Walter Scott, their cultural and legendary impact as custodians of native tradition became all the greater. It was not surprising that pressure for identity in Scotland took an overtly political and institutional form, culminating in the successful campaign for a revived Scottish Office acknowledged by Gladstone in 1885. It was not surprising also that it was through leading figures in the native aristocracy, men like the Duke of Argyll and the Earl of Fife, that the pressure for a Scottish Office was expressed. As Arthur Balfour observed, "The finest salmon river in Scotland would get you a long way." The successful achievement of a Scottish Office, 80 years before a similar landmark in Wales, testified to a distinctive Scottish tradition of social leadership and hierarchy and a separate sense of Scottish citizenship.

In Wales, by contrast, there was no clearly defined sense of citizenship. Its identity was expressed in cultural and religious terms, and mediated through its own language which until the industrial era was spoken by the vast majority of the population. The most important event in the development of the Welsh identity had been the translation of the Bible into Welsh by Bishop Morgan back in 1588. By contrast, pressure for devolution or any form of political separatism was weak. The last distinctive Welsh institution, the Courts of Great Session, popular because of their widespread use of the Welsh language, were abolished in 1830, local protests being ignored by Westminster. Modern Wales, after all, was a product not of an Act of Union in 1707 but of a process of military conquest over 400 years earlier. Under Henry VIII its political and administrative structure had been merged into that of England. The four Welsh dioceses were an integral part of the Province of Canterbury. The *Encyclopaedia Britannica* contained the famous entry, "For Wales, see England." The Welsh aristocracy were in the main symbols of Englishness, Anglican, anglophone, usually Tory. There was no Welsh version of Walter Scott to extol or invent their mighty deeds. Sometimes they bore Scottish names like Bute or Cawdor. The lost leader, Owain Glyndŵr, his revolt crushed in the early fifteenth century, never generated the legends associated with Bruce or Wallace. He has never inspired a Welsh "Braveheart," though that may be as well.

Yet the industrial age did see a mounting pressure on behalf of the Welsh identity. Unlike Scotland, it arose from pressure from below. The social upheavals of the 1830s and 1840s — the Merthyr rising, Chartism, the Rebecca riots — had very limited distinctively Welsh characteristics. However, the explosion of protest released by the so-called "treason" of the Blue Books in 1847, when ill-informed English educational commissioners poured derision on the language, culture, and religious complexion of the Welsh people, stung Welsh nationalism awake. For the first time, Welshness took political, though not yet separatist form. After the parliamentary reforms of 1867 and 1884, a new Liberal ascendancy in Wales gave Welsh national awareness irresistible democratic force. There were effective campaigns for disestablishment of the Church of England in Wales, for a national unsectarian system of secondary and higher education, for reform of the land system, for temperance reform, for recognition for the Welsh language. Further, the voices of this national awareness were commonly young, forceful men, like the philosopher-nationalist Tom Ellis, the belligerent coal owner D.A. Thomas, and the rising radical tribune David Lloyd George. There were disturbing similarities, in the mind of many Unionists, between the so-called '"Welsh Party" and the Irish Nationalist Party. Some ventured to call the youthful Ellis the "Parnell of Wales." Through effective pressure within the Liberal Party, they gained a remarkable series of victories. The *Welsh Sunday Closing Act* of 1881 was the first act of parliament to apply a quite different legislative principle to Wales as distinct from England, basing itself on the distinctive national identity and will of Wales as expressed through its parliamentary representatives. The *Welsh Intermediate Education Act* of 1889, followed by the national federal University of Wales in 1893, created a distinctive educational system. It was far more democratic than that of England, still skewed decisively by the private "public" schools, an institution almost unknown in Wales (as also in Scotland).

There was administrative devolution for Wales, for education in 1907 and later in health and agriculture. A National Museum was instituted in Cardiff, in the heart of that Edwardian metropolis, and a National Library high up on a hill in rural, sea-girt Aberystwyth. Above all, the disestablishment of the Church in Wales, bitterly contested by Anglicans and Unionists, was passed through the Commons in 1914 and finally became law in 1919, at a time when a Welsh Baptist was resident in 10 Downing Street. With all its limitations, it was in Wales the equivalent of Irish home rule. Scots, divided over disestablishment whereas the Welsh were united on it, never came near a similar political achievement, though of course they had their own department of state.

At the *fin de siècle*, Britain as a polity showed a strong element of pluralism. Encouraged by the fall-out from the Liberal schism over Home Rule in 1886, which gave new political possibilities to the Scots and Welsh, as well as to labour, land reformers, urban radicals and others, Victorian and Edwardian Britain revealed a new awareness of its multiculturalism at the heart of a mighty worldwide empire. It chimed in with the Victorian passion for national autonomy and for the rights of small nations, to which Gladstone especially responded. The cult of Switzerland, the model of local, federal, civic independence, from William Tell downwards, was especially powerful to the late Victorians, as were other, usually mountainous, peoples such as Norway or the Tyrol.

But this was far short of anything resembling devolution. The Scots and the Welsh, unlike a growing number of the Irish, sought equality within the United Kingdom and the Empire, not separation from it. The *Cymru Fydd* (Young Wales) movement within the Liberal Party in the mid-1890s, in which the young Lloyd

George briefly tried to turn the Welsh Liberal Party into a movement committed to Welsh home rule, collapsed almost without trace. Apart from other factors, the deep political and cultural divisions between the Welsh-speaking rural and industrial hinterland and what Lloyd George called "the Newport Englishmen" along the southern littoral in the ports of Newport, Cardiff, Barry, and Swansea, proved to be unbridgeable. Thereafter the differences between the Welsh and the nationalist Irish became ever more manifest, especially as the Welsh took pride in the rapid ascent of their countryman, David Lloyd George, to the pinnacle of power in Westminster.

During the Boer War, most Welshmen at first (though not Lloyd George himself) were supportive of the war, and took pride in the alleged Welsh antecedents of Lord Roberts and Baden-Powell, as they had previously done in the deeds of the 24th Welsh at Rorke's Drift during the Zulu Wars in 1879. The Scots, powerful forces in the spread of empire, variously as soldiers, shipbuilders on the Clyde, missionaries, doctors, and educationalists, were even more vehemently imperialist, and actually swung toward the Unionist government during the 1900 "khaki election." The same was emphatically true of the Ulstermen, a strong force in the British higher command in South Africa, as again in two world wars later on. In total contrast, the Irish Nationalists, Parnellite and Anti-Parnellite alike, cheered the news of the British defeats at Colenso and Magersfontein in the "black week." Unlike the relatively loyalist Welsh and Scots, the Irish wanted the Boers to win.

The subsequent course of comparative Celtic history was to magnify the difference. In Wales and Scotland before 1918, there was no Sinn Fein, no Easter Rising, no "time of troubles," no Republican Army. They generated no Parnell, Griffiths, Collins, Pearse, or de Valera. In 1920, when the Irish "troubles" were at their worst, with Lloyd George making wanton use of the violent "Black and Tans," the Welsh were placidly celebrating the advent of Church disestablishment — assuming they knew that it was actually happening. But the disestablishment and disendowment of the Church of England (a fact which in time the Church leaders themselves came strongly to endorse) were an alternative to home rule, not a precursor of it.

The twentieth-century history of Britain, from the First World War onwards, was a time in the main of unrelenting centralism and Unionism. The integrating effects of two world wars and the class impact of worldwide industrial depression and mass unemployment during the interwar years reinforced this process. For a time, until the early 1920s, the Conservatives actually called themselves the Unionists; they continued to do so in Scotland until the sixties. There were moves just before and during the First World War for forms of "home rule all round," treating Ireland on the same basis as Scotland, Wales, and of course England, but these got nowhere, in part because of the obvious intractability and massive dominance of England whose population had no interest whatsoever in the question. Alternatively there were attempts from the 1880s onward to promote within Britain some variant of the imperial federation urged by Unionist propagandists such as Joseph Chamberlain.

It was promoted with some rhetorical force by the journal *Round Table*, whose editor, F.S. Oliver, advocated the cause in a biography of the early American federalist, Alexander Hamilton. It attracted youthful disciples from amongst the young men inspired by Milner's "kindergarten" in South Africa after the Boer War — men like Philip Kerr, Lionel Curtis, Mark Sykes and Leopold Amery, many of them to end up in Lloyd George's so-called "garden suburb" of private advisers during the First World War. The federal systems of Australia, Canada, and South Africa were held up as examples of what might be achieved, and the model of the federal United States was cited somewhat loosely by F.S. Oliver and others. But in Britain, with the obviously different features of Irish, Scottish, Welsh, and English identity, these ideas got absolutely nowhere. The Speaker's Conference on federalism in 1919 proved to be a dead letter.

One possible deviation from the centralist norm had been the early Labour Party. In its early period prior to 1914, there were many elements in the Labour and socialist movement who favoured decentralization and devolution. The Independent Labour Party backed localism and the politics of the local community. Keir Hardie, its first leader, championed Scottish and Welsh home rule. He wrote on behalf of a self-governing Wales in his pamphlet of 1911, "The Red Dragon and the Red Flag," *Y Ddraig Goch a'r Faner Goch*. Ramsay MacDonald, a youthful member of the Scottish Home Rule movement, took a similar view. Again, the Fabians advocated "municipal socialism" and championed the growth of a vigorous autonomy on the London County Council. Socialists in Britain tended to endorse a vivid local democracy in contrast to what they saw as the dead bureaucratic centralism of the Prussian-dominated German Social Democratic Party. In the latter stages, Labour figures like Arthur Henderson and Philip Snowden tried to breathe life into the inert cause of British federalism.

But after 1918 it was a lost cause. The interwar years, with their mass unemployment and massive social distress in all the older industrial regions of Britain, saw a class-conscious Labour Party, with its Trade Union allies, as implacably British-centred as the Tory enemy. The localism of pre-war Labour focused on sustaining local government as civic champions of the social message of the national Labour Party, not on any kind of devolution. In a national social and economic crisis, a centrally run, nationally conceived movement to defend the workers seemed the only sensible response. Events like the hunger marches in south Wales were part of a wider people's movement mirrored in Jarrow in the northeast and elsewhere. Such nationalist separatism as there was in Scotland and in Wales came in the form of the Scottish National Party (1928) and Plaid Cymru (1925), both mainly clusters of intellectuals. Yet the national identities diverged even in this puny form. The SNP favoured localized radical protest, as with the ex-Communist Hugh MacDiarmid, prophet of the Scottish literary renaissance, and much-expelled socialist dissenter. The Scottish Nationalists briefly held the Motherwell seat in 1945. By contrast, Plaid Cymru, initially focused only on protecting the Welsh language, was led by the far-right Roman Catholic Saunders Lewis, a poet whose neo fascist sympathies, admiration for Mussolini, and apparent concessions to anti-semitism proved obstacles to progress in so radical and democratic a nation as Wales. A dramatic episode in 1936 when Lewis and two other nationalists admitted to committing arson in an RAF aerodrome in Caernarfonshire, did not broaden their appeal, especially when Lewis declared his ideological neutrality between the Allies and Hitler in 1940.

The climax of British unionism was reached during the Second World War. Opinion in Wales and Scotland on behalf of the national war effort was virtually unanimous: dissidents, whether political or religious, were far less numerous than in 1914-18. The whole impact of war propaganda was to uphold the unity of the United Kingdom. ABCA classes for the army in the African desert or the jungle of southeast Asia emphasized the integrating force of the "mother of parliaments" and other national symbols. The Labour Party, no less than Churchill's Tories, fully shared in this ethos. Government ministers like Attlee, Bevin, Morrison, and Dalton strongly emphasized the central power of national government, collectively, in defending the nation, clearing up after the blitz and planning for a better postwar world. The Beveridge Report on social insurance was a wholly unionist, integrative document. A famous socialist, Douglas Jay, had written in 1937 that, in terms of social and economic planning, "the gentleman from Whitehall knew best." All too often, this gentleman turned out to be a product of somewhere like Winchester and New College, Oxford, like Jay himself: other Oxford socialists like Evan Durbin, Hugh Gaitskell, Harold Wilson, Denis Healey, and Anthony Crosland, the intellectual spearhead of the postwar social democratic generation, felt much the same. So now did Harold Laski, his early enthusiasm for pluralism in *Grammar of Politics* days set aside. On the far left, Aneurin Bevan in 1944 poured scorn on the entire idea of having a "Welsh Day" debate in Parliament. What was the point? Welsh sheep grazed on the same grass as did English sheep. The Labour government of 1945-51 made few concessions to Celtic, especially Welsh sentiment. Crosland's *Future of Socialism* in 1956, with its call for social equality and revisionist socialism, was as centralist in its message as anything written by Karl Marx. In Crosland's humane view, the entire British Isles, from the Old Man of Hoy down to John O'Groats, was identical, with no cultural, social, or national variation to be detected anywhere. Devolution was not even remotely on his program.

On the other hand, the Second World War did confirm how much further along the devolutionist road Scotland was, compared to Wales. Tom Johnston, an old socialist at the Scottish Office, was able to persuade Churchill of an alleged Scottish Nationalist threat. As a result the power of the Scottish Office was built up massively, with the assistance of major Scottish public figures like the distinguished agricultural planner, Sir John Boyd Orr. A Scottish Council of State and Council of Industry were set up to promote social and economic development, new planning powers accrued to the Scottish Office instead, and a North of Scotland Hydro-Electric Board was created. Postwar reconstruction in Scotland was to derive much of its impetus from locally based planning and investment. By contrast, Wales got almost nothing, only a nominated Council for Wales in 1949 which limped along for 17 years with little to show for its efforts. Even so, the general conclusion can only be, down to the election of the Labour government under Wilson in 1964, that Celtic devolution was making less headway at this period than it had for over a half-century.

The great transformation came in the 1960s, that great, half-mythical crucible of change and redefinition in Britain as in many other countries. It led to a great reassessment of region, nation, and international standing. Institutions of all kinds, traditions, cultural and moral norms, faced intense challenge. A slow process began in the break-up of the Victorian system of government, along with the monuments to Victorian canons of morality. A climax came in the third week of July 1966, soon after Harold Wilson's Labour government had been returned with a majority of nearly 100, when London basked in the happy, mini-skirted consumer frivolity of "swinging Britain," just after England had thrilled the majority of British people by defeating the hated Germans in winning the football World Cup. The period 14 to 21 July was a time of near chaos when Wilson and sixties socialism almost came tumbling down. The key ministers in the government, Wilson, George Brown, James Callaghan, seemed hopelessly at odds. Rumours abounded of a *putsch* (organized, some speculated, at the elegant home of the libertarian wife of the author of the James Bond novels!) to get rid of the prime minister while he was away in Moscow, discussing possible peace moves in Vietnam. There was new global pressure on the British economy, leading to a humiliating devaluation of the pound sterling in November 1967. There were changes in Britain's world perception in the renewed application to join the European Common Market. Further afield, the last remnants of the Victorian empire were stripped away with the withdrawal of the British military and naval presence from east of Suez by 1971.

At home, there was a sharp loss of faith in the imperatives of the Labour government, and indeed in the political system generally. What happened in Wales and Scotland was a part of this. In Wales, the electorate, unimpressed by the creation of a Welsh Office in 1964, returned Gwynfor Evans for Carmarthen as the first Plaid Cymru MP in July 1966, during that very period of political and economic turmoil. Soon after, the Scottish Nationalist Party won an emphatic by-election victory at Hamilton, and Labour suddenly seemed unexpectedly vulnerable in its own Celtic heartlands. The aftermath, noted by other chapters in this volume, was a profound change in the social and political culture of modern Britain, and a transformation in its age-old forms as a polity, in which the nostrums of political commentators from A.V. Dicey and Sir Henry Maine in the late-Victorian era to Crossman and Crosland in recent times were rudely dispatched.

Since that time, Celtic nationalism and the perceived needs of the Celtic nations have been central features of the history of the British Isles. Of course, the roots of these movements in both Scotland and Wales went back many centuries, almost to the dawn of Britain itself. But they were fostered by a clutch of movements given new expression in the 1960s: pacifism, concern for the environment, sympathy for folk cultures, and the cult of youth. Celtic nationalism, in short, was the unexpected offspring of the so-called "permissive society," another facet of generational revolt. It was not surprising that in Wales the lead should be given by the youthful student members of *Cymdeithas yr Iaith Cymraeg*, the Welsh Language Society, picketing post offices, shinnying up television masts, or defacing road signs in their impatient, but undeniably effective, campaigns of direct action.

Devolution henceforth remained on the public agenda as it had not been previously in modern times. The subsequent course of events is well-known and other chapters in this volume allude to it. There was the establishment of the Crowther-Kilbrandon Commission on the constitution and its various reports broadly in favour of a Scottish parliament and a Welsh assembly. There was the fragmentation of politics in the 1970s which left the Wilson-Callaghan governments of 1974-79 in a minority position and thus inevitably forced to pay heed to the demands of the handful of Scottish and Welsh nationalist MPs and the forces they represented. There was the difficult passage of separate bills for Scotland and for Wales in 1978. And finally there was the calamitous outcome of the referendums of 1 March 1979 which saw Welsh devolution overwhelmingly defeated, even in Welsh-speaking Gwynedd, and Scottish devolution scrape home with a majority far too small to enable a Scottish parliament to go ahead. The Callaghan government was defeated in the Commons by just one vote four weeks later on 28 March, the result of the decision of the Scottish Nationalists (though not the Welsh) to join the Tories and Liberals in voting it down.

The defeat of devolution in 1979 was predictable. The cause of Welsh devolution at this time was inevitably weak as it had been for much of the century. Important elements in the dominant Welsh Labour Party, including figures like Neil Kinnock and Leo Abse, were strongly hostile. Scottish devolution was stronger, though here also there were powerful countervailing factors both among Unionists and among members and supporters of the Scottish Labour Party where Tam Dalyell emerged as a formidable critic. In any case, the government showed little enthusiasm for the devolution measures it had cobbled together. Prime Minister Callaghan made only one token speech in Scotland and one in Wales, and other leading government ministers showed little more enthusiasm. In any event, the broader unpopularity of the government at this period of the so-called winter of discontent with its almost uncontrollable union unrest, meant that the devolution campaign was conducted in streets full of uncollected refuse and against a background of closed schools and hospital wards, and even undug graves.

The defeat of devolution, then, was inevitable. But the issue was certainly not going to disappear. On the contrary, even under the centralizing, indomitably Unionist, regime of Mrs. Thatcher, the cause continued to make progress, especially in the later 1980s as government and prime minister became increasingly unpopular. In Wales, the Welsh Office became unexpectedly vigorous in the Thatcher period, especially under the centrist figure of Peter Walker, and its activities served to reinforce the sense of the territoriality of Wales. In Scotland, resentment at a Tory, centralist government out of sympathy with almost every shade of Scottish opinion, led to devolutionist sentiment hardening, including in the Labour Party. Politicians like John Smith or Robin Cook, previously resistant to devolution, now changed their stance. The professional middle class in Scotland, whether as academics, civil servants, medical men or, increasingly, businessmen, became increasingly separatist in their view of Scottish affairs, while the historic working class, traditionally solid for unionism and class solidarity, dissolved in its allegiances and structure as unemployment and recession mounted. The astonishing decision to try out the poll tax first in Scotland, a policy apparently endorsed by leading elements in what remained of Scottish Conservatism, marked a climax of Scottish rejection of Westminster's diktats. The despairing, defeatist *demi-monde* of the John Major years merely confirmed this pattern.

In 1997 devolution was triumphant. No Conservative was elected at all in either Scotland or Wales; Tory Celts like Malcolm Rifkind were cast into oblivion. The dominant force in all this, without doubt, was Scottish national sentiment, with the rejection of Thatcherism leading to the all-party consensus over a Scottish parliament with some tax-raising powers generated by the Scottish Constitutional Convention chaired by Canon Kenyon Wright. In Wales, as always, devolutionary pressure was far less strong and no Constitutional Convention took place to prepare the way for a putative Welsh assembly. Even here, though, Welsh Labour became more strongly devolutionist as it had never been in 1992, while the existence of unrepresentative, non-elected "quangos" over wide areas of Welsh life at a time when elected local authorities were in the doldrums added momentum to the pressure for some kind of local source of decision making. In the referendums of September 1997, Scotland voted by a two-thirds majority for a parliament with tax powers. In Wales, devolution scraped home by the narrowest of margins, only 0.3 percent of the vote on a low poll.

On the other hand, even here there was a considerable swing of opinion of up to 30 percent compared with 1979. Notably, the Welsh valley constituencies in the south, along with the major town of Swansea, now voted for devolution, no doubt in part because of disillusion with the ability of Westminster and Whitehall to generate new economic activity in the old mining valleys. One notable feature, a contrast with 1979 and indeed with *Cymru Fydd* in the 1890s for that matter, was that the Welsh language no longer had the capacity to divide Welshmen as they contemplated the future scenarios for their nation. Twenty years of successful pressure on behalf of good Welsh-language schools, primary and secondary, along with the recognition of the Welsh language on television and other media, had seen to that. Even the burning of English-owned "second homes" had come to an end.

After the outcome of the referendums in September 1997, however mixed, a new force was given to the pluralism inherent in Britain throughout the industrial age. The idea of Britishness was in the melting pot, and an integrative British culture under challenge, as never before. The Scottish Parliament and the Welsh Assembly came into being after elections in May 1999. In neither did Labour achieve an overall majority as a result of the partly proportional voting system, and in Wales indeed Plaid Cymru won no less than 17 seats, coming in a strong second to Labour's 28. The early experiences of the Scottish and Welsh bodies were not particularly inspiring. The Scottish Parliament was marked by a variety of disputes over local issues. Its leader, Donald Dewar, died suddenly. The Welsh Assembly saw the unexpected resignation of Ron Davies, its prospective first secretary, after a sex scandal, and then Tony Blair's unwise attempt to pressure the Welsh Labour Party into having Alun Michael as its head instead of the more popular Rhodri Morgan. Eventually, in early 2000, Michael was forced to resign as first secretary, and Morgan took over after all, perhaps inaugurating a more self-confident and inclusive period for the new Welsh Assembly.

Despite these adventures, however, the pattern of British public life and culture began to look increasingly different. A more diverse, pluralist, many-sided polity was beginning to emerge within the United Kingdom. The level of autonomy achieved by the Northern Ireland Assembly within the structure of asymmetrical devolution might also have its impact in time, although the age-old sectarian animosities in Ulster, which led to the Assembly being suspended after only a few weeks of activity, inevitably minimized the impact of Ireland. Another feature of growing significance was a more diverse approach to the European Union (EU). Scotland and Wales both showed clear signs of responding to the idea of a "Europe of Nations" in which a small, mainly rural nation like the Republic of Ireland had done so well, along with many local regions. Both Scotland and Wales began to frame internal and external strategic alliances within the EU, drawing inspiration and advice from regions such as Lombardy, Catalonia, and Baden-Württemburg which had flourished in the European context through their "motor scheme." Finally, the wider impact of globalization in the world economy, with a miscellany of local, rapidly moving centres of decision making also testified to the importance of decentralized, locally based strategies rather than uniquely central direction mediated by the time-worn mechanisms of the nation-state.

One major aspect of local and national identity stirred up by the impact of devolution and its wider implications, was the growing identity crisis of England. The dominant element within the British Isles, the English seemed increasingly at a loss to know how to respond to the changing devolutionary scene. Indeed, the relative lack of concern among the English at the consequences of Tam Dalyell's unanswerable "West Lothian question," whereby Scots and Welsh MPs could intervene in English matters whereas the English had no such comparable power, was remarkable. Clearly, though, there was a conceptual problem, with many important political implications. The old totems of Englishness were in marked decline. The end of Empire had removed an essential area for the deployment of English power and sentiment; the Union flag and the national anthem were losing their appeal in consequence. Equally, memories of war, especially of the highly English resonance of the Battle of Britain, the retreat from Dunkirk, and the legend of Churchill in the summer of 1940, were slowly fading and unable to fan the flames of English patriotism. No longer would works of reference declare "For Wales, see England," Indeed, "For Wales, see Scotland" seemed a more likely slogan for many now. English nationalism certainly existed, notably at the level of football matches and other mass sport where the flag of St. George was increasingly observed; but it remained unfocused. In 1997 attempts by the Conservatives to act as the voice of a beleaguered English nationalism in the face of the varied threats of Europe and of Celtic devolution were markedly ineffective. Nationalism in England remained the dog that did not bark, or perhaps the love that durst not speak its name. Even so, a healthy British polity demanded some kind of logical and understood role for the dominant English element within it. Asymmetry, like patriotism, was not enough. Whether this role would take the form of new regional experiments within England, an expanded series of civic autonomies along the lines of London with its newly elected mayor, or different methods of asserting the particular perspectives of the English within the EU, remained to be seen.

At the new millennium, what the outlook for the future of Britain would be after the constitutional revolution of devolution was uncertain. The historian Norman Davies, in a widely discussed synoptic historical work, *The Isles* (1999), seemed to take the break-up of the United Kingdom for granted. But the evidence for this appeared slight indeed. In Wales in particular, for all the presence of 17 Plaid Cymru members in the Cardiff Assembly, separatist sentiment was very slight, while Plaid Cymru now claimed (most dubiously) that historically its objective had never been national independence at all. Centrist theorists like David Marquand toyed with ideas of a federal solution, but no practical scheme emerged that could accommodate the overwhelmingly important role of England within one. Separatist pressures in Britain remained far less powerful than in, say, Spain with its centuries-old regional divisions, Austria, or Belgium with the massive confrontation between the Flemish and French speakers, the last two countries with sinister neo-fascist components as the Euro-elections of 1999 revealed.

Nevertheless, even if on a more subdued level, a fundamental debate about regional and national identities within Britain was under way in the year 2000. A central dialogue about the workings of the British state had been triggered by the reforms of the Blair government, in which its reforms of the House of Lords, debates over a bill of rights, and the relations with European law all played their part. The dualism in the soul of New Labour, in which ideas of local accountability and devolution lay uncomfortably alongside Millbank *dirigisme* and a post-socialist emphasis on national social standards, was being laid bare. Perhaps Labour was returning to its devolutionary roots in the days of Hardie and MacDonald before 1914. A redefinition of relationships and identities was underway which would blast away impartially the philosophies of Dicey and the Webbs, Tony Crosland and Margaret Thatcher. Scotland and Wales, so long seen dismissively and derisively as marginalized survivors, patronized or just tolerated by their dominant English neighbours, lay on the cusp of modernity. After centuries of "unhistoric" national ambiguity, they might be prophets of the political and cultural future, harbingers not of the legendary mists of an introverted Celtic twilight, but of the irresistible radiance of the Britain that is to be.

# 3

# Managing the Multinational State: Constitutional Settlement in the United Kingdom

*Michael Keating*

## THE NEW CONSTITUTIONAL AGENDA

During 1998 and 1999, the voters of Northern Ireland, Scotland, and Wales elected devolved national assemblies, a belated step forward in the process started by Prime Minister William Ewart Gladstone in 1886 to convert the United Kingdom from a centralized state to a federation of self-governing nations and regions. This is the most radical constitutional change since the abolition of the House of Lords' veto in 1910 and forms part of a broader program of constitutional change now on the agenda, including reform of the House of Lords, freedom of information, and referendums on proportional representation and the European single currency. As usual in the UK, the process is piecemeal, with little regard to consistency or any overall plan but, once set in train, it could be irreversible. Devolution represents a radical change for the UK but, in another sense, it can be seen as a recognition of deep-seated and historic features of the British state, and of the need to modernize the system to take account of current realities.

This is a revised and updated version of Michael Keating. 1998. "Reforging the Union: Devolution and Constitutional Change in the United Kingdom," *Publius: The Journal of Federalism*, 28(1):217-34. It is produced here by permission.

## THE UNION STATE

The United Kingdom is often described as a unitary state. In the absence of a written constitution, parliamentary sovereignty is the supreme law, allowing no room for rival authorities above or below it. This theory, based in the parliamentary practice of England, was fully articulated by A.V. Dicey (1885) in his works in the late nineteenth century. The modern party system and the norm of majority government means, as observers from Walter Bagehot onward have noted, that parliamentary sovereignty gives the Cabinet largely untrammeled power. Many academics in the 1950s and 1960s argued, further, that underlying this unitary constitution was a homogeneous political culture (e.g., Finer 1970; Blondel 1974), a claim based upon unfamiliarity with the UK outside the English heartland. This unitary reading of the constitution has not been confined to academics. The British political class has also tended to see power as concentrated. The Labour Party, once it had begun to penetrate the political system, saw concentrated authority as an instrument to be used in its plans to transform society (Jones and Keating 1985). Right-wing radicals like Margaret Thatcher have similarly seen parliamentary sovereignty as absolute power, giving them the authority to push through large-scale social change without winning a majority of the popular vote.

Yet there has always been another interpretation of the British state, which sees it as a balanced constitution, in which no one element can be pushed to extremes at the expense of the others. Parliamentary sovereignty is balanced by a limitation in the scope of the state, by respect for the independent institutions of civil society, and by conventions of restraint. Important public matters, such as the universities, the professions, the legal system, and the City of London, were left to the self-regulating institutions of civil society. Local government, while lacking constitutional entrenchment, was given a large degree of freedom, as long as it did not challenge the principle of parliamentary sovereignty.

Another interpretation that challenges the unitary state doctrine is that of the "union state," one built by the incorporation of diverse territories through treaty and agreement. While administrative standardization prevails over most of the territory, pre-union rights and structures continue to exist in other parts (Rokkan and Urwin 1983; Mitchell 1996). So the Union of England and Scotland in 1707 involved the abolition of both English and Scottish parliaments and their replacement by a new parliament of Great Britain. For the dominant classes in contemporary Scotland, this was a bargain in which they surrendered their parliament in return for the preservation of their civil society, notably in the form of the established Church of Scotland, the education system, the legal system, and the burghs or self-governing municipalities. During the eighteenth century, Scots notables were given a free hand in running local affairs (Harvie 1994) while from the late nineteenth century, the modern, interventionist state took a distinct administrative form in Scotland. The Scottish Office was created in 1885, headed by a Scottish politician from the ruling party. It has been argued that, in this way, the Scots bargained for as much autonomy as was available within the imperial order, while playing full parts in the politics of the UK as a whole (Kellas 1984; Midwinter, Keating and James 1991; Paterson 1994). During the twentieth century, these institutions were greatly expanded, serving to maintain Scottish political identity and focus political debate within a Scottish context.

Wales, united with England in 1536, has always been more closely integrated. It shares the English legal system and has fewer distinct civil institutions than Scotland. Yet some distinctiveness persists, reinforced in the nineteenth century by nonconformist religion and the resistance to linguistic assimilation in the Welsh heartland. Since 1965 the Welsh Office has provided a focus for a Welsh politics and a growing political identity.

Ireland's position within the United Kingdom was different again, always more colonial than that of Scotland and Wales. Until 1800 there was an Irish Parliament, but subject to control from Westminster and dominated by the Anglo-Irish Protestant minority.[1] After the union of 1800 Ireland sent MPs to Westminster but the country was not administratively integrated as was Wales, nor administered by a locally elected member of the ruling party, as in Scotland. Instead, power was shared by the Lord Lieutenant and the Chief Secretary, sent over from the mainland. From the 1870s, the Irish largely broke with the British party system.

The Union has undergone periodic crises, calling for adjustment or renegotiation of its terms but, given the doctrine of parliamentary supremacy, it has proved very difficult for British governments to negotiate or to undertake radical constitutional reform. Instead, adjustments are made to administrative arrangements, local government is reformed, or policy concessions are granted. The late nineteenth century saw a rise of nationalism across Europe, challenging multinational states and empires. Expansion of the interventionist state brought government, central bureaucracy, and educators into peripheries with their own culture and tradition (Keating 1988). Agrarian and industrial class conflicts broke out as a new division of labour was imposed, often assuming a territorial dimension. In the late nineteenth century, Irish home-rule crises broke the British party system, consigning the Liberals to long periods of opposition and bringing the country to the edge of civil war by 1914. It was resolved only with the concession of what became full independence to the southern part of the country and the establishment of the UK's only previous example of devolved government in the north. Scotland proved more tractable, and rises in home rule and nationalist sentiment in the late nineteenth century and after the two world wars were contained by administrative devolution and economic concessions. Wales was less of a problem for the state. The rise of nonconformist religion led to pressure for the disestablishment of the Church of England there, finally successful after the First World War. Later, language demands were met though policy concessions.

Since the nineteenth century, a number of integrating factors have been at work. The first is the development of common values, especially in the development of the welfare state and social citizenship. Second is a shared economic interest. The economic effects of the union on Scotland continue to be debated (Lee 1995) but most observers agree that access to British and imperial markets was important for the industrial development of Scotland, Wales, and Northern Ireland.[2] Since the 1930s, the relative industrial decline of the peripheral industrial areas has made them dependent on transfers from the south of England, and from the 1960s elaborate national regional policies were put in place to encourage reindustrialization and growth. The party system has been another unifying element as Scotland and Wales, but not Northern Ireland, voted overwhelmingly for British parties which from the 1920s, focused on the need to gain power at the centre rather than campaign for self-government in the periphery. More generally, the entire political and administrative elite recognizing a trade-off between autonomy for the minority nations and access to the centre, chose the latter (Keating 1975), resisting reductions in Scottish and Welsh parliamentary representation, despite declining population relativities, and developing the Scottish and Welsh Offices as mechanisms allowing some inflections of policy to suit local circumstances but, more importantly, as channels of access into the central decision-making apparatus. Northern Ireland was less tightly integrated although, until 1974, MPs from the dominant Unionist Party took the Conservative whip at Westminster.

## THE NEW TERRITORIAL POLITICS

Since the late 1960s, this territorial settlement has gradually been breaking down and is giving way to a radically new dispensation in the 1990s. One factor, common to other European states, is the crisis of the nation-state itself in the face of globalization and Europeanization. These, combined with the rise of neo-liberal ideology, have undermined many of the instruments of territorial management, including tariffs, diversionary regional policies, and state-directed investment strategies. The relationship between territory and function has changed with the emergence of the region as a key level of policy and strategy (Keating 1998). In those states with existing national and cultural fault lines, the weakening of the state's integrative capacity and the new regionalism have led old identities to be refurbished and pressed into new use. A related element is a democratic impulse to confront the new networks of policy making with more effective mechanisms for citizen participation and accountability and to establish a new public domain and forums for democratic deliberation. Minority nationalism was often dismissed in the past as tribal and atavistic, given the pejorative label of "ethnic" to distinguish it from the civic nation-building of the large states. This attitude still persists among some metropolitan intellectuals (see, for example, Dahrendorf 1995) but, in Scotland and Wales nationalism is seen more as a search for civic community, for new principles of solidarity and cohesion in the face of the international market. Scotland and Wales have also seen cultural revivals, in which distinctly national, if not always nationalist, themes have featured strongly. This new culture, linking local and cosmopolitan themes, also allows nationalist and home rule movements to escape the charge of parochialism by placing their demands in a broader global and European context. Indeed, nationalist intellectuals are fond of taunting southern English opinion-formers for their narrow-minded nationalism, anti-Europeanism and "little Englander" mentalities.

The conflict in Northern Ireland, always present but repressed, burst out again in the late 1960s, as the Catholic community chafed under the Protestant hegemony. Initially, this took the form of a civil rights movement claiming the rights to which Catholics should have been entitled as British citizens, and drawing inspiration from events in the southern United States and colonial empires. Soon, however, it adopted the more historic form of a confrontation between a Catholic-nationalist and a Protestant-unionist community. This dual nature of the Northern Ireland problem, involving divisions within the community as well as between Ireland and Britain, marks it off from the issues of Scotland and Wales. Northern Ireland is also unique within the UK in giving birth to political violence at the extremes of both the nationalist (republican) and unionist (loyalist) communities.

Europe has had a profound effect on territorial politics in the UK. At the time of British accession to the European Community in 1973 both elite and mass opinion in the peripheral nations tended to be hostile to the Community. The Labour Party was against membership and Scottish and Welsh Labour even more so, while the nationalists regarded Brussels as even more remote and therefore objectionable than London (Keating and Jones 1995). Northern Ireland Protestants were vigorously anti-Europe,[3] while the nationalists had yet to discover it. This changed dramatically in the late 1980s, not least in response to Margaret Thatcher's anti-European rhetoric, which convinced many Scots and Welsh that there must be something to be said for it! By 1988, both Labour and the nationalists had adopted Europe, albeit in rather different ways. The Scottish National Party (SNP) sees Europe as lowering the costs of secession and campaigns for "independence in Europe," while Labour and the Liberal Democrats support home rule within the UK, but with a European dimension, tapping into the "Europe of the regions" theme. Plaid Cymru, the Welsh nationalist party, supports a Europe of self-governing peoples without the trappings of statehood. The moderate nationalists of the Northern Ireland Social Democratic and Labour Party (SDLP) see Europe as a framework for internationalizing the conflict and taking it out of the UK context, although the Unionists, especially the more extreme ones, remain hostile.

Party politics have also undermined the old territorial settlement. In the mid-1970s, advances by the SNP, which in 1974 won 30 percent of the Scottish vote and 11 parliamentary seats, and to a lesser extent by Plaid Cymru, frightened Labour into reverting to its old policy of Home Rule for Scotland and Wales.[4] Labour's attempts to set up assemblies in Scotland and Wales were unsuccessful, undermined by dissent within its own ranks, by parliamentary obstruction and by a referendum requirement. The Welsh proposals were defeated by a margin of 80 percent, reflecting the divisions in Welsh society and the lack of trust between the Welsh-speaking north and the English-speaking south. The Scottish proposals won a narrow majority but failed to meet the parliamentary requirement of the support of 40 percent of the entire electorate. In opposition in the 1980s, Labour stuck with the Home Rule policy, reinforcing it as they lost ground in England and were driven back to the periphery. Throughout the years of Conservative government, Labour regularly gained the plurality of the vote and the majority of seats in Scotland and Wales. In Scotland at least, this represented a marked contrast to earlier periods of Conservative rule; as recently as 1955 the Conservatives had won more than 50 percent of the vote in Scotland. By 1997, they were reduced to 18 percent and no seats.

In contrast to their attitude to Scotland, the Conservative governments constantly sought to restore self-government to Northern Ireland but failed to gain cross-community consent or to convince Unionists of the need to share power. At the same time, they sought to frame the issue as one of security, with the result that community divisions polarized further. This represented a continuation of the traditional strategy of trying to distance Northern Ireland from mainstream British politics. By the late 1980s, the British were prepared to countenance a role in the conflict for the Republic of Ireland and the United States, further evidence of a willingness to disengage themselves. In the Downing Street Declaration of 1993 the government went so far as to say that they had "no selfish strategic or economic interest in Northern Ireland," a statement which would have been inconceivable in relation to Scotland.

## THE HOME-RULE COALITION

Thatcher's attacks on the self-governing institutions of civil society, including the trade unions, universities, and local government, were widely seen as an abuse of parliamentary sovereignty and therefore a violation of the unwritten norms of the constitution. This sentiment was especially strong in Scotland, where the union is still seen as a compact, while in Wales there was much criticism of the "quango state," the erosion of local government in favour of appointed agencies staffed by Conservative placemen. This brought into the home-rule coalition organizations and individuals who in the 1970s were hostile, fearing that Scottish and Welsh assemblies might encroach on their own autonomy. In Scotland, this was formalized in the Campaign for a Scottish Assembly and its offshoot, the Scottish Constitutional Convention. By the 1992 election, the Convention had produced a scheme for home rule and, while the Conservatives won yet again, the parties of the Convention gained an absolute majority of the Scottish vote and 58 of Scotland's 72 parliamentary seats. With this wide base of support, the Convention questioned the legitimacy of the Conservatives' mandate in Scotland and insisted on the inherent sovereignty of the Scottish people and their right to renegotiate their own position in the Union. Cooperation between Labour and the Liberal Democrats, itself a remarkable innovation in British politics, produced further agreements, notably on a system of proportional representation in the new assembly, which was now to be called a Parliament. Agreement was also reached on limited taxation powers. Pressure from Scotland ensured that devolution was a Labour manifesto commitment, despite Neil Kinnock's active opposition to Welsh devolution in 1979. By 1992 this had become a promise to establish a Scottish assembly in the first year of a Labour government. The commitment was further reinforced by the election as Labour leader of John Smith who, as a minister in the last Labour government, had piloted the devolution legislation through the Commons and referred to it as "unfinished business."

Progress in Wales was slower but during the 1980s and early 1990s, a new form of Welsh identity seemed to be emerging, focused less on the cultural issues that had characterized Welsh nationalism in the past, than on the promotion of Wales as a European region. While conflicts over language did continue, Conservative policy was quite generous, with the establishment of a Welsh television channel, a Welsh language commission, and a separate Welsh national education curriculum. Together with continued administrative devolution to the Welsh Office, this helped reinforce a sense of Welsh political identity, while the nomination of a series of English MPs as secretary of state (which would be unthinkable in Scotland) created a certain alienation. The Labour Party in Wales was much more divided on devolution than was its Scottish counterpart, and there was no cross-party organization. Nonetheless, by the late 1980s Labour was coming back to the idea of a Welsh assembly and this did feature in the 1992 manifesto.

Much of the opposition to devolution in the 1970s had come from English MPs in the northern region, who feared that Scotland and Wales would be further advantaged if they had their own assemblies. The government had tried to mollify them by various spending commitments, and some vague proposals for English regional government which, while it has been Labour policy since 1976, has never been taken very seriously. John Prescott, now deputy prime minister, produced his own proposals while spokesman on regional affairs in the mid-1980s, but they ran into opposition from municipal leaders more interested in stronger city government, and from those steeped in the party's centralist tradition.

By the time of Tony Blair's accession to the leadership in 1994, Scottish and Welsh devolution was a firm part of Labour Party policy and his main contribution was an insistence on pre-legislative referendums in Scotland and Wales. Following the 1997 election, Labour moved quickly, overcoming last-ditch opposition by some of the English Cabinet ministers, publishing White Papers on Scotland and Wales in July and naming referendum dates in September. In Scotland, the referendum campaign was quite one-sided. The "no" forces were led by a demoralized and disorganized Conservative Party while the business community, not wanting to be caught on the losing side, largely sat on the sidelines. The principle of a Scottish Parliament was approved by a margin of 74.3 percent, while the tax-raising powers gained the support of 63.5 percent. With a turnout depressed by the use of a relatively old electoral roll this meant that both questions would even have passed the old 40 percent hurdle. There was a large "yes" majority in all regions of Scotland, varying from 84 percent in Glasgow to 57 percent in Orkney, and the tax-raising powers were rejected only in two areas (Orkney and Dumfries and Galloway).

In Wales, matters were more difficult. Labour was still internally divided and the cultural division between the regions of Wales had not been bridged. The assembly proposals passed by a bare majority of 50.3 percent and, significantly, were rejected in the city of Cardiff, capital of Wales, site of the future assembly, and the most modern and dynamic part of the principality. The narrow result in Wales sealed the chances of movement in England and John Prescott announced that there would be no proposals for English regional government in this parliament.

The Northern Ireland question is more complicated than that of Scotland or Wales. There is the issue of Northern Ireland's relationship to the UK, but also to the Republic of Ireland. There is the division within the province between nationalists and unionists, largely corresponding to that between Catholics and Protestants. There are divisions within each community. The nationalist side is divided between moderate nationalists (the SDLP) and republicans (Sinn Fein), who support IRA violence. On the unionist side are the relatively moderate Official Unionists and the more extreme Democratic Unionists of Ian Paisley, as well as a fringe of extreme unionists or "loyalists" linked to paramilitary terrorist groups. From the early 1970s, British governments repeatedly sought consociational solutions based on cross-community power-sharing between the moderates on each side, but without success. The IRA and loyalist ceasefires of 1996 provided the first opportunity to bring all sides into a renewed effort, although the dependence of the Major government on Unionist support meant that it was only after Labour came to power in 1997 that progress could be made. After difficult negotiations, agreement was finally reached on Good Friday 1998 to establish a power-sharing assembly. The agreement covered a wide spectrum of political forces from Sinn Fein, through the SDLP to the official Unionists and the loyalist paramilitaries. The main absentee was Ian Paisley's Democratic Unionist Party, while a substantial section of the official Unionists bucked the leadership of David Trimble to oppose it. The proposal was put to a referendum in Northern Ireland, where it gained overwhelming support among the Catholics and, it appears, a bare majority among the Protestants. A parallel referendum in the Republic of Ireland replacing the claim to sovereignty over the north with a commitment to unity by consent, gained massive support.

## THE SETTLEMENT

The *Scotland Act* of 1998 establishes a Scottish Parliament and an executive headed by a first minister.[5] The Parliament has primary legislative powers; this has been a feature of most proposals for Scottish devolution, given the existence of Scots law and the large body of separate Scottish legislation handled by Westminster. In contrast to the proposals of the 1970s and even those of the Constitutional Convention,[6] only the powers reserved to Westminster are defined, with the Scottish Parliament free to make its own laws and to change existing laws outside this field. Major reserved powers include defence and foreign affairs, taxation and monetary policy, company law and regulation of financial institutions, employment legislation, social security,[7] and a range of regulatory matters. The main areas thus devolved to Scotland include health, education and training, local government, social work, housing, economic development, transport, criminal law, civil law except in reserved matters, judicial appointments, the environment, agriculture forestry and fishing, and sports and the arts.

As in the 1970s, the Labour government has insisted that sovereignty remains with Westminster, which will thus be able to legislate in non-reserved matters or override Scottish legislation. This is in contradiction to the Scottish Convention declaration, signed by the Labour representatives, that sovereignty lies with the Scottish people. The list of reserved items is reasonably clear, largely following existing areas of Scottish law and administration, although there has been some criticism of the details.

The main reserved matters are given in Table 1.

TABLE 1:   Reserved Matters in Scotland

---

- the Crown, the Union of the Kingdoms of Scotland and England, the Parliament of the United Kingdom
- international relations, including foreign trade except for: observing and implementing EU and European Convention on Human Rights matters
- defence and national security; treason; provisions for dealing with terrorism
- fiscal and monetary policy, currency, coinage and legal tender
- immigration and nationality, extradition
- the criminal law in relation to drugs and firearms, and the regulation of misuse of drugs;
- elections, except local elections
- official secrets, national security
- law on companies and business associations, insurance, corporate insolvency and intellectual property, regulation of financial institutions and financial services
- competition, monopolies, and mergers
- employment legislation including industrial relations, equal opportunities, health and safety
- most consumer protection; data protection
- post office, postal and telegraphy services
- most energy matters
- railways and air transport; road safety
- social security
- regulation of certain professions, including medical, dental, nursing and other health professions, veterinary surgeons, architects, auditors, estate agents, insolvency practitioners and insurance intermediaries
- transport safety and regulation
- research councils
- designation of assisted areas
- nuclear safety, control and safety of medicines, reciprocal health agreements
- broadcasting and film classification, licensing of theatres and cinemas, gambling
- weights and measures; time zones
- abortion, human fertilization and embryology, genetics, xenotransplantation
- equality legislation
- regulation of activities in outer space

---

Everything else is devolved, meaning in practice the functions listed in Table 2.

TABLE 2:   Functions Devolved to the Scottish Parliament

---

* health
* education and training
* local government, social work, housing, and planning
* economic development and transport; the administration of the European Structural Funds
* the law and home affairs including most civil and criminal law and the criminal justice and prosecution system; police and prisons
* the environment
* agriculture, fisheries, and forestry
* sport and the arts
* research and statistics in relation to devolved matters

---

The financial powers of the Parliament, by contrast, are very weak. The main source of funding will be a block grant from Westminster. It may raise or lower the basic rate of income tax by three percentage points. The Parliament also has full control of local taxation, which presently is limited to property taxes set by local governments for residential property and by the central government for commercial property, but in practice there is little scope for changing this. If it is tempted to raise money for itself by squeezing transfers to local governments, there is provision for Westminster to claw back block grant funds.

In a radical departure, the Labour government conceded that the Parliament should be elected by proportional representation. Along with Labour's introduction of proportional representation for European Parliament elections, it marks a serious breach in the plurality system for British elections, and may have implications in due course for Westminster. The system used is a modification of the German additional-member system, with regional party lists competing in the eight European constituencies in Scotland, providing 56 members to top up the 73 elected in the constituencies. A divisive issue in the Convention was a proposal for gender equality, which some wanted to be written into the devolution legislation. At the insistence of the Liberal Democrats, who objected to the state interfering in the affairs of political parties, the final report did not recommend a statutory requirement, but Labour and the Liberal Democrats pledged to achieve gender equality in their lists of candidates.

The Government of Wales Bill, like its predecessor in the 1970s, provides for a much more limited devolution of power. There is a National Assembly for Wales with executive powers and some powers of secondary legislation,[8] corresponding to existing ministerial powers. There is no definitive list of powers but rather a list of existing Welsh Office powers which can be transferred over time to the Assembly. It has no powers of taxation but depends entirely on block grants. The organization of the Assembly in some ways resembles the local government model, with subject committees drawn from all the parties having executive responsibility. In practice, the Assembly delegates its executive powers to a first secretary and departmental secretaries who together form a Cabinet. The electoral system is the same as in Scotland. The executive responsibilities of the secretary of state for Wales transferable to the Assembly include economic development; agriculture, forestry, fisheries and food; industry and training; education; local government; health and personal social services; housing; environment; planning; transport and roads; arts, culture, the Welsh language; the built heritage; sport and recreation.

While the Scottish and Welsh arrangements form part of a process for decentralizing a unitary state, the Northern Ireland settlement looks in some ways more like the sort of provision the UK made with its former colonies and dominions, allowing them to evolve to full independence or whatever other arrangement they might choose. It is explicitly stipulated in the *Northern Ireland Act* that, should a majority of the electorate wish at some time in the future to join a united Ireland, then the secretary of state must lay an order to do this. The role of the republic in the meantime is recognized, and a whole range of institutions are put in place to allow the people of Ireland to express multiple loyalties and forms of identity. The Act establishes a Northern Ireland Assembly with both legislative and executive powers, elected by proportional representation but using the single transferable vote, rather than the semi-proportional mechanisms used in Scotland and Wales. Members are invited to designate themselves as nationalist or unionist and certain matters require qualified or concurrent majorities. There is an executive headed by a first minister and deputy first minister, and in which all parties represented in the Assembly are entitled to have ministers. There is a North-South Ministerial Council to link Northern Ireland and the Republic, an Intergovernmental Conference linking the British and Irish Republic governments, and a British-Irish Council (sometimes referred to as the Council of the Isles) bringing together the British and Irish governments, the Northern Ireland Assembly, the Scottish Parliament, the National Assembly for Wales, and even the Channel Islands and the Isle of Man.

Competences are divided into excepted matters, which remain with the UK Parliament; reserved matters, which may be devolved to the Assembly provided it

TABLE 3:   Reserved and Excepted Matters in Northern Ireland

---

*Excepted Matters*

- the Crown, the Parliament of the United Kingdom
- international relations, but not:
    the surrender of fugitive offenders between Northern Ireland and Republic of Ireland;
    participation in the all-Irish institutions;
    observing and implementing European Union and European Convention on Human Rights matters.
- defence and national security; treason; provisions for dealing with terrorism or subversion
- dignities and titles of honour
- immigration and nationality
- taxes under UK laws or existing stamp duties in Northern Ireland
- social security
- the appointment and removal of judges and director of Public Prosecutions for Northern Ireland
- elections, including local elections
- coinage, legal tender, and bank notes
- the National Savings Bank
- national security
- any matter for which provision is made by this Act or the *Northern Ireland Constitution Act* 1973

*Reserved Matters*

- navigation, but not harbours or inland waters
- civil aviation but not aerodromes
- the foreshore and the sea bed and subsoil and their natural resources
- domicile
- postal services
- qualifications and immunities of the Assembly and its members
- criminal law; the surrender of fugitive offenders between Northern Ireland and Republic of Ireland
- public order, police, firearms and explosives, civil defence
- the *Emergency Powers Act* (Northern Ireland) 1926 or any similar enactment.

---

*... continued*

TABLE 3 (cont'd.)

---

- court procedure and evidence

- foreign trade

- regulation of building societies; banking; friendly societies; the investment and securities business

- competition, monopolies and mergers

- some consumer protection matters

- trade marks, copyright, patent and topography rights, weights and measures

- telecommunications and wireless telegraphy

- xenotransplantation; human fertilisation and embryology; surrogacy; human genetics.

- consumer safety, some environmental matters, data protection

- nuclear installations

- designation of assisted areas

- research councils

- regulation of activities in outer space

---

asks for them by concurrent majority; and transferred matters, which covers everything else. Powers will be transferred over time as the Assembly develops. This is derived from the old Stormont system (which has also influenced the *Scotland Act*). The excepted matters are similar to those reserved in the *Scotland Act*, but there are differences in substance and tone. The Scottish legislation is more unionist in tone, stressing the need for integration and consistency, especially in social and economic matters; on the other hand, it is rather permissive on matters of criminal law and policing. The list of reserved powers in Northern Ireland covers most matters to do with security and policing, a highly sensitive area in which competences will be transferred only when the Assembly has demonstrated its ability to use them without discrimination; the *Northern Ireland Act* also has lengthy sections devoted to equal rights and non-discrimination provisions. On the other hand, it is silent on many "common market" and "common standards" matters. It is notable that there is no commitment to maintaining a single currency as in Scotland, merely an exception of coinage, legal tender and bank notes.[9] So Northern Ireland could probably move into the single currency without the rest of the UK (O'Leary 1999). The conclusion is that in the case of Scotland, maintaining the economic and social union is paramount, while the British government's main concerns in Northern Ireland are related to security. The list may also reflect the fact that the former Stormont parliament (1922-72), established before the interventionist welfare state, was not barred from a wide range of economic and social fields and developed parallel provision; Scotland on the other hand has always had its own criminal law. The list of reserved powers in Scotland is longer and more detailed than its Northern Ireland counterpart, reflecting successful battles by Whitehall departments to retain functions which had not in the past been administered by the Scottish Office. In both Scotland and Northern Ireland, the legacy of past traditions of separate legislation and administrative development are thus apparent.[10]

TABLE 4:  Functions Devolved to the Northern Ireland Assembly

- health
- education and training
- social work, housing, and planning
- economic development and transport; the administration of the European Structural Funds;
- the environment
- agriculture, fisheries, and forestry
- sport and the arts

## THE ELECTIONS

Elections to the Northern Ireland Assembly took place in June 1998 and to the Scottish Parliament and National Assembly for Wales in May 1999. The purpose of the Northern Ireland elections was to produce a majority in favour of the Good Friday Agreement, which could then form a power-sharing executive. On the Unionist side, voters were almost exactly divided between supporters and opponents of the agreement but transfers yielded a bare majority in the Assembly for pro-agreement forces willing to make the settlement work. On the nationalist side, Sinn Fein advanced to its largest ever share of the vote, although the moderate SDLP was still ahead. David Trimble of the Ulster Unionists and Seamas Mallon of the SDLP were elected first minister and deputy first minister respectively, although progress on forming a government stalled on the issue of decommissioning paramilitary weapons.

The stakes in the Scottish and Welsh elections were quite different as the UK parties were in competition, against each other and against nationalists. Here a serious contradiction emerged in the "New Labour" program. While committed to constitutional devolution, Blair's Labour Party has been highly centralizing and disciplined in its own organization and has failed to match parliamentary devolution with devolution in its own affairs. After the unrest in the Scottish party over Blair's referendum edict, a coup was organized to replace members of the Scottish executive considered too left-wing, "old Labour," or suspected of nationalist leanings and a number of prominent members, including Westminster MPs, were kept off the panel of approved candidates. When Labour's candidate for Welsh first secretary, Ron Davies, resigned over a bizarre incident on Clapham Common, huge efforts were put into ensuring his replacement by a faithful Blairite, Alun Michael, a Welsh MP who had initially chosen not to run for the Assembly, rather than the more charismatic but independent-minded Rhodri Morgan.

In Scotland, opinion polls between the referendum and the election showed the SNP making great progress at the expense of Labour. In the event, the result largely reflected the 1997 UK election, with the nationalists making a modest advance, the Conservatives falling back further and the Liberal Democrats just about holding their own. Labour dissident Denis Canavan, a Westminster MP who had been excluded from the panel of potential candidates, won a huge majority running as an independent in his constituency. One list seat each was won by the Greens and the Scottish Socialist Party, a Trotskyist offshoot formed when the Militant Tendency was expelled from the Labour Party. Labour in particular was affected by a transfer of votes in the proportional part of the ballot to smaller parties. As expected, no party gained a majority and a coalition government was formed between Labour and the Liberal Democrats. As a result of Labour's commitment to parity, 38 percent of the members were women.

It was Wales that yielded the greatest surprise. On a turnout of barely half the electorate, Labour's vote slumped, notably in its South Wales heartlands and the nationalists of Plaid Cymru advanced to become the second party of Wales, picking up seats in the constituencies as well as on the lists. Labour's poor showing was widely attributed to its insistence on parachuting in London's candidate for first minister and its control tendencies in general. Failing to gain its expected majority, it chose to form a minority administration rather than a coalition.

The Scottish and Welsh results show how far these two nations have now developed their own party systems, as well as a possible tendency for nationalist parties to do better in these elections than in UK elections, as happens in Spain. The results in the two cases are remarkably close, with a leading but not hegemonic Labour Party and the nationalists forming the opposition. The Conservatives won only one constituency in Wales and none in Scotland, taking the rest of their seats on the proportional lists. The Liberal Democrats, who in England desperately need proportional representation to have any chance of a breakthrough, are well enough dug-in locally in Scotland and Wales to win constituency seats.

TABLE 5:   Scottish Parliament Election Results

|  | Constituency % Vote | List % Vote | Total Seats | Constituency Seats | List Seats |
|---|---|---|---|---|---|
| Labour | 38.1 | 33.6 | 56 | 53 | 3 |
| SNP | 28.7 | 27.2 | 35 | 7 | 28 |
| Conservative | 15.6 | 15.4 | 18 | 0 | 18 |
| Liberal Democrat | 14.2 | 12.4 | 17 | 12 | 5 |
| Other | 3.4 | 11.4 | 3 | 1 | 2 |

TABLE 6:   National Assembly for Wales Election Results

|  | Constituency % Vote | List % Vote | Total Seats | Constituency Seats | List Seats |
|---|---|---|---|---|---|
| Labour | 37.6 | 35.4 | 28 | 27 | 1 |
| Plaid Cymru | 28.4 | 30.5 | 17 | 9 | 8 |
| Conservative | 15.9 | 16.5 | 9 | 1 | 8 |
| Liberal Democrat | 13.4 | 12.6 | 6 | 3 | 3 |
| Other | 4.7 | 5.1 | 0 | 0 | 0 |

TABLE 7:   Northern Ireland Assembly Election Results

|  | First Preference Votes | Seats |
|---|---|---|
| Ulster Unionists | 21.3 | 28 |
| SDLP | 22.0 | 24 |
| Democratic Unionists | 18.0 | 20 |
| Sinn Fein | 17.7 | 18 |
| Alliance | 6.5 | 6 |
| UK Unionists | 4.5 | 5 |
| Anti-agreement Unionists | 3.0 | 3 |
| Progressive Unionists | 2.5 | 2 |
| Womens' Coalition | 1.6 | 2 |

## INTERGOVERNMENTAL RELATIONS

The proposals provide for a differentiated and highly asymmetrical system of government. The question of relations with the central government and, nowadays, with Europe, is thus a key issue. The settlement retains the offices of secretary of state for Scotland, Wales, and Northern Ireland, to act as a link with Cabinet and Westminster. Clearly, the secretary of state for Wales will have a continuing role, sponsoring Welsh business in Parliament and presiding over the Welsh Office in the long process of transferring its powers. Some surprise was expressed by the decision not only to retain the office of secretary of state for Scotland, but to keep two junior ministers as well. The secretary of state for Northern Ireland has a key role in the peace process and in managing the gradual transfer of powers. In the long run, it is difficult to see a role for the three secretaries of state and they may be combined into a single office.

The three devolved assemblies will be subject to the terms of the legislation setting them up, to European Union law, and to the European Convention on Human Rights. Jurisdictional disputes are to be handled by the Judicial Committee of the Privy Council, the body that used to settle such disputes in the self-governing colonies and in Canada. This will have the power to rule Scottish and Northern Irish legislation and Welsh secondary legislation *ultra vires* but not to strike down Westminster legislation going beyond the reserved matters because Westminster has retained its full sovereignty. Although Parliament has now incorporated the European Convention on Human Rights into British and English law, it has not accepted full judicial review on this matter either. This creates the interesting situation that Scottish and Northern Ireland citizens of the United Kingdom have more direct access to and redress from the Convention than their English co-citizens.

Representation in the decision-making instances of the European Union has become one of the main preoccupations of devolved governments in Europe, and the issue is given considerable attention in the UK. At present, there is provision for ministers and officials of the Scottish and Welsh Offices to participate in negotiations and delegations and the devolution proposals try to retain the same arrangements for the devolved administrations, excepting various EU matters from the definition of the reserved field of international relations. It is possible that Scottish and Northern Ireland ministers could form part of the UK delegation and, using article 146 of the Maastricht Treaty, could even speak for the UK in the Council of Ministers. This could pose great difficulties. The countries where this provision has been used — Germany, Austria, and Belgium — are federations, and the regional level forms a significant counterweight to the centre, with its guaranteed powers.

There are also long traditions of corporatist and consociational accommodation, which contrast with the British tradition of adversary politics. Although it is possible to imagine a Labour central government cooperating in Europe with a Labour-Liberal Democrat Scottish government, it is much more difficult to see a Euroskeptic Conservative central government doing so. The Scottish government has, under the Act, set up its own office in Brussels, as a more explicitly political presence than the existing Scotland Europa. Given the existing Scottish activity in Europe and the high name-recognition of Scotland in Europe, this could make the Scottish executive an important player in the Europe-of-the-Regions movement and create more tensions with the UK central government. The proposals are much weaker on Welsh representation in Europe, merely noting that the Assembly will be able to make its view known to the UK government, notably via the secretary of state. In the case of Northern Ireland, the interesting thing will be the possibility of developing common approaches with the Republic of Ireland on matters of mutual interest.

Central-local conflicts in Britain have usually assumed a partisan form and it is likely that the parties will be a key element in relations between the centre and the devolved administrations. Labour's "control freak" tendency proved a liability in the Scottish and Welsh elections and, to compete with the nationalists, its local branches will have to demonstrate more independence. Relations will be more difficult should the Conservatives return to power at Westminster, or a non-Labour coalition takes power in the Scottish Parliament or Welsh Assembly.[11]

## FINANCE

The biggest potential source of conflict remains finance. Here the proposals are least clear and build on a variety of existing systems for the various parts of the UK. Under the Stormont regime, Northern Ireland was assigned the product of the main taxes and had devolved control over some others. It made a payment, known as the "imperial contribution" to London for common services. By the 1930s, Northern Ireland's economic problems rendered the imperial contribution negative and after the Second World War British governments undertook to finance the foundation and development of the welfare state in Northern Ireland (Birrell and Murie 1980).

For many years, Scottish expenditure levels were governed by the Goschen formula, named for a nineteenth-century Chancellor of the Exchequer, which gave Scotland more or less its population share of expenditures. The formula gradually fell out of use in this century, surviving in education until some time after the Second World War. By this time, failure to recalculate the base to take account of Scotland's falling population share had increased Scottish per-capita spending relative to that of England. As the formula was abandoned, secretaries of state were able to build further on this advantage, bargaining service by service, making significant gains when Labour was in power and when Scotland was politically crucial to the fortunes of the government of the day. The devolution proposals of the 1970s brought a backlash by English MPs, who feared that a devolved assembly would benefit the Scots even more, although anti-devolution Scots took the opposite view, that devolution would imperil their access to the Treasury. So the Labour government introduced a new system, known as the "Barnett formula" and applied it to both Scotland and Wales; later it was extended to Northern Ireland. Scottish, Welsh, and Northern Ireland expenditure is divided into two parts, one of which applies to expenditure driven by UK and European policy and the other, known as the block, was handed over to the secretaries of state, who had full discretion to reallocate within it. The total of the block is determined by historic expenditures, with any increase or decrease in the corresponding English expenditures being reflected in a more-or-less population-based change in the Scottish, Welsh, and Northern Ireland blocks.

Thus there are two principles at work, for the base and for the margin. In time, especially given inflation, this should have produced a convergence of spending across the four units. In practice, the operation of the system, including the definition of the corresponding English totals, has been shrouded in mystery (Heald 1992), while the size of the block has increased by putting new items into it. Estimates of the advantage that Scotland and Wales gain in public expenditure vary and are highly contested, but it does seem that Scotland gains up to 20 percent and Wales perhaps 10 percent as measured by identifiable expenditures (Midwinter, Keating and James 1991).

These raw figures, however, must be heavily qualified by the impact of expenditures which are not regionally identified but which benefit the south of England, such as research and defence spending, and by tax expenditures such as mortgage-interest relief (which has now been phased out). On the income side, the equation is very sensitive to the treatment of North Sea oil revenues. In 1997, the SNP managed to extract a parliamentary answer from the Treasury showing that Scotland had a notional net budgetary surplus of £26.7 billion over the years 1978-79 to 1994-95; but this in turn was based entirely on two years of booming oil revenues, with net tax flows in the rest of the period going the other way. In the late 1970s, in preparation for the devolution proposals of the time, the Treasury conducted a Needs Assessment Study, purporting to show that Scotland and Wales gained more than their relative need would indicate, but the study's methodology has been widely questioned. David Heald and his colleagues, who have made the most exhaustive studies of the issue, judge that "Our best guess is that, on devolved services ... a needs assessment exercise might show that Scotland's expenditure relative is higher than its needs relative, necessitating a downwards adjustment through time' (Heald, Geaughan and Robb 1998).

The devolution legislation simply decrees that the secretary of state will transfer funds to the new assemblies.[12] In practice, the government intends to use the Barnett formula to determine the amounts. Because this does nothing more than institutionalize a historic accretion of spending patterns, it has come in for a great deal of criticism. There has been a strong reaction from English MPs, and it is likely that the regular voting of the Scottish and Welsh transfers will be an occasion for continued attacks on alleged Scottish and Welsh advantages. Northern Ireland expenditure has not so far been an issue in the UK Parliament, given the delicate security situation and the small absolute sums involved. The power of the Scottish Parliament to alter income tax by up to 3p in the pound might provide something of a safety valve, giving a Scottish government a small room for manoeuvre but in practice such a change could only be upwards, because reducing taxation in Scotland while continuing to transfer resources from Westminster would cause irresistible pressure among English MPs to revise the settlement. The Northern Ireland Assembly does not have significant taxation powers, but has inherited property taxes formerly levied by local governments and this may become a significant issue, given its limited room for fiscal manoeuvre.

## REMAINING ISSUES

Constitutional change usually comes to the UK piecemeal, as a result of short-term political pressures and without any overall design. Scottish and Welsh devolution has been better prepared than most, having been debated and analyzed almost continuously for the last 30 years.[13] There is, however, still no overall plan for the UK as a whole or even, given the very different circumstances of Northern Ireland, for mainland Britain. The proposed arrangement is highly asymmetrical. Opponents have focused on this feature, reviving the old West Lothian Question, posed in the 1970s by anti-devolution Scottish Labour MP Tam Dalyell, who asked why, as a Scottish MP, he should be able to vote on matters affecting English towns but not on those affecting his own constituency. The same question had been raised repeatedly in relation to the Irish Home Rule bills of 1886, 1892, and 1912. The new settlement addresses one part of this by requiring the boundary commission to reduce the number of Scottish MPs, which hitherto has been higher than the population would warrant but while this reduces the magnitude of the problem, it does not address the principle.[14] Yet, short of federalizing the whole country, for which there is no significant support in England, the question has no answer.

It is unlikely that this will be the last word on constitutional change in the UK. Far too much is already changing to allow the line to be held here. European integration has called into question the myth of parliamentary sovereignty. The Scottish Parliament, in a European context, will not content itself with the role of subordinate government. This is not to say, as some used to argue, that devolution will inevitably lead to independence; but Scotland will join those stateless nations and strong regions looking for a special place in the European Union. The narrow result in the referendum has dispirited those wanting a stronger Welsh assembly, but once the body is up and running, it may become the focus of a more coherent Welsh identity and for demands for more powers. Centralizing elements in the Labour Party have resisted regional government for England, but there are pressures, especially in the northeast, which are likely to magnify once a Scottish Parliament is in operation. The Northern Ireland settlement of 1998 introduces another asymmetrical element into the UK constitution and is explicitly framed as a process rather than a final settlement, allowing movement toward a united Ireland or, possibly, new forms of joint sovereignty. Londoners have voted, albeit on a very low turnout, to have a directly elected mayor. In Cornwall, a peripheral region with a distinct culture, there are regionalist stirrings.

Many have criticized the UK constitutional reforms as incoherent, asymmetrical, and failing to follow an overall plan. Yet, for all the anomalies they produce, this feature might be of most interest for outside observers interested in the conditions for peace and stability. The United Kingdom has not one constitutional problem but several, concerning Ireland, Scotland, Wales, England, and the European Union. Rather than look for a single formula, a majority of the political class has now settled for complexity. This should not be seen as the product of some primordial British genius for consensus and pragmatism, or an aversion to doctrine. The refusal to grant Ireland home rule brought the country to the brink of civil war in 1912-14 and led to a secession. Persistent demands from Scotland were stonewalled for generations. In the 1980s and 1990s, the Conservatives were prepared to risk electoral extinction rather than concede the case for Scottish devolution. Pressure for home rule has certainly increased in the 1990s, but the response is to be explained by a weakening of old dogmas, a loss of faith in the old forms of British nationalism and the centralized state. In the debates of the 1980s and 1990s there were many echoes of debates a hundred years before and the new settlement might be seen as a belated triumph of the old Gladstonian coalition over the dogmatic unitarists. Yet this is no mere short-term political victory, as the new constitutional settlement has now been embraced by the Conservative Party, although the latter have not yet come to terms with Europe. The loss of faith in the old nation-state form is not unique to the UK, and it may be that the experiments here might be of interest to other societies looking for institutional mechanisms for managing conflicts.

NOTES

1. From 1793 Catholics were allowed to vote for the Irish Parliament but remained ineligible for election.
2. The effects of the union on the economy of southern Ireland were more negative. In the northeast, it stimulated the industrial revolution and the shipbuilding and heavy engineering industries.
3. Some of them saw a dark meaning in the fact that the EEC was founded by the Treaty of Rome.
4. Home Rule, which has officially been Labour Policy for its entire history except for the period 1958-74, was a dead letter after the early 1920s, as the party focused on gaining power at Westminster.
5. This title is chosen to distinguish him/her from the prime minister of the UK, although the effect will be lost on foreigners (for whom it was presumably intended) since in other European languages the terms are the same.
6. The Convention had agreed on limiting the Parliament to specified powers in order to make its scheme acceptable to the Labour Party!
7. In the UK, this includes welfare, unemployment benefits, family support, and pensions.
8. Secondary legislation, or statutory instruments, are delegated powers given by Parliament to the executive, allowing ministers to change the details of law or the timing of its introduction.
9. In Scotland and Northern Ireland, private banks issue their own currency notes, so that this is not a state monopoly as it is in England.
10. Extraterrestrial readers may take comfort from the fact that both the Scottish Parliament and the Northern Ireland Assembly are explicitly excluded from intervening in outer space.
11. While the prospects of the Conservatives winning in Scotland or Wales are remote, a Liberal Democrat-Nationalist coalition is not out of the question.
12. A provision linking Northern Ireland revenues to the product of taxes there appears to have disappeared from the original draft of the bill. This would have made little difference, as there was also provision for a transfer at the discretion of Westminster.
13. It was in 1969 that Harold Wilson's Labour government set up the Royal Commission on the Constitution, later known as the Kilbrandon Commission, whose 1973 report recommended Scottish and Welsh assemblies.
14. The overrepresentation of Scotland and Wales in Parliament is an historic accident, but since the Second World War has been seen as an element in the territorial management package. Northern Ireland was underrepresented until the late 1970s, ostensibly because it had its own Parliament until 1972; in practice the British parties wanted to exclude Northern Irish issues from the House of Commons. There has been no suggestion that the Northern Ireland MPs should be reduced after the new Northern Ireland Assembly is established. For a discussion of Scottish and Welsh representation at Westminster, see McLean (1995) and Rossiter, Johnston and Pattie (1997).

REFERENCES

Birrell, D. and A. Murie. 1980. *Policy and Government in Northern Ireland: Lessons of Devolution.* London: Gill and Macmillan.

Blondel, J. 1974. *Voters, Parties and Leaders.* Harmondsworth: Penguin.

Dahrendorf, R. 1995. "Preserving Prosperity," *New Statesman and Society*, 8 (15 December):36-41.

Dicey, A.V. 1885. *Law of the Constitution.* London: Macmilllan.

Finer, S. 1970. *Comparative Government.* Harmondsworth: Penguin.

Harvie, C. 1994. *Scotland and Nationalism: Scottish Society and Politics, 1707-1994.* London: Routledge.

Heald, D. 1992. *Formula-Based Territorial Public Expenditure in the United Kingdom.* Aberdeen Papers in Accountancy, Finance and Management, W7. Aberdeen: University of Aberdeen.

Heald, D., N. Geaughan and C. Robb. 1998. "Financial Arrangements for UK Devolution," in *Remaking the Union: Devolution and UK Politics in the 1990s*, ed. H. Elcock and M. Keating. London: Frank Cass.

Jones, B. and M. Keating. 1985. *Labour and the British State.* Oxford: Oxford University Press.

Keating, M. 1975. "The Role of the Scottish MP." PhD thesis. Glasgow: Glasgow College of Technology and London: CNAA.

_____ 1988. *State and Regional Nationalism: Territorial Politics and the European State.* London: Harvester-Wheatsheaf.

_____ 1998. *The New Regionalism in Western Europe: Territorial Restructuring and Political Change.* Aldershot: Edward Elgar.

Keating, M. and B. Jones. 1995. "Nations, Regions and Europe: The UK Experience," in *The European Union and the Regions*, ed. B. Jones and M. Keating. Oxford: Clarendon.

Kellas, J. 1984. *The Scottish Political System.* 3d ed. Cambridge: Cambridge University Press.

Lee, C.H. 1995. *Scotland and the United Kingdom: The Economy and the Union in the Twentieth Century.* Manchester: Manchester University Press.

McLean, I. 1995. "Are Scotland and Wales Over-Represented in the House of Commons?" *The Political Quarterly*, 66(4):250-68.

Midwinter A., M. Keating and J. Mitchell. 1991. *Politics and Public Policy in Scotland.* London: Macmillan.

Mitchell, J. 1996. *Strategies for Self-Government: The Campaigns for a Scottish Parliament.* Edinburgh: Polygon.

O'Leary, B. 1999. "The 1998 British-Irish Agreement: Power-Sharing Plus," *Scottish Affairs*, 26(Winter):14-35.

Paterson, L. 1994. *The Autonomy of Modern Scotland.* Edinburgh: Edinburgh University Press.

Rokkan, S. and D. Urwin. 1983. *Economy, Territory, Identity: Politics of West European Peripheries.* London: Sage.

Rossiter D., R. Johnston and C. Pattie. 1997. "The Evolution and Partisan Impact of Scottish and Welsh Over-Representation in the Redrawing of British Parliamentary Constituencies," *Regional and Federal Studies*, 7(3):49-65.

# 4

# Recent Trends in Federalism and Intergovernmental Relations in Canada: Lessons for the UK?

*Richard Simeon*

## INTRODUCTION

Canadians marvel at the enormous pace and scope of recent constitutional innovation in Britain. To us, the speed with which constitutional ideas in Britain have moved from proposal to enactment and implementation is extraordinary. Britain passed 11 bills of a constitutional nature in 1997 and 1998 alone. In Canada, a succession of rounds of "mega-constitutional" debate, to use Peter Russell's term, from the 1960s to the present has produced only one, albeit hugely important, set of major constitutional changes. That was the patriation of the constitution, adoption of an amending formula, and enactment of the Charter of Rights and Freedoms in 1982. In 1987, federal and provincial governments unanimously agreed on the Meech Lake Accords, designed to provide modest recognition of Quebec's distinct status within Confederation, but it was defeated in 1990 by a wave of hostile popular mobilization in English Canada. Another attempt, this time broadening the agenda in an attempt to build support across different groups in Canadian society, resulted in the Charlottetown Accord in 1992. But once again, the unanimous agreement among governments was rejected, this time in a national referendum.

A version of this chapter appeared in *Round Table*, April 2000, No. 354. It appears here by permission.

The result of all these disappointments has produced in Canada a pronounced constitutional fatigue. Given the deep conflicts between competing visions of the Canadian federation, and the high hurdle to constitutional change posed by the amending formula, Canadians have come to believe that successful constitutional change is impossible in the foreseeable future. Hence, attention in the last few years has turned to non-constitutional mechanisms to renew the federation. So it was no surprise that when a senior British official came to Ottawa to outline Britain's plans to Canadian officials, he was greeted with disbelief, and a fervent cry: "Don't try it; you must be mad."

Indeed, one of the puzzles we might wish to discuss is what explains this difference between the impasse in Canada and such rapid progress in the UK. Institutional factors are no doubt important: the British changes have been made through the normal parliamentary process, driven by a powerful government; in Canada constitutional debate occurs largely in intergovernmental forums and requires the agreement of Ottawa and either seven or ten provinces to be adopted. Second, the British debate has proceeded on an ad hoc, issue-by-issue basis in several different forums, whereas in Canada, recent attempts at constitutional change have tended to take on the character of "package deals," including a wide variety of elements, each of which alienated at least some part of the population. But the big puzzle that remains is why there has, at least so far, been so little popular mobilization around constitutional issues in the UK. A constitutional revolution seems to be passing largely unnoticed, in stark contrast to the mobilization in Canada on issues such as citizen rights and Quebec's status in the federation. However, the popular beast was slow to mobilize in Canada; could it soon begin to play a much greater role in the UK?

I will focus on two distinct, though closely related issues. The first is the evolution of the debate about the status of Quebec in the Canadian federation. This is where the parallels between Quebec and the devolution of authority to Scotland and Wales are most striking. How sustainable are asymmetrical models of federalism? Is devolution, or in Canada special status for Quebec, a stable solution or the start of a slippery slope toward eventual independence? If it were to come to secession in either country, what rules should govern such a step? Second, while these debates about the very existence of the country continue in Canada, the day to day functioning of the Canadian federation has continued to evolve. There is a renewed focus on "collaborative federalism," seeing governance in Canada as partnership between two equal levels of government. Canadians appear to be relieved that governments are emphasizing cooperation over confrontation, but there remain deep concerns about the democratic and policy deficits that accompany the collaborative model.

Let me look first at the Quebec-Canada relationship.

## DEBATING THE FUTURE OF QUEBEC IN CANADA

The status of Quebec in Canada is of course the single most critical political question for Canada: only this division has the potential for ending the Canadian experiment. Since the 1960s, the debate within Quebec has been between options that call for a "renewed federalism" that devolves further powers to Quebec and recognizes the distinct status of its government as the primary political expression of the Quebec nation, and those that call for independence, with varying degrees of association with the remaining country. Federalist options range from minor adjustments to the status quo to more radical proposals for increased powers that fall just short of independence, to proposals for a general decentralization of power to all provinces. The sovereignist options range from recognition of sovereignty combined with a close economic and political "partnership" to outright independence with a future relationship no more and no less close than that between any two independent countries. Over many years, the bulk of Quebec public opinion has been clustered around the two options of "renewed federalism" and "sovereignty-association" or sovereignty partnership. Support for outright independence and status quo federalism are distinctly minority positions. Over time, Quebec public opinion has been quite evenly divided between the sovereignist and federalist options, with support for sovereignty peaking at times, such as after the rejection of the Meech Lake Accord, when Quebec is perceived to have been humiliated, rejected, or excluded by the rest of the country. Quebec elections have alternated between the Quebec Liberals, advocating renewed federalism, and the Parti Québécois (PQ), advocating sovereignty-association. One of the most worrying current differences of interpretation in the present context is that Quebecers tend to see the line between special status and sovereignty-association as merely steps along a continuum, and many move easily between these two. But for most Anglo-Canadians sovereignty is the Rubicon, with all the federalist options on one side and all the sovereignist variants on the other.

How has the rest of Canada responded? During the 1960s considerable progress was made toward a non-constitutional, *de facto* special status, as in the adoption of separate, but closely coordinated Canada and Quebec pension plans. But a primary goal of Pierre Trudeau when he became prime minister was to halt the growth of Quebec nationalism, and to arrest this trend toward what he saw as special status. The constitutional changes enacted in 1982 reflected his views and made no concession to Quebec as a distinct society. Trudeau asserted two principles in opposition to Quebec nationalism. First was the "equality of the provinces" rejecting asymmetrical federalism. Second was the "equality of citizens" reflected in the new Charter of Rights and Freedoms, a national project to be enforced by a national institution, the Supreme Court. Ironically, these ideas developed far more resonance among Canadians outside Quebec than they did within the province. They were central to the defeats of the Meech Lake and Charlottetown Accords, in 1990 and 1992. English-Canadian opinion became increasingly hostile not only to the idea of sovereignty, but also to the idea of distinct society for Quebec within Canada.

This is the background to the Quebec referendum of October 1995, where as we all know, the sovereignists came within less than 1 percent of winning. The narrow federalist victory sharply intensified the debate. Suddenly Canadians realized how close they might be to a breakup. There was sharp criticism of the federal government for lacking an effective strategy to counter secession and for lacking a strategy to deal with a positive referendum outcome. Anti-Quebec opinion in the rest of the country hardened. Divisions within Quebec, especially in the bilingual city of Montreal intensified, as many English-speaking residents began to advocate "partition," asserting that if Quebec had the right to leave Canada, federalist regions had the right to leave Quebec.

The result was a rethinking that came to be known as Plans A, B, and C. Plan A was designed to explore ways to ensure Quebecers would wish to remain in the federation. Given the demonstrated impossibility of achieving constitutional agreement and the hostility to special status, these options were limited. They focused primarily on finding ways to demonstrate to Quebecers, and other Canadians, that the federation could work effectively. Plan B was the stick. It was designed to demonstrate to Quebecers that secession was no easy matter to achieve, that it could only be accomplished with great difficulty and at great cost. It was designed to demonstrate that the "soft sovereignists" were wrong to believe that after secession nothing would really have changed. They could not expect a new partnership — the PQ could propose it, but it would be up to the rest of Canada to agree. Central to Plan B was the belief that it was now essential to clarify the rules that would govern any Quebec secession. Remarkably these questions had been virtually ignored before both the 1980 and 1995 referenda; now that secession seemed to be a distinct possibility, they came to the fore. The federal government took the lead. Its most important step was the referral of three questions to the Supreme Court of Canada: Did Quebec have the right to secede under existing Canadian law? Under international law? And if the two conflicted which should prevail?

The Court decided in the summer of 1998. It asserted that neither Canadian nor international law allow Quebec to secede unilaterally. Secession could only be achieved through a process consistent with the Canadian constitution. Since nothing in the written constitution spoke directly to the point, the court asserted a number of broad principles that underpin the constitution, and that should govern in any secession debate: constitutionalism and the rule of law, federalism, democracy, and respect for minorities. The federalist victory, however, was tempered by the Court's conclusion that if Quebec were to vote for secession by a clear majority, on a clear question, then the rest of Canada would have a constitutional obligation to negotiate with Quebec. Thus both extreme positions — that Quebec could leave unilaterally, according to rules it set for itself, and that under no circumstances would the rest of Canada agree to secession — were ruled out. Both sides could therefore claim some comfort.

But the decision left a host of questions unanswered. What was a clear majority? Fifty percent plus one, as advocated by the PQ, or some super-majority of more than 50 percent? And if a super-majority, how high should the bar be set? What was a clear question? Federalists assert that "soft" questions linking sovereignty to future partnership and association are dishonest. They offer Quebecers something that Quebec alone cannot deliver, and they lure Quebecers into believing secession would be painless. They want a question that asks for a simple "yes" or "no" to independence. The PQ reply is that sovereignty-partnership is the goal, not outright independence, so the question should reflect that. Both sides realize referendum outcomes could be greatly dependent on the wording of the question.

Many other questions would need to be answered. Who would determine the rules governing the conduct of the campaign, especially those governing the participation of those from outside Quebec? If the "yes" were to win, then how is the obligation to negotiate to be met? Who would be at the negotiating table? Would provinces or Aboriginal peoples have a vote? What would be negotiated, some form of renewed federalism, or would negotiations be limited to the terms of secession? What decision rules would apply? If the current amending formula was unworkable, what other formula could be invented?

The PQ has consistently asserted that the decisions are for Quebecers alone to make, and that the National Assembly must set the rules. The Government of Canada asserts that because the interests and well-being of all Canadians will be affected by the decision it has the right, indeed the obligation, to set the rules. This impasse is highly dangerous, since the potential for social and economic upheaval would be much greater if the country faced another referendum in which the rules, and hence the results, would be contested. Yet it is impossible politically for either side to be seen to be negotiating on these issues.

Hence the federal government is now trying to decide whether or not to introduce its own legislation setting out the terms of the referendum. Advocates of this strategy suggest it is a federal responsibility to clarify the rules. Doubters argue that such an assertion of federal power, seen as challenging Quebecers' right to self-determination, might just help provide the PQ with the "winning conditions" for a successful referendum. The question has divided the federal Cabinet, as well as split the federal and Quebec Liberal parties.

In the meantime a recent survey shows that a majority of Quebecers have accepted much of the federal argument.

- Support for sovereignty-partnership has declined from the almost 50 percent of 1995 to 38 percent today.

- Majorities agree with the Supreme Court on the need for a clear question and a clear majority (72 percent) on the idea that a unilateral declaration of independence (UDI) would be illegal (55 percent); on the need for Aboriginal peoples to be included in the negotiations (61 percent); and on the obligation of the rest of Canada to negotiate (74 percent).

- Ninety-three percent agreed that it was reasonable to demand a clear question and 61 percent agreed that the 1995 question was not clear.

- Majorities also felt that the question should be set jointly, including the opposition parties in Quebec, the Government of Canada and the rest of Canada.

- Most Quebecers (60 percent) say that 50 percent plus one is not a sufficient majority; while 70 percent thought 60 percent would be sufficient.

- Most respondents believe that Quebec would keep its current borders, but three-quarters believe that it would be "reasonable" for northern Aboriginal communities to remain in Canada, and almost half believe that other areas of the province where a majority voted "no" could remain in Canada.

- Strong majorities call for negotiation rather than UDI after a referendum victory.

- While two-thirds agree that it would be difficult to negotiate a new partnership, majorities agreed that it would be possible to negotiate agreements on an economic association, with freedom of movement; minority rights, and on other areas (including half who believe that Quebecers could retain a common Canadian citizenship and passport).

These and similar data showing that Quebecers have little stomach for yet another referendum suggest that no new referendum is imminent. The PQ has begun to discuss alternatives to a one-shot, all or nothing referendum. There is some possibility that the trend is toward diminished support for sovereignty, but such predictions have been made before, only to see support rise after some perceived shock.

Several comparative questions arise from this story. First, one of the striking elements in Canada is the increased hostility to asymmetry, at least in a symbolic or constitutional sense. "Equality of the provinces" has trumped "special status." Fewer and fewer Canadians appear prepared to see Canada as a multinational country. Yet in Britain, the once exemplary unitary state, there seems to be widespread acceptance of its multinational character, and little expressed resistance to representing this fact in the form of devolved institutions. This is a puzzle we might address.

Among the possible reasons we might note:

- the high degree of regional identity in a number of other provinces, leading to the view that "we are distinct too." Strong regional identity in Quebec has been one factor stimulating the growth of other provincial identities. Might Scotland and Wales have a similar effect on England proper?

- the existence of provincial governments that institutionalize this regionalism. Whatever the potential for regionalism in the rest of Britain, it has not yet been given institutional form.

- simultaneously the growth, via the Charter, of a more universalistic and abstract sense of citizen equality that is hostile to institutionalizing differences, despite the language and other group rights found in the Charter. One manifestation was the intense hostility to some Quebec language laws designed to enhance the status of the French language, which were seen to infringe on freedom of expression and the rights of the English-speaking minority.

- the growth in the salience of identities and interests other than regional, that render preoccupation with the Quebec-Canada less relevant and pressing.

- increasing awareness of the divisions within Quebec itself, not only between francophones and anglophones, but also between the majority and Aboriginal groups.

The result is that even a relatively minor degree of special status is seen to offend the now dominant conceptions of equality and fairness in English Canada.

The question is whether such resentments against Scotland and Wales will arise in the UK. This could take two forms: resistance to any accretion of powers in Scotland or Wales or emulation of Scotland and Wales in the English regions. Just as questions about the continued role of Quebec MPs in Ottawa with respect to powers devolved in Quebec is an issue in proposals for special status in Canada, one wonders if the "West Lothian" question might be one of the flash points for popular mobilization in Britain.

The second parallel between Scotland and Quebec relates to the conditions under which federalism, or devolution, constitute a stable, enduring arrangement, or whether, instead, they are way stations toward some other outcome. There is a fascinating similarity in the Canadian and UK debates here. In Canada, a key element in Pierre Trudeau's opposition to special status for Quebec was his belief that it would create a slippery slope. Quebec would ask for greater and greater powers, while Quebecers' links to the national government were progressively being cut. The only logical stopping place, he argued, was secession. Supporters of the Meech Lake Accord made precisely the opposite prediction: if some measure of distinct status was *not* accorded to Quebec, then Quebecers would opt for secession sooner rather than later. These, then, were two diametrically opposed predictions about the consequences of constitutional engineering.

Precisely the same debate has taken place in the UK. Supporters of devolution argue that only by recognizing the national aspirations of the Scots and the Welsh can the push toward independence be arrested; devolution is thus essential to the preservation of the British Union. Opponents have argued the opposite: that endowing Scotland with its own institutions sets up a dynamic that will give secessionists a stronger platform from which they can argue for greater powers and set the stage for eventual secession. Who is correct: the government which asserts that devolution "will not only safeguard but also enhance the union," or Tam Dalyell, when he says that devolution is a "motorway without exit to an independent state"? The interesting thing for Canada is that I do not think we yet know which prediction is correct. Nor does Britain.

The third comparative question asks about the rules of the game for secession. How should such fundamental questions be decided? Like Quebec, Scotland has no legal authority to alter the British constitution, or, indeed its own. Yet the Scottish National Party has promised a referendum on independence, and the government has acknowledged that politically it could not be ignored. Moreover, the Northern Ireland agreement explicitly states that its rights of self-determination can be exercised by a majority of the people, with no suggestion of the need for a super-majority. Why should this logic not apply also to Wales and Scotland?

Surely, however, if the possibility of an actual vote for secession in Scotland ever got as close as it got in Canada, in 1995, the issues now being debated in Canada would become prominent in the UK? These would not only include the rules to govern the process, but also the whole range of more practical questions that arise when deeply intertwined societies contemplate breakup — national debts, the division of assets, future economic relationships, citizenship, and so on.

## NEW PATTERNS OF INTERGOVERNMENTAL RELATIONS

Intergovernmental relations have long been at the heart of the Canadian policy-making process; the creation of new regional authorities in Scotland, Wales, and Northern Ireland is about to give them greater prominence in the UK as well. Perhaps, then, the Canadian experience can provide some models and some cautionary tales. As Richard Cornes points out, intergovernmental relations will be a "significant new aspect" of the study of governance in the UK. This is because the devolution of powers in the UK emphasizes shared rather than divided competences. Hence the need to develop new machinery to handle intergovernmental relations.

Canada and the UK, however, have very different starting points. In Canada, provinces exercise a high degree of jurisdictional and fiscal autonomy. Ten provinces (and three territories) are equal partners with the central government. But there are fundamental institutional similarities as well. Notably both are Westminster-type parliamentary systems. Hence their relationships are likely to take the form known in Canada as executive federalism: bargaining and negotiations among the senior executives of the two orders of government.

Many adjectives have been attached to the Canadian pattern of intergovernmental relations — cooperative federalism, competitive federalism, and so on. The term that David Cameron and I have used to describe the current relationship is "collaborative federalism." By this we mean an intergovernmental process through which national policies are achieved not by the federal government acting alone, nor by its coercing provincial action through its spending power, but rather by some or all the 11 governments and territories acting collectively.

It can take two forms. First is collaboration among federal, provincial, and territorial governments, seeking an appropriate balance among their roles and responsibilities. It is based on the premise that since both levels possess strong jurisdictional tools, effective governance depends on coordination among them. Second is collaboration among the provincial and territorial governments, with Ottawa on the sidelines. This introduces a more confederal dimension in that it is based on the view that since the constitution allocates major responsibilities for fields such as health, education, and welfare to the provinces, then "national" policies and standards are for them, not Ottawa, to decide. In some important areas, collaborative federalism is seen to be an alternative to constitutional change: governments can achieve by informal agreement what they cannot achieve in the constitutional forum.

The prototype for this approach was the 1994 federal-provincial Agreement on Internal Trade designed to reduce domestic barriers to the mobility of goods, services, capital, and people within Canada. Early in 2000, Ottawa and all the provinces but Quebec signed the Framework to Improve the Social Union for Canadians, the result of a provincial initiative designed to balance common national standards for social policy against the variations that federalism encourages. Developed in the aftermath of drastic cuts in federal transfers to the provinces, the agreement also sought to clarify how the federal spending power is to be exercised. The final text of the agreement was considerably less provincialist than earlier drafts. It explicitly endorsed the federal spending power, while ensuring due notice provisions and prior provincial consent for new programs or changes in existing ones. Governments also committed themselves to public accountability and transparency and to procedures for dispute avoidance and resolution.

The British have already developed a memorandum of understanding or concordats with similar features. They cover agreement on a Joint Ministerial Committee, and Concordats on Co-ordination of EU policy issues, on financial assistance to industry, on international relations, and on statistics. Here too, it is not intended that they be justiciable, but it has been suggested that they may indeed create "legitimate expectations" that might be enforced by the courts. (Research paper 99/84, Parliament and Constitution Centre, House of Commons Library, 21-22.)

Other examples of the collaborative approach are the National Child Benefit, which clarified federal and provincial responsibilities relating to child poverty (1998), and the Canada-Wide Accord on Environmental Harmonization (1996), negotiated by the Canadian Council of Ministers of the Environment and aimed at ensuring that roles and responsibilities will be undertaken by the order of government best situated to effectively discharge them. It also embraced a large measure of provincial enforcement of federal environmental laws.

Accompanying these sorts of initiatives is a significantly greater institutionalization of intergovernmental processes. First Ministers' Conferences, bringing together the prime minister and the premiers remain at the apex of the system, but have in fact occurred much less frequently under the current Chrétien government than under that of his predecessor. By contrast, the Annual Premiers' Conference (APC), chaired by premiers on a rotating basis, has become a major event on the intergovernmental calendar. Frequently the APC delegates tasks to the wide variety of Councils of Ministers that have emerged to cover most policy fields. The increasing use of intergovernmental accords also indicates greater institutionalization.

However, it is important to realize that the intergovernmental machinery remains largely informal and ad hoc. Apart from logistical arrangements, they have little bureaucratic support. There are no formal voting procedures. Agreements are not formally binding or legally enforceable. The frequency and character of intergovernmental meetings is strongly dependent on the will of the prime minister and the premiers. And of course it has no legislative, or even statutory, basis. It thus differs greatly from the highly institutionalized interlocking or shared federalism of Germany.

A number of observations can be made about this process:

- Unlike earlier postwar cooperative federalism, it stresses the equality of Ottawa and the provinces. Many councils and meetings are co-chaired.

- Agreements leave constitutional powers intact; the goal is to exercise assigned powers in a coordinated manner.

- Relationships can take different forms in different policy areas, including voluntary provincially determined standards, enforced simply by consensus, voluntary federally established standards, allowing for provincial variations; and jointly negotiated standards. Only in a few areas, notably the enforcement of national health-care standards through the *Canada Health Act*, are the rules set unilaterally by Ottawa.

- Many of the new relationships are influenced by ideas associated with the New Public Management. There is much emphasis on the need to minimize duplication and overlapping to achieve greater efficiency and cost saving. Agreements typically emphasize the need to share "best practices," to develop performance indicators, and to monitor results.

- All agreements pay at least lip service to the need for greater transparency and accountability. An increasing number acknowledge the need to "engage stakeholders," and to "build linkages to other structures in the broad social and economic environment."

- Frequently a framework agreement is negotiated with all provinces, to be followed by individually negotiated bilateral agreements.

- Many of these initiatives were designed to demonstrate to Quebecers, and indeed to all Canadians, that federalism works. However, Quebec's participation has been highly variable. It believes that intergovernmentally established national standards can be as much a threat to its autonomy as unilateral federal initiatives.

- Other governments also approach the process with different interests. Stronger provinces, notably Ontario and Alberta, seek to wrestle the initiative from Ottawa, limit its ability to intrude into areas of shared jurisdiction, and assert their autonomy. The rapidly declining proportion of their revenues derived from federal transfers greatly weakens the federal bargaining position.

- For the smaller, poorer provinces, autonomy is less important than ensuring the continued flow of federal dollars.

- Ottawa is anxious to retain its influence and visibility and, in particular, attempts to ensure its direct links to citizens by providing programs that benefit them individually rather than indirectly, through the provinces. A good example is the recently established Millennium Scholarship Fund, flowing money to postsecondary education through direct grants to students.

- While this process involves a higher degree of intergovernmental harmony than at many earlier periods, it is by no means conflict free. Governments continue to disagree on the basis of regional interests (Prairie conflict with Ottawa over aid to farmers is a recent example); over ideology (as in numerous battles between the national Liberals and Conservative regimes in Ontario and Alberta). Fiscal arrangements remain sources of disagreement, as provinces continue to absorb the impact of federal budget cuts in the mid-1990s and now pressure Ottawa for a greater share of growing federal surpluses. The federalism of growth can be as conflictual as the federalism of restraint. More generally, it is an inherent feature of the system that governments will compete to win credit for positive developments and avoid, or transfer, blame for negative ones.

We can expect some of the same intergovernmental dynamics to develop in Britain.

A few years ago, it was widely believed that these and other trends in Canadian federalism were pushing the country toward a more regionalized, decentralized, and confederal pattern. In the work of writers like Tom Courchene (1995), globalization and localization went hand in hand. The changes in global and North American trading patterns were gradually undermining the importance of economic linkages across Canada, as each region integrated differently into the wider environment. This would make national policy harder and harder to develop and would, over time, undermine common identities and willingness to redistribute. Ottawa was losing critical economic powers both upward to international institutions, and downward to provinces. Moreover, debts and deficits had weakened Ottawa's ability to take new initiatives. The federal share of provincial spending in areas such as health and welfare was rapidly declining and provinces increasingly argued that if Ottawa was no longer paying the piper what right did it have to call the tune. Hence, Courchene and others like Andre Bruelle (1995) argued that increasingly provinces would go their own way. If the Canadian economic and social union was to be sustained, it would come about through collaboration among the provinces. In addition, the continuing need to demonstrate flexibility toward Quebec, while maintaining provincial equality would tip the balance toward continued decentralization.

Recent evidence suggests that this picture may have been exaggerated. In a detailed analysis of Canadian identities, Frank Graves and his colleagues (1999) conclude that the recent crisis of federalism linked to fiscal and unity woes has had the ironic impact of strengthening national attachments while weakening provincial attachments, though both remain strong and are, outside Quebec, mutually reinforcing. At the economic level, despite major changes in trading patterns, John Helliwell finds that the intensity of economic linkages within Canada remains much greater than the linkages between Canadian provinces and the outside world (1999). Now that the federal government has eliminated the deficit, and looks forward to substantial surpluses in future years, its sense of impotence has faded. Once again it can exercise the spending power. While the last budget did restore some of the transfer payments to the provinces, and provinces continue to call for more, the federal government is likely to give the highest priority to spending programs that enhance its visibility and its direct contact with Canadians. All this suggests that we should be exceedingly cautious about predicting long-term trends in either direction.

What relevance might this description have for thinking about intergovernmental relations in the UK? First, it may help us identify some of the factors that are likely to shape the character of intergovernmental relations, whether in a conflictual or a cooperative direction. Second, it may help identify some of what Ron Watts calls the "pathologies of federalism," that designers of intergovernmental mechanisms in the UK might seek to avoid (1999).

The Canadian experience suggests a number of observations about some of the factors that shape intergovernmental relationships, whether in Canada or the UK. At the most general level are trends toward global or regional integration. The European Union, and the possibility of a direct Scottish relationship with it, is a far greater and more direct influence on Britain than the North American Free Trade Agreement is for Canada, since NAFTA lacks the broad institutional and policy scope of the EU.

A second set of factors is institutional. Whether or not the "slippery slope" prediction proves correct will depend not only on the steps toward regional autonomy, but also on the continued representation of Scotland and Wales within central institutions. "Building out" must be accompanied by "building in." This concern has shaped much of the Canadian debate about reforming the Senate and may become an issue in further reforms to the British House of Lords.

Third are trends in identities. As the Graves research shows, attitudes and identities can be remarkably independent either of policy trends or of broad trends in the political economy, at least in the short run (1999). Critical to the sustainability of either the British or Canadian models will be the maintenance of dual, or nested, identities, with the understanding among most citizens that national and regional identities are mutually compatible.

A fourth influence will be emerging policy agendas. The Canadian case shows that intergovernmental conflict and pressures for decentralization are low when the dominant policy agendas cut across regional differences, as in the postwar period of the construction of the welfare state. Conflict is high when the issues are regionally divisive, as in the Canadian "energy wars" of the 1970s.

Fifth is the evolution of the party system. Conflict is minimized when the governing party can maintain support across the country; failure to do so increases conflict and leads excluded regions to turn to their provincial governments to pursue their interests. Hence the critical question facing the Canadian party system is whether the regional fragmentation of party support continues to intensify. And lastly, there is the character and aspirations of the leadership that emerges at both levels in the two countries.

Finally, a few words on the "pathologies" of intergovernmental relations that the British might seek to avoid in the design of their intergovernmental relations. First is the "democratic deficit," a term we have imported from Europe. It focuses on the extent to which intergovernmental relations are dominated by senior executives, many of them intergovernmental strategists in central agencies; the inherent secrecy and closed door nature of most intergovernmental relations; the difficulties of maintaining accountability when responsibilities are shared and governments spend funds that they have not taken responsibility for raising, and so on. Such criticisms have long been addressed to Canadian intergovernmental relations and were a major factor in the citizen revolts against the Meech Lake and Charlottetown Accords. Declining deference to elites and demands for greater citizen participation sustain a powerful critique of the intergovernmental process.

In Canada, we need to clarify roles, responsibilities, and lines of accountability and increase transparency. Intergovernmental committees and councils need to find better ways to incorporate consultation with affected groups. And we need to find better ways to involve legislatures in monitoring and debating intergovernmental issues. Revitalizing legislatures is part of the British constitutional agenda, and it would be highly desirable to extend this to greater participation in intergovernmental relations — something that will not be easy in the Westminster model, as the Canadian experience demonstrates.

Indeed, legislatures were not involved in the development of the recent Concordats, and, according to a 1998 report of the Scottish Affairs Select Committee on multi-layer democracy, there is no provision for parliamentary oversight of them. Nor is there "any provision for an open forum at parliamentary level for the public discussion of matters of common concern" (United Kingdom. House of Commons 1998).

The second pathology has also been given a label that originated in Europe — the "joint decision trap." It suggests that there may be high costs associated with a collaborative model that places a high value on consensus. It can lead to high transaction and decision costs as decisions are worked out. It can lead to policy that represents a "lowest common denominator." The institutional interests of the governmental actors can dominate the process. The emphasis on agreement may undermine the very virtues of experiment and innovation that federalism is designed to achieve.

A number of the agreements I have described seek to address these concerns. But it remains the case that many groups in Canada, notably social policy and environmental activists, are deeply suspicious of the policies that emerge from the intergovernmental process.

Perhaps as the British design their intergovernmental process, starting with a clean slate, they may find more effective ways to manage the inevitable interdependencies that arise in systems of multi-level government. Multi-level government has been described as a process not an event. As grizzled veterans of the constitutional wars, Canadians will watch British developments with interest. Perhaps we may learn from your fresh approach to constitutional reform, just as you may anticipate pitfalls and possibilities by considering the Canadian experience.

## REFERENCES

Bruelle, A. 1995. *Le mal canadien.* Montreal: Fides.

Courchene, T.J. 1995. "Glocalization: The Regional/International Interface," *Canadian Journal of Regional Science*, 18(1):1-20.

Graves, F.L. with T. Dugas and P. Beauchamp. 1999. "Identity and National Attachments in Contemporary Canada," in *Canada: The State of the Federation 1998/99. How Canadians Connect*, ed. H. Lazar and T. McIntosh. Montreal and Kingston: McGill-Queen's University Press for the School of Policy Studies, Queen's University.

Helliwell, J.F. 1999. "Canada's National Economy: There's More to it than you Thought," in *Canada: The State of the Federation 1998/99*, ed. Lazar and McIntosh.

United Kingdom. House of Commons. 1998. Scottish Affairs Select Committee. "The Operation of Multi-Layer Democracy." Minutes of Evidence. 25 February. HC460.

Watts, R.L. 1999. *Comparing Federal Systems.* Kingston: Institute of Intergovernmental Relations, Queen's University. Ch. 11.

# 5

# Oxymorons: The Scottish Parliament, the European Union and International Relations?

*Trevor C. Salmon*

## IT OUGHT TO BE CLEAR BUT ....

The *Scotland Act* 1998 appears to answer the question of the role of the Scottish Parliament and Executive in foreign policy; foreign, international, European Union (EU) or external relations very clearly and directly. Schedule 5.7.- (1) entitled "Foreign affairs etc." says "International relations, including relations with territories outside the United Kingdom, the European Communities (and their institutions) and other international organisations, regulation of international trade, and international development assistance and co-operation are reserved matters."

Elsewhere matters identified by Schedule 5 as "reserved" include:

The defence of the realm

The naval, military or air forces of the Crown ...

Treason ...

Fiscal, economic and monetary policy, including the issue and circulation of money, taxes, and excise duties ... the exchange rate and the Bank of England

The currency ...

Money laundering ...

Immigration and nationality ... including asylum ... free movement of persons within the European Economic Area; issue of travel documents.

National security, interception of communications, official secrets and terrorism ...

Extradition.

Competition. Regulation of anti-competitive practices and agreements, abuse of dominant position; monopolies and mergers

Control of nuclear, biological and chemical weapons and other weapons of mass destruction.

Regulation of activities in outer space.

although

financial assistance to commercial activities for the purpose of promoting or sustaining economic development or employment

is *not* reserved.

Elsewhere in the Act it is made clear that the Parliament and Executive do have to comply with and fulfill the obligations of European Communities membership and the European Convention of Human Rights.

Thus, the role of the Scottish Parliament and Executive in international relations appears to be clear: it is nil. It is a reserved area, where all the "reserved matters" are carefully enumerated. This, however, is clearly an oxymoron, since it is already outmoded both empirically and theoretically. Given the nature of the contemporary political system, even the provisions of the *Scotland Act cannot* rule out the Scottish Parliament's involvement in international or foreign relations.

The question thus arises as to how much is different after the creation of the Scottish Parliament and Executive in 1999. Previously Scots had little direct influence on European Union and international relations issues, since it was Her Majesty's Government in London that held the power. Scottish Office input was diluted into an HMG *British* position, or disappeared into the corridors of Whitehall. On European Union matters, for example, the secretary of state for Scotland, although a member of the Committee on Defence and Overseas sub-committee on European questions, OD(E), was part of *British* policy making, and HMG did not always recognize that there were distinctive Scottish interests. This despite the problems over beef/BSE, the Common Agricultural Policy (CAP) in general, fishing, the duty on whisky and Edinburgh's fears of the European Central Bank/ Frankfurt challenge to its position as a financial centre. Although the Conservatives argued in the 1990s that Scotland possessed more influence as part of the powerful or large whole, not all were convinced.

Scottish interests in the European Union are substantial — just over 60 percent of Scotland's export trade is with EU member states, and that generates £12 billion and 70,000 jobs. In the first 20 years or so of membership and until the eve of devolution, Scotland received some £1,600 million in Regional and Structural

Fund aid, and a further £2,700 million from the European Investment Bank. Individual parts of Scotland also benefited: the west by £260 million and the east by £110 million in the last five years of the 1990s to help them overcome unemployment. In the same period, the Highlands and Islands received £240 million, as an Objective 1 area. Remarkably in the 1999 shake up of the Structural Funds in light of the putative enlargement of the EU, the Highlands and Islands were treated as one of the "Particular Situations 2000-2006," it being agreed that "In view of the particular structural problems resulting from the low population density matched with a high degree of poverty, the Highlands and Islands of Scotland will receive a special phasing-out programme totalling EUR 300m (£180 million)" (Bulletin of the European Union 3/2000).

While the EU has provided redistributed funds and an export single market, it is also true that nearly 40 percent of Scottish exports go to states outside the EU and are thus bound by the EU's Common Commercial Policy (CCP), and that produces some £7 billion plus and over 40,000 jobs.

Given this extra British dimension, for some years Scots have sought to bypass London and deal directly with Brussels and other centres of power, for example, with US cities for tourist traffic. But as Hooghe (1995) and others have suggested, such links can only complement HMG activity, although some (Bomberg 1994; Mitchell 1995; McAteer and Mitchell 1996) have argued that informal lobbying of the EU can be reasonably effective, although not always an unmitigated success. Scots have continued to believe that their interests did not receive adequate attention. Part of the endeavour to rectify this saw the creation of Scotland Europa in 1991, a privately funded presence to facilitate private and public sector links with Europe, but emphatically not an official governmental Scottish presence. Scotland Europa Ltd. represented, and informed through intelligence gathering, nearly 50 subscribing members: industry, councils, and universities. Scotland, like many other "sub-national actors" (SNAs) or "non-central governments" (NCGs) had some influence but no direct power. (For the latter term, see Hocking 1993.) Despite the expectations raised by devolution, the legal and constitutional settlement, as seen above, did not appear to change the situation significantly.

## THE CONTEXT OF WAR

It is sublimely ironic that as Iain Macwhirter wrote in April 1999

> WELL, what no-one expected was a khaki election. The campaign to elect Scotland's first parliament in 300 years has inevitably been eclipsed by the conflict over Kosovo — and not just because of Alex Salmond's condemnation of Nato airstrikes. War — even undeclared war — changes everything. The common currency of party political debate becomes devalued when matters of life and death are at stake (*Sunday Herald*, 11 April 1999).

While the force of outside events could not be excluded from the campaign, they doubly intruded given that Alex Salmond, the leader of the Scottish National Party, chose to condemn British and NATO policy at the outset of the election campaign, when he was given the right to reply to a prime ministerial broadcast. Salmond accused Prime Minister Blair and NATO of pursuing a "misguided" policy of "dubious legality and unpardonable folly." He went on to apparently compare NATO bombing to the Nazi blitz on London and Clydebank during the Second World War. (*The Scotsman*, 30 March 1999).

Whatever the specific merits of the argument, the broadcast had important consequences. It led to at least the first half of the election campaign focusing on his words and the response from Belgrade (which used it as a propaganda tool); and it clearly lost him support, not just because a third of his own party supported the air strikes but because about a quarter of the electorate claimed it would make them less inclined to vote SNP. This in itself was important given that the final outcome produced no single party overall majority. Muslim opposition to his stance may even have contributed to the SNP failing to gain a key Glasgow seat they had targeted. In addition, it raised questions over Salmond's judgement and statesmanship.

The khaki election and the "unpardonable folly" remarks ensured that the classic components of international relations — war and the use of force and power — would have a profound effect on the Scottish body politic not just in the election itself but in the life of the first Scottish Parliament the electorate voted for at the end of the campaign.

These episodes demonstrate the difficulty of maintaining the alleged separation of international relations from mainstream politics. Whatever the *Scotland Act* says, it is difficult to see how the Parliament can avoid at least debating such major issues in the future. As early as May 1999 Alex Salmond himself called for the Parliament to debate the consequences of NATO and British policy, despite the fact that it had no responsibility for foreign affairs. At that time, however, the Parliament was not fully functioning and members (MSPs) were not allowed to put down motions, so the issue was moot. Such issues are unlikely to be moot in the future. Indeed, when the Scottish Affairs Committee of the House of Commons investigated "The Operation of Multi-layered Democracy" in 1998, Anne Begg, MP asked Dr. Charles Jeffrey, an expert witness:

Do the sub-national assemblies debate reserved powers ...?

DR. JEFFREY:
Yes, they do debate reserved powers. They can debate anything they like (United Kingdom. House of Commons 1998, col. 51).

When finally published in the autumn of 1999 the Memorandum of Understanding between Her Majesty's Government and Scottish Ministers and the Welsh Cabinet accepted that:

> The devolved legislatures will be entitled to debate non-devolved matters, but the devolved executives will encourage each devolved legislature to bear in mind the responsibility of the UK Parliament in these matters (United Kingdom. Scottish Executive 1999).

## THE ANACHRONISTIC NATURE OF THE SEPARATION THE SCOTLAND ACT PURPORTS TO UPHOLD

The foundation of international relations lies in the fact that there are many different societies or groups of individuals scattered all over the globe, and these scattered societies have some form of contact with one another. International relations, even foreign relations, involve the study of the interactions that take place between these societies or entities, and the factors that affect those interactions. This broad definition allows for the time before the emergence of the modern state system, and also for the potential situation where the state is superseded by some new form of government. For much of the twentieth century, international relations has actually been concerned with the study of relations between states. However, this has come increasingly into question given the emergence of entities such as the European Union, which is neither a state nor a nation, and of sub-national actors or as Hocking prefers non-central governments. Both these developments plus technological change, global market forces, and changing social patterns, have affected the nature of the actors in international relations at all levels.

The very word "international relations" infers of course a particular concern with relations between nations, but it does not have to be so confined. For most of the twentieth century, the main actors in international relations were seen as states, but "relations" implies all the various types of interaction between geographically separate entities, whether these be governmental or private. They range from the great issues of war and peace to tourism, trade, commerce, communications, and even letters that cross state boundaries. So there is no particular characteristic specified as to the nature of the interaction. Thus, contrary to the narrow traditionalist realist view of international relations and foreign policy/relations, which focuses on the physical security and protection of the territory of the state and its people, one needs to look wider.

The traditional view implicit in much of international relations literature follows the assumption of Bodin that social and political order and legality are the highest values of a society and that it followed, along lines pursued by Hobbes, that in every given territory sovereignty must be united in one clear, secular authority to establish and maintain order. Following this, the Treaty of Westphalia, and the evolution of international diplomacy since 1648, there was a situation where sovereign rulers exercised theoretically and actually the unchangeable right of law-making. Law-making and foreign relations were for centuries the preserve of the state. Thus only those holding authority on behalf of states could have political relations with each other. A generation ago, as Wallace noted, it was still possible for some to assume that "The separation of foreign policy from domestic policy is fundamental to the traditional concept of the nation-state" (1971, p. 8). Or as Henry Kissinger put it: "In the traditional conception ... the domestic structure is taken as given; foreign policy begins where domestic policy ends" (1969, p. 261).

Foreign policy was seen as providing the bridge between domestic and international politics. It was seen as state-centric. But in the intervening period the increasingly indistinguishable separation between domestic and international politics has been widely, if not universally accepted. Wallace himself and others were coming to the view that "The difference between 'national' and 'international' now exists only in the minds of those who use the words" (Mosely 1961, p. 43 ff.) not least because as Rosenau observed:

> In certain respects national political systems now permeate, as well as depend on, each other and that their functioning now embraces actors who are not formally members of the system. These non-members not only exert influence upon national systems but actually participate in the process through which such systems allocate values ... Most important, the participation of non-members of the society in value-allocation and goal-attainment is accepted by both its officialdom and its citizenry (1980, p. 146).

These are "penetrated" political systems, that is, a political system in which "Non-members of a national society participate directly and authoritatively, through actions taken jointly with the society's members, in either the allocation of its values or the mobilisation of support on behalf of its goals" (ibid., pp. 147-48).

All this is self-evidently true of those elements of British and Scottish policy that are touched by British membership of the European Union. The *European Communities Act* of 1972 gave domestic effect to the Treaty of Accession. It provided that:

> All such rights, powers, liabilities, obligations and restrictions from time to time created or arising by and under the Treaties, and all such remedies and procedures from time to time provided for by or under the Treaties, as in accordance with the Treaties are without further enactment to be given legal effect or used in the United Kingdom ... (*European Communities Act* 1972 c.68, part I).

This becomes all the more potent given that since 1972 the European Communities have moved into new fields of policy, the Single Market has been virtually completed and 12 states have adopted a single currency, and the Communities have been transformed into the European Union. It might be argued that the European Union has substantially moved in the direction of President Jacques Delors' prediction of 1988: "the quiet revolution that is taking place, as a result of which 80 per cent at least of economic, financial and perhaps social legislation will be flowing from the Community by 1993" (Salmon and Nicoll 1997, p. 208).

Whatever about "80 percent," it is true that swathes of what was traditionally British or Scottish law now flows from or increasingly is even determined by the decision-making procedures of the European Union. This confirms that there can be no simple division of power between Edinburgh, London, and the European Union. Virtually all departments of the new Scottish Executive have forged links with their European counterparts in the Commission, in the member states and in other sub-national or non-central government authorities. Ironically the long awaited devolution of power from London is in a new framework of constraints accepted as part of European Union membership. These constraints would apply, of course, even in an independent Scotland, especially given the wish of some leading members of the Scottish National Party to adopt the EU's single currency.

More broadly, it is increasingly apparent that the number of government departments (central, regional, and local) which may wish to conduct relatively low-level negotiations or to exchange technical information with their opposite numbers in other states is virtually equivalent to the number of departments which actually exist at any given time. It has certainly become increasingly true that each major department of central government has its "foreign ministry." As Roy Jones noted, a consequence is that

> They develop their own norms and procedures, their own styles of cross-national conduct ...The extension of this process has the effect of gradually reducing the role of politics in world society ... the role of diplomacy is gradually supplanted by the activities of sets of non-technical experts (Jones 1970, p. 147).

It is thus not surprising that terms such as micro-, para-, proto-, and pluri-national diplomacy have entered the conceptual language in the attempt to categorize the emerging international role of SNAs and NCGs, although it is clear that both the concepts and what they refer to are still contested (Aguirre 1999).

It is clear that the Weberian definition of a government, portraying it as a formal state structure granted with legitimate authority over a society inhabiting a defined territory, is increasingly being eroded, both by the involvement of subnational as well as supranational actors (Rhodes 1995). The government described by Weber cannot function in the contemporary world, due to the magnitude of internal and external factors forcing it to be more flexible. More contemporarily, it is now recognized that there is "A complex, multi-layered, decision-making process stretching beneath the state as well as above it; instead of a consistent pattern of policy-making across policy areas, one finds extremely wide and persistent variations" (Marks 1992, pp. 221-23).

According to Marks, multi-level governance explains systems of policy making "among nested governments at several territorial tiers," which take place as "…the result of a broad process of institutional creation and decisional reallocation" (Marks 1993, pp. 391-410).

The capacity of SNAs or NCGs to participate effectively in the new multi-level governance system depends

> Not merely on constitutional structures but on the nature of territorial civil societies economic resources, the capacity for political mobilisation and the capacity to project the territory internationally, especially within international regimes (Keating 1992, p. 45).

Clearly Scotland does have a significant resource base (financially and administratively) to allow it both to operate as and to become a more significant international actor, as long as one moves from the narrow view of international or foreign relations. Thus the simple propositions in the *Scotland Act* will not do.

## THE SCOTTISH PARLIAMENT AND EXECUTIVE, THE EUROPEAN UNION AND INTERNATIONAL RELATIONS

The British government acting outside the *Scotland Act* has itself acknowledged that there is an international role for the Parliament, namely its responsibilities and role in BIC, the "British-Irish Council," that was part of The Agreement arrived at on Good Friday 1998 between the various parties involved in the attempt to resolve the Northern Ireland crisis. In The Agreement and subsequently, Her Majesty's Government have accepted that the Council, which has met, comprises

> Representatives of the British and Irish Governments, devolved institutions in Northern Ireland, Scotland and Wales, when established, and, if appropriate, elsewhere in the United Kingdom, together with representatives of the Isle of Man and the Channel Islands (United Kingdom. Northern Ireland Assembly 1998).

And that the Council may meet at "summit level," and in "Specific sectoral formats on a regular basis, with each side represented by the appropriate Minister; in an appropriate format to consider cross-sectoral matters." In addition, it is to "Exchange information, discuss, consult and use best endeavours to reach agreement on co-operation on matters of mutual interest within the competence of the relevant Authorities."

The 1998 agreement states that

> Suitable issues for early discussion in the BIC could include transport links, agricultural issues, environmental issues, cultural issues, health issues, education issues and approaches to EU issues. Suitable arrangements to be made for practical cooperation on agreed policies.

Although "Individual members may opt to participate or not in such common policies and common action..." It will be open to the British-Irish Council "...to agree on common policies or common actions" and

> It will be open to two or more members to develop bilateral or multilateral arrangements between them. Such arrangements could include ... mechanisms to enable consultation, co-operation and joint decision-making on matters of mutual interest; and mechanisms to implement any joint decisions they may reach. These arrangements will not require the prior approval of the BIC as a whole and will operate independently of it.

There was also the possibility of interparliamentary links.

Although it might seem as if the BIC is a version of domestic politics, that interpretation is insulting to the Irish Republic, and it is instructive that the Irish Republic opened a Consulate-General in Edinburgh in September 1998; that Bertie Ahern, the Irish Taoiseach (prime minister), visited Scotland twice in 1999, in addition to visits by the Tanaiste (deputy prime minister) and foreign minister. In November 1999, President McAleese visited Scotland. Just days earlier, the Irish government gave Donald Dewar, the first minister, on the occasion of his visit to Dublin, the full trappings of a state visit (although technically it was not) with a six-car cavalcade led by two police outriders. While this treatment was related to the delicate situation in the peace process and the Irish attempt to influence Unionist perceptions of Dublin, it does point up that the Scottish role in the BIC gives the new Executive and Parliament a very significant international responsibility and an added responsibility because of the ties between Scotland and Northern Ireland. In the first year of the new Scottish administration, other Scottish ministers also visited Dublin, including, for example, Wendy Alexander, minister for communities, who was accompanied by a deputy minister, two civil servants, one private secretary, a press officer, and a visitors' officer from the British Dublin Embassy, as she sought to learn more about Dublin's anti-poverty strategy.

Edinburgh is now home to 13 full-time career consuls and to the representatives of about 40 different states. The most recent consulates to be established include the Irish, Taiwanese, Mongolian, and Indian. The Indian Consul referred explicitly to the need to have "close contact with members of the Scottish parliament and executive." While the honorary consul of Austria has referred to governments wanting to be "as close as they can to the seat of power" (*The Scotsman,* 10 November 1999).

While some of the consulates have been in Scotland for some time, with some in Glasgow, the creation of the Holyrood Parliament has had an impact on both their numbers, their moving to Edinburgh, and their modus operandi.

Mention has already been made of Scotland Europa. In July 1999 "Scotland House" opened. Scotland Europa and the new office of the Scottish Executive came together to form it, while retaining their own identities. The Scottish Executive's Office has six members of staff. It does not aim to replace other Scottish representation in Brussels such as Scotland Europa, but to complement it. Interestingly, the six staff are tasked to cover Industry, Agriculture, Fisheries, Regional and Social Policy, the Environment, Transport and Energy, as well as Justice and Home Affairs.

This raises the issue of whether in addition to "Scotland House" in Brussels, there will need to be "Scotland Houses" elsewhere. The Labour regimes in Edinburgh and London are cautious because of the association in some minds of overseas representation with diplomatic recognition and statehood. The foreign secretary, Robin Cook, has pointed out that the United Kingdom has 221 embassies around the world, at least four times the Irish number (Ireland being a model the SNP often likes to cite). He also noted that Ireland had no diplomatic representation in Hong Kong, Oslo, Sofia, or Skopje, nor in states like Slovenia. Nonetheless, over time the question of the representation of specifically Scottish interests is bound to arise, not least because Scotland has key economic interests to protect and advance, such as agriculture, tourism, and energy. There may well be potential for friction with London here, since such offices would surely be tasked with specific responsibilities such as promoting tourism to Scotland and inward investment. Whatever the current arrangements, or the initial agreement in the Concordat on International Relations and the Concordat on Co-ordination of European Union Policy Issues (see below), there is certain to be evolution in these areas, not least because MSPs will be answerable to a local electorate, and members of the Executive will be answerable to the MSPs. After awhile, it is difficult to see how either can hide behind the provisions of a Concordat, especially when it comes to attracting jobs to or defending jobs in local areas. Even before devolution ministers were asked in the Commons about when they would meet representatives of Scotland's financial services industry to discuss Edinburgh's position or the Confederation of British Industry (CBI) in Scotland to discuss prospects for investment in Scotland.

So far some broad criteria for establishing Scottish links with "foreign" actors have been identified, and they include:

• shared interests in the economic, social, cultural and environmental fields;

- shared geographic and demographic similarities (peripherality and population sparsity);

- exchanges of information and expertise on the role of regional legislatures;

- good potential to bring benefits to Scotland without prejudice to UK interests, including access to new markets or funding, achieving added insight into common issues and increased Scottish influence.

## IS THE INTERNATIONAL DIMENSION EXAGGERATED?

Beyond membership of the European Union, it is perhaps important not to overemphasize the significance of the external dimension. In the early life of the Scottish Parliament it has become clear that these broader international possibilities can be exaggerated. Although, as will be shown below, issues with an international dimension have been raised in the Chamber, there has actually been more evidence of a parochial tendency, noted with respect to the House of Commons and public opinion in the 1950s, when George Jeger MP remarked:

> When I was in my constituency last weekend I asked my constituents ... which they would rather I did — endeavour to catch Mr. Speaker's eye in the grand foreign affairs debate tomorrow or raise the question of their bus shelter, which is only a local problem. They told me any fool can speak on foreign affairs and no doubt several would, but that if I did not speak about their local bus shelter, then nobody else would (Wallace 1975, p. 95).

In addition, therefore to the formal limitations on the Parliament, there are the political imperatives of responding to constituent concerns, and the general question of the interest of voters and MSPs in international issues. It is interesting to note that the "international" issues that have been raised in questions or touched on in debates in the Scottish Parliament have overwhelmingly tended to have a constituent economic or job dimension. Thus questions have been raised about the Seattle World Trade Organization negotiations and their impact on the Scottish economy and local businesses; for example, a series of questions about whether the minister had consulted Scottish Natural Heritage, the Scottish Landowners Federation, Convention of Scottish Local Authorities, Scottish CBI, the Federation of Small Businesses and representatives of Scottish registered companies. The answer from Henry McLeish, (minister for enterprise and lifelong learning) was that:

> The negotiation of International Trade Agreements, including World Trade Organisation talks is a reserved matter and consultations with interest groups, including industry, is a matter for the UK Parliament ... The Scottish Executive is in regular contact with DTI on Trade issues and the WTO talks and how these may impact on

the Executive's responsibilities (Scottish Parliament Official Report, 13 December 1999).

While the debacle in Seattle has in the short term rendered some of MSPs' concerns moot, the impact of international disputes and international dispute procedures on trade was dramatically brought home by the protectionist conflicts between the EU and the US, especially by the conflict over the EU post-colonial preference to imports of bananas from the Caribbean. This disadvantages banana growers in Latin America, where production is in the hands of US food giants. They egged on the US government into making a complaint to the World Trade Organization, which repeatedly sustained the complaint. Early in 1999 the US produced a "hit-list" of $320 million worth of imports from the EU which would be subject to 100 percent increases in duties. Particularly badly hit initially were cashmere sweater manufacturers in the Borders of Scotland, it being calculated that up to 30 manufacturers — most of them in Hawick and Innerleithen — could be forced out of business. While this was legally a problem for Her Majesty's Government in London, the EU and WTO, clearly elected local MSP were required to become involved in lobbying and seeking solutions amenable to local concerns; failure to do so would provoke questions about their role and purpose. The potential economic and employment impact of the international dimension is also illustrated by

- The issue of the implications of the Multilateral Agreement on Investment (MAI) for Scotland's trading position, to which the answer from Henry McLeish was basically the same as that above on the WTO negotiations, although he did acknowledge that anything that adversely affected Scotland's world trade position would be a matter of concern.

- Takeovers of Scottish companies, some by other British concerns, but some by overseas corporations.

- The retention of RAF Buchan, near Peterhead and the jobs associated with the base, given that the Ministry of Defence in London was looking to rationalize the functions that Buchan performed and it became a choice between it and a similar base in East Anglia.

Other questions have focused on the local and Scottish consequences of Britain's international policy, for example,

- While defence is a reserved matter, the attitude of the Scottish Executive to the presence of the Trident missile and submarine installations in Scotland, has become a running issue. It has been argued that their presence was contrary to the wishes of 85 percent of the Scottish people, the STUC, and the Scottish parties. This set of questions was made all the more poignant given that Sheriff Gimblett of Greenock Sheriff Court had acquitted three anti-nuclear protesters who allegedly caused £80,000 damage at Faslane Naval Base, which houses the British nuclear deterrent, on the grounds that she accepted the defence argument that the International Court of Justice had declared that nuclear weapons were illegal. This ruling allowed Alex Salmond, the leader of the SNP, and others to raise the nuclear question in the Parliament.

- The issue of the impact of accommodation costs for Kosovo refugees on local councils and whether they would receive additional support to meet the additional costs, as well as associated questions about the implications for Scotland of asylum-seekers.

- The decision of the British home secretary, Jack Straw, to allow the former heavy-weight champion of the world, Mike Tyson, to enter the United Kingdom and to fight in Glasgow despite Tyson's criminal convictions and the entreaties of the Scottish minister of justice, Jim Wallace, who coincidentally happened to be acting first minister at the time, and the Scottish Parliament. Straw was acting within the law and the legal framework created by the *Scotland Act*, but demonstrably against the wishes of the Scottish people.

There has also been a general awareness that Scotland's voice needed to be heard on issues such as climate change, especially following a report in December 1999 that warned of "...rising sea levels, a 20 per cent increase in rainfall, worsening public health and the loss of many wild species" (Kerr *et al.* 1999) and raised issues that clearly demonstrated the need for cooperation between London and Edinburgh to meet international obligations and to formulate positions.

## THE CONCORDATS OR MEMORANDUM OF UNDERSTANDING AND SUPPLEMENTARY AGREEMENTS

On several occasions when some of the above issues were raised in the Scottish Parliament, reference was made to the concordats, especially those on "Coordination of European Union Policy Issues – Scotland," and "International Relations," which were officially designed to ensure that the Scottish Executive was fully involved on all European Union and international issues which touch on devolved matters. These documents were finally unveiled in the autumn of 1999, two years after the publication of the White Paper on Scotland's Parliament and nearly a year after the *Scotland Act* was passed. They were negotiated between the constituent parts of the United Kingdom and Her Majesty's Government in London. It is still not entirely clear how fiercely they were negotiated, but undoubtedly that was made easier by the political complexion of the regimes in Edinburgh and Cardiff, with a Labour preponderance if not majority in both.

Such agreements were necessary because, as has been made clear above, Scotland has a clear interest in many matters that were "reserved" and on many issues there is some blurring of responsibility between the two governments. Ambiguities result also from the fact that while the 1997 White Paper suggested how Her Majesty's Government envisaged operation of the new system, the *Scotland Act* did not legislate on many of these matters and how the relationship was to actually work and evolve. In fact, the handling of day-to-day matters is a matter of politics and practice, precedent and convention, although within a certain framework, thus the need for concordats. The concordats attempted to set out the working practices that will apply in the relations between London and Edinburgh (with others referring to Wales, and where appropriate Northern Ireland), including the procedures to ensure that Scottish interests and views are taken fully into account in formulating the overall UK approach. The memorandum of understanding recognizes that the Scottish Executive has a responsibility for ensuring that the interests of Scotland "in non-devolved matters are properly represented and considered," but it went on to make clear, and this has been repeated by Scottish ministers in the Scottish Parliament, that the

> memorandum is a statement of political intent, and should not be interpreted as a binding agreement. It does not create legal obligations ... It is intended to be binding in honour only ... Concordats are not intended to be legally binding, but to serve as working documents (United Kingdom. Scottish Executive 1999).

Officially central to the arrangements between the different administrations are

- good communication between those administrations
- the attempt not to constrain the discretion of the devolved institutions, but to seek to ensure that they have time to make representations
- to alert each other to developments, to take into consideration the views of others, and as appropriate to consider joint action
- the need to respect the mutual confidentiality of discussions and information supplied
- that there must be adherence to the resultant UK line
- that the devolved administrations are responsible for implementing international, European Court of Human Rights (ECHR), and EU obligations
- that most of the contact is on a bilateral or multilateral basis, directly between departments with most business being conducted through normal administrative channels, but that
- some central coordination system was necessary. A Joint Ministerial Committee (JMC) consisting of UK, Scottish, and Northern Ireland ministers and

members of the Welsh Cabinet has thus been created. The JMC can meet at prime minister/first minister level (probably once a year), but also in what are termed "functional" formats, that is, agricultural or environmental ministers. The major meetings of the JMC are to be chaired by the prime minister or his deputy. It is presumed that issues will only go to the JMC when there has been a lack of success in bilateral exchanges at ministerial level, and it is necessary for a higher level to seek to resolve disputes. In December 1999 Gordon Brown, the Chancellor, apparently announced Joint Ministerial Action Committees without full consultation with elements of the Edinburgh coalition. The JMC is shadowed by a committee of officials, comprising a core group of at least one official from each administration, with others invited to attend as appropriate. The JMC also has a joint secretariat — comprising staff of the Cabinet Office in London and officials from the devolved administrations. One of its tasks incidentally is to liase with the joint secretariat of the British-Irish Council.

Specifically in the Concordat on International Relations – Scotland, and the Common Annex (shared with Wales), having reiterated the formal position making clear Her Majesty's Government's responsibility, there is recognition that:

> The conduct of international relations is likely to have implications for the devolved responsibilities of Scottish Ministers and that the exercise of those responsibilities is likely to have implications for international relations. This Concordat therefore reflects a mutual determination to ensure that there is close co-operation in these areas (United Kingdom. Scottish Executive 1999, D3).

The Concordat on Co-ordination of European Union Policy Issues – Scotland makes the same point, "As all foreign policy issues are non-devolved, relations with the European Union are the responsibility of the Parliament and Government of the United Kingdom, as Member States" (ibid., B1.3).

But goes on to state:

> However, the UK Government wishes to involve the Scottish Executive as directly and fully as possible in decision making on EU matters which touch on devolved areas (including non-devolved matters which impact on devolved areas and non-devolved matters which will have a distinctive importance in Scotland) ... (ibid., B1.3).

> Participation will be subject to mutual respect for confidentiality of discussions and adherence by the Scottish Executive to the resulting UK line without which it would be impossible to maintain such close working relationships (ibid., B1.4).

The Concordat on International Relations covers

- exchange of information

- formulation of UK policy and conduct of international negotiations

- implementation of international obligations

- co-operation over legal proceedings

- representation overseas

- secondments and training co-operation

- visits

- public diplomacy, the British Council and BBC World Service

- trade and investment promotion

- diplomatic and consular relations (ibid., D1.1).

In addition to these general issues, it was made clear that only the UK government could enter into legally binding treaties or other international agreements, although the devolved administrations would be allowed, in cooperation with the Foreign and Commonwealth Office (FCO) to:

> make arrangements or agreements with foreign national or sub-national governments or appropriate counterparts in international organisations, to facilitate cooperation between them on devolved matters, provided that such arrangements or agreements do not purport to bind the UK in international law, affect the conduct of international relations or prejudice UK interests (ibid., D3.7).

It was also agreed that it "may be appropriate" for Scottish ministers or officials to be part of a UK delegation, but that they would have to support the single UK line. It is the UK lead minister who retains "Responsibility for the negotiations and ... determine(s) how each member of the team can best contribute" and indeed determines whether a Scottish minister is to be part of the team, a matter which has already caused some difficulty in the environmental area (ibid., D3.8). The devolved administrations can establish offices overseas dealing with devolved matters.

The international concordat also states that "The devolved administrations are responsible for implementing international, ECHR and EU obligations which concern devolved matters. In law, UK ministers have powers to intervene in order to ensure the implementation of these obligations" (ibid., part 1, no. 20).

The Concordat on Co-ordination of European Policy Issues covers the same general points drawing specific attention to

- provision of information;

- formulation of UK policy;

- attendance at Council of Ministers and related meetings;

- implementation of EU obligations; and

- infraction proceedings (ibid., B1.2).

Emphasis is again placed on "confidentiality and adherence to ... the resulting UK line." It specifies three key objectives:

- full and continuing involvement of Ministers and officials of the Scottish Executive in the processes of policy formulation, negotiation and implementation, for issues which touch on devolved matters;

- ensuring that the UK can negotiate effectively, in pursuit of the single UK policy line, but with the flexibility that fast-moving negotiations can require; and

- ensuring EU obligations are implemented with consistency of effect and where appropriate of timing (ibid.).

Most of the coordination is through interdepartmental consultation, but the JMC and its supporting system is in the background. It is to be the responsibility of the lead UK department and the United Kingdom Permanent Representation to the European Communities (UKREP) to inform officials of relevant EU business, and there is an EU subcommittee of the JMC.

> Decisions on Ministerial attendance at Council meetings will be taken on a case-by-case basis by the lead UK Minister ...[who] will take into account that the devolved administrations should have a role to play in meetings of the Council of Ministers at which substantive discussion is expected of matters likely to have a significant impact on their devolved responsibilities (ibid., B3.13).

But all will be required to

> support and advance the single UK negotiating line which they have played a part in developing. The emphasis in negotiations has to be on working as a UK team; and the UK lead Minister will retain overall responsibility for the negotiations and determine how each member of the team can best contribute to securing the agreed policy position. In appropriate cases, the leader of the delegation could agree to Ministers from the devolved administrations speaking for the UK in Council, and that they would do so with the full weight of the UK behind them (ibid., B3.14).

Similar arrangements apply to officials. In March 2000, Ross Finnie, minister for rural affairs (Scottish Executive) attended an Agricultural Council meeting as part of the UK team, which was led by Nick Brown the UK minister for agriculture, fisheries and food and included Christine Gwyther (agriculture and rural development secretary, National Assembly for Wales). A few weeks later, Nicol Stephen, deputy minister for enterprise and lifelong learning in the Scottish Executive was *the* British representative at an Education Council meeting, although significantly perhaps some other member states were represented by their deputy permanent representatives at that meeting. In November 1999 Alex Salmond of the SNP asked why there was no dedicated European Union minister in the Executive, although some have claimed that Jack McConnell, minister of finance, has partly played that role. The concordat gave approval to the devolved administrations creating their own offices in Brussels, which, as noted above, they have done. However, it was also made clear that "The status and functions of the UK Permanent Representation in Brussels as the institution representing the United Kingdom within the European Union will be unchanged" (ibid., B3.26). Any devolved administration office was to conform to UK policy lines and work closely with UKREP.

The devolved institutions can monitor EU policy. They receive Explanatory Memoranda from the UK lead department and can pass on their views via London. In the Scottish Parliament there is a 13-strong European Committee, with some experienced Westminster hands, but so far they appear to have been rather overwhelmed by the volume of material, and for the most part decide to take no action on what comes before them. Moreover, as yet, they have been reactive rather than proactive. Indeed as Alex Wright has noted

> there is no evidence that the EAC's "Opinions" will be transmitted direct to Brussels — as the members of the committee were surprised to discover in August 1999.
> ... there is nothing to prevent the EAC's views being diluted long before they reach the EU and even then they may arrive too late in the day because the Council has already reached agreement (2000, p. 138).

In many ways the most controversial concordat proved to be the Concordat on Financial Assistance to Industry, specifically the financial assistance offered to inward investors. Building on existing practices, there will be an arrangement covered by the concordat, providing for consultation and agreement between interested parties where two or more parts of the UK are in competition for a major investment.

The constituent parts of the United Kingdom of Great Britain and Northern Ireland had long been competitors for such investment, particularly since parts of Scotland, Wales, Northern Ireland, and England suffered high levels of unemployment with the slump of traditional industries. Previously Scottish and other UK government departments had concurrent powers to promote exports and inward investment, and this has continued. With regard to inward investment the concern was to stop different parts of the United Kingdom engaging in competitive bidding against each other, as had happened in 1997 when there was a bidding war between the Welsh Development Agency and its northeast of England rival. Under the concordats, a JMC comprising representatives from: Departments of Environment, Transport and the Regions, Treasury, Trade and Industry, the FCO and the devolved administrations are to agree on general policy on such issues as the levels of assistance to be offered, and a Committee of Overseas Promotion (COP), comprising representatives of the UK government, the Scottish Executive, the Cabinet of the Welsh Assembly, and the Northern Ireland Executive to coordinate the attraction of investors and adherence to the guidelines. The key issue had been who or what would adjudicate when Scotland was fighting it out with areas south of the border for grant aid on the siting of new industries, and the development or attraction of new industries. Initially it had been feared that the British Department of Trade and Industry would be the final arbiter, but this role was ultimately accorded to the JMC. There are also to be agreed limits covering major schemes of financial assistance to companies. Both the SNP and the Conservatives attacked these arrangements, arguing in particular that Locate in Scotland would now face more restrictions on its operations than before devolution, and would waste time in fighting its corner in the COP system.

## CONCLUSION

Scotland does have other models to follow of course, although the particular role and powers of other SNAs or NGCs varies with their own political and constitutional position. One of the most powerful models is that of the Länder in Germany, but there is the crucial difference that the Länder operate in a federal system with a written constitution and entrenched rights. In the case of Spain, the 1978 constitution assigned exclusive jurisdiction over international relations to Madrid. Hocking (1998) argues that in the period up to 1989 the central Spanish Constitutional Court took a broad view of international relations, so that it constrained the Autonomous Communities' international ambitions, but that, since 1989 it has defined international relations more narrowly, such that it is now seen as focused on war powers, conclusion of treaties, recognition of foreign governments, and overseas representation. Even here, as seen above, there can be problems of definition.

The experience of other systems raises the question of whether the consultation is genuine and how much the views of SNAs and NGCs are taken into account. While lawyers may pay attention in formal models of foreign policy, political analysis requires the examination of practical implications and other processes, often informal. In relations between the London and Edinburgh administrations they are still finding their way. The real test will come when the political complexion of the regimes in Edinburgh and London are significantly different.

The new Scottish Parliament and Executive will not only be dealing with Her Majesty's Government, the BIC, the EU, and other macro-international institutions. In order to maximize Scotland's influence, they will wish to establish links with other regions and even states. This will raise a number of issues about the strategic basis of such links and the role of each body in pursuing and maintaining them. An example of the sort of contact and issues involved can already be seen: in recent years Scotland has forged links with a number of EU (Sweden and Finland) and non-EU states (Norway and Iceland). These links, which in Scotland's case have focused largely upon the Highlands and Islands, are based upon common features (e.g., geographical peripherality) and socio-economic interests (e.g., regional development). Four areas of cooperation have been pursued (IT, SMEs, forestry, and further education) with informal links having been developed in the environment area as well. Further cooperation on a range of other issues will surely follow (e.g., rural development). Many devolved matters thus now have not only an EU but also a broader European and international dimension.

The foregoing has demonstrated the ubiquity of international relations, and how wide-ranging their impact can be on Scotland. For the Parliament, it also means that committees like Enterprise and Lifelong Learning, Rural Affairs, and Transport and Environment will have a strong international dimension.

In an era of globalization, the local is increasingly international and vice versa. That is, the boundaries delineating territorially defined political arenas are becoming increasingly fluid (Rosenau 1997). As Hocking has observed, the notion that there is an accepted and uncontested hierarchy of interface with the international arena is challenged as SNAs or NGCs of various kinds respond to forces generated by domestic and international change (1993). The attempts by central governments to assert control over a fragmenting international political environment whilst at the same time recognizing that new policy agendas create mutual dependencies between actors, both public and private, which demand constructive management strategies, are fraught with difficulty. These difficulties and tensions have clearly not been fully confronted in the UK/Scottish case. The longer term answer will depend upon how the practice of the concordats evolves, but it will also be crucially dependent on the aspirations of the Scottish people and their representatives.

REFERENCES

Aguirre, A. 1999. "Making Sense of Paradiplomacy? An Intertextual Inquiry about a Concept in Search of a Definition," in *Paradiplomacy in Action: The Foreign Relations of Subnational Governments*, ed. F. Aldecoa and M. Keating. London: Cass.

Bomberg, E. 1994. "Policy Networks on the Periphery: EU Environmental Policy and Scotland," *Regional Politics and Policy*, 4(1):45-61.

"Climate Change: Scottish Implications Scoping Study." 1999. Quoted by *The Scotsman*, 3 December 1999.

Hocking, B. 1993. *Localizing Foreign Policy: Non-Central Governments and Multi-layered Diplomacy*. London: Macmillan.

———. 1998. "Foreign Policy and Devolution," Conference Paper, British International Studies Association, 24th Annual Conference. December 1999.

Hooghe, L. 1995. "Subnational Mobilisation in the European Union," *West European Politics*, 18:175-98.

Jones, R. 1970. *Analysing Foreign Policy: An Introduction to Some Conceptual Problems*. London: Routledge and Kegan Paul.

Keating, M. 1992. "The Rise of the Continental Meso: Regions in the European Community," in *The Rise of Meso Government in Europe*, ed. L.J. Sharp. London: Sage.

Kerr, A. *et al.* 1999. "Climate Change: Scottish Implications Scoping Study." Edinburgh: Scottish Executive Central Research Unit.

Kissinger, H. 1969. "Domestic Structure and Foreign Policy," in *International Politics and Foreign* Policy, ed. J. Rosenau. New York: Free Press.

Marks, G. 1992. "Structural Policy in the European Community," in *Euro-Politics: Institutions and Policy-making in the New European Community*, ed. A.M. Sbragia. Washington, DC: The Brookings Institution.

———. 1993. "Structural Policy and Multi-level Governance," in *The State of the European Community: The Maastricht Debates and Beyond*, Vol. 2, ed. A. Calfuny and G. Rosenthal. London: Longmans.

McAteer, M. and J. Mitchell. 1996. "Peripheral Lobbying! The Territorial Dimension of Euro Lobbying by Scottish and Welsh Sub-Central Government," *Regional and Federal Studies*, 6(3):1-27.

Mitchell, J. 1995. "Lobbying Brussels: The Case of Scotland," *European Regional and Urban Studies*, 2(4):164-91.

Mosely, P.E. 1961. "Research on Foreign Policy in Brookings Dedication Lectures," Research for Public Policy. Washington, DC: The Brookings Institution.

Rhodes, M., ed. 1995. *The Regions and the New Europe: Studies in Core and Periphery Development*. Manchester: Manchester University Press.

Rosenau, J. 1980. *The Scientific Study of Foreign Policy*. London: Pinter.

———. 1997. *Along the Domestic-Foreign Frontier: Exploring Governance in a Turbulent World*. Cambridge and New York: Cambridge University Press.

Salmon, T. and W. Nicoll, 1997. *Building European Union: A Documentary History and Analysis*. Manchester: Manchester University Press.

United Kingdom. House of Commons. 1998. Scottish Affairs Select Committee. "The Operation of Multi-Layer Democracy." Minutes of Evidence. 25 February. HC460.

———. Northern Ireland Assembly. 1998. *The Agreement*. Agreement reached in the multi-party negotiations. 10 April. Available at <www.nio.gov.uk/agreement.htm>.

———. Parliament. 1997. "Scotland's Parliament." Presented to Parliament by the Secretary of State for Scotland by Command of Her Majesty, July. Cm 3658.

_____ 1998. *The Scotland Act 1998*. HMSO.

_____. Scottish Executive. 1999."Memorandum of Understanding and supplementary agreements between the United Kingdom Government, Scottish Ministers and the Cabinet of the National Assembly for Wales." October. SE/99/36. <www.scotland.gov.uk/library/memorandum>

_____. Scottish Office. 1998. "Report of the Consultative Steering Group on the Scottish Parliament." London: HMSO.

Wallace, W. 1971. *Foreign Policy and the Political Process*. London: Macmillan.

_____ 1975. *The Foreign Policy Process in Britain*. London: Royal Institute of International Affairs.

Wright, A. 2000. *Scotland: The Challenge of Devolution*. Aldershot: Ashgate.

# 6

# The Nation-Building Role of State Welfare in the United Kingdom and Canada

*Nicola McEwen*

## INTRODUCTION

Rokkan and Urwin identified two territorial objectives of the state: (i) to preserve the integrity of the state and (ii) to ensure legitimacy within its boundaries through popular support and acquiescence to its political authority (1983, p. 166). In achieving these objectives, democratic states have relied upon a claim to represent the nation. This is rendered more difficult where the state's claim to represent one nation is contested by sub-state national groups. In such cases, in particular, states are compelled to engage in nation-building, that is, to foster a sense of belonging to the national state and a shared national identity and solidarity among "the people" it claims to represent.[1] Nation-building is evident at both the state and the sub-state levels in the UK and Canada, where nationalism in Scotland and Quebec poses a territorial challenge to the integrity and legitimacy of the existing state structure.[2] This chapter focuses on the nation-building strategies of the state. In particular, it considers the extent to which successive state governments have attempted to strengthen "nationality" by drawing upon notions of social citizenship embodied in the discourse and policies of the welfare state.

The author would like to thank Michael Keating, Siobhan Harty and James Mitchell for helpful comments on an earlier draft.

The first section of the chapter develops the theoretical framework in which the analysis is set. The empirical study which follows addresses three central themes. First, it considers the extent to which a state-wide system of welfare developed in the UK and Canada and whether this encouraged a sense of belonging to the state among Scots and Quebecers. Second, it considers whether neo-liberalism and the welfare retrenchment it engendered weakened the attachment of Scots and Quebecers to the state and augmented demands for constitutional change. Finally, it examines the effectiveness of renewed efforts of the state to revert to a nation-building strategy which draws upon the discourse and policy of the welfare state.

## NATION-BUILDING, "NATIONALITY" AND SOCIAL CITIZENSHIP

Whether at state or sub-state level, nation-building contributes to reinforcing consent among "the people" by strengthening their identification with and attachment to the nation. It involves promotion of a nationalist discourse and reliance upon practical strategies to accommodate territorial demands within the existing state structure. In the first instance, nationalist discourse promotes the shared meanings which underpin the collective dimension of national identity and contribute to defining who we are as a people and what it is we represent. As Gellner observed, these "shared meanings" or characteristics are "a contingency, not a universal necessity" (1983, pp. 6, 56) and thus prevailing conceptions of national identity are open to challenge by competing representations of nationhood. Despite efforts to secure the people's consent and loyalty by promoting a political discourse, an element of will remains regarding the extent to which one identifies with and gives consent to the conceptions of nationhood it articulates. In practice, nation-building is often more pragmatic, involving elaborate systems of territorial and class accommodation within the existing state structure via institutional and material means (Keating 1988). Deutsch suggested that the working class may be more inclined to feel a sense of national belonging and fraternity with their compatriots where the opportunity to improve living standards is afforded within the national state; "if they find not merely factories and slums but schools, parks, hospitals and better housing ... there the ties to their own people ... will be strong in fact" (Deutsch 1966, p. 99). In a similar vein, territorial or ethnic minorities may feel a stronger sense of belonging to a national state which guarantees their material well-being through the provision of social and economic security and services.

Membership of a state is also defined by the status, rights, and obligations of citizenship. According to Marshall, social rights, including the right to a minimum standard of economic and social security, represented the fullest expression of citizenship as without social rights, citizens could not fully exercise their civil and political rights (Marshall [1949] 1963, pp. 100-15). Citizenship and national identity are closely related (Heater 1990, pp. 57-58; Soysal 1996, p. 18). Miller argued that in the absence of a national identity and the solidarity that entails, citizenship would reflect a relationship of strict reciprocity whereby a citizen would expect to benefit from membership in the state in proportion to the contribution he or she makes. This would preclude the redistributive policies associated with the welfare state (Miller 1995, pp. 71-73). Similarly, Keating argued that the heightened profile of nationalist discourse during the Second World War in part facilitated the creation of the welfare state. The rationale upon which it was founded was "underpinned by a notion of national solidarity which in turn depends on some sense of common identity" (Keating 1996, p. 34).

Justifying public policy in the name of "the nation" presupposes a shared national consciousness. Yet the sense of belonging to the state may also be reinforced by the substantive recognition of rights afforded by one's citizenship status. In other words, public policy designed to recognize citizenship rights may in turn reinforce the national identity upon which they are founded. As Balthazar observed, while a strong sense of nationhood facilitates the intervention necessitated by the welfare state, such intervention in the daily lives of the population may also strengthen allegiance to the nation (Balthazar 1986, pp. 30-31). It is not coincidental that the terms "citizenship" and "nationality" are often employed interchangeably in political discourse. The rights afforded to the community of citizens by virtue of its membership of the state contribute to giving the state its "national" character.

Miller suggested that because of the degree of social solidarity they rely upon, redistributive policies aimed at social justice are easier to implement in states where citizens are united by a strong and uncontested national identity (Miller 1995, pp. 92-98). Yet, in multinational states, where there exists a nation or nations within the state, the recognition of social and other citizenship rights may serve an important integrative function, reinforcing an attachment to the national state which can complement an identification with an historical-cultural nation within the state's boundaries. Within multinational states, national boundaries are often contested and overlapping; for example, the boundaries of the Quebec nation are submerged in the vision of a Canadian nation. In such circumstances where nation-building actors at state and sub-state levels may compete for the loyalty of "the people," the social rights of citizenship embodied in welfare services can enhance the ability of government at the centre to appeal directly to citizens throughout the state territory. This may encourage a loyalty to the state as the source and guarantor of the social rights of citizenship. In addition, the social protection and security offered by the welfare state can be contrasted to the uncertainty and insecurity of secession. The nation-building role of the welfare state goes beyond providing a rational, material basis sustaining the state's territorial integrity. Welfare institutions can serve to provide not just common social services but a common heritage and project for the future, which together contribute to reinforcing the consent, "the clearly expressed will to continue a life in common," which for Renan was the defining feature of nationhood ([1882] 1990, p. 19).

In states, such as the UK and Canada, which witnessed the emergence of neo-liberalism in public policy making, the capacity of the state to promote national unity built upon the security and solidarity of the welfare state became more limited. The promotion of a deregulated, flexible, free-market economy with minimal state intervention implied a partial "rolling back" of the welfare state and diminished the continued appeal and security offered by national states vis-à-vis the uncertainty of enhanced sub-state autonomy. A substantial degree of state intervention remains evident in the states in question and the rhetoric of neo-liberalism has often exceeded the implications of public policy. Nevertheless, the promotion of a "minimal state" may influence public perceptions regarding the extent to which states can guarantee social and other citizenship rights. This is exacerbated within a federal or devolved system where alternative conceptions of citizenship may find expression within sub-state parliaments. As the guarantors of some citizenship rights, autonomous sub-state governments may be in a position to divert the loyalty of their citizens away from the centre. Sub-state citizenship thus limits national state citizenship by circumscribing the state's ability to inspire loyalty to the polity through the recognition and distribution of rights.

The following section examines the development and nation-building implications of the postwar welfare state in Scotland/UK and Quebec/Canada. Subsequent sections then explore the territorial impact of welfare retrenchment and the recent efforts of the Labour and Liberal governments to reinvoke the welfare state in reinforcing state nationality.

## THE DEVELOPMENT OF THE WELFARE STATE IN THE UK AND CANADA

In the UK and Canada, the governments which emerged from the war brought a commitment to social reform and Keynesian-inspired economic management. The welfare state developed differently in each case and its nation-building consequences varied as a result.

## Reinforcing Britishness: The UK Welfare State

The first majority Labour government elected in 1945 set in stone the major pillars of the postwar welfare state. Social security provision was consolidated and extended into a comprehensive universal system, large-scale investment expanded and renovated the public housing stock, and equal access to free health care was established with the National Health Service (NHS) (Morgan 1990; Fraser 1984; Glennerster 1995).[3] In so doing, it drew upon a national solidarity engendered in war, declaring in its manifesto, for example, that the task of building the welfare state would require "the spirit of Dunkirk and of the Blitz sustained over a period of years" (Labour Party, [Great Britain 1945] 1975). Williams suggested that the postwar welfare state, in turn, became an important symbol of Britishness helping to replace the unifying appeal once provided by the British Empire (1989, p. 162). Bennie, Brand and Mitchell suggested that the welfare state provided a new set of recognizably British institutions which in greatly improving the living standards of working-class Scots, "probably more than the Empire helped cement the Union" (1997, pp. 5-6).

Within the postwar constitutional framework, all legislative decision making rested with the Westminster Parliament. However, the Scottish Office retained administrative authority over a number of areas of welfare policy, including health, housing, and education, while separate Scottish legislation was often passed at Westminster to accommodate distinctive needs.[4] The Scottish Office was also responsible for implementing legislation and Paterson argued that this permitted to Scotland as much autonomy as afforded to other small nations within federations, facilitating the development of a distinctively Scottish welfare state (1994, p. 103). Comparisons with Quebec, which enjoyed autonomy over the design as well as the implementation of substantial areas of social policy, suggest this view is somewhat exaggerated. Furthermore, the Scottish Office ceded its existing responsibility for administering poor relief and pensions in spite of Scottish Office warnings that centralization of social security would exacerbate "the growing intensity of feeling in Scotland against Scottish business being decided in London" (SRO, HH1/2574, 12 April 1943, p. 4).

There was some scope for the Scottish Office to take the initiative in social policy. A notable example is the *Social Work (Scotland) Act* of 1968, which pioneered the replacement of juvenile courts by children's panels (Macdonald and Redpath 1980). But in high profile cases where the subject of legislation was ideologically motivated, the scope of the Scottish Office to exercise autonomy was much more restricted (Midwinter, Keating and Mitchell 1991, pp. 78-83).

Indeed, Midwinter, Keating and Mitchell suggested that limited autonomy was the quid pro quo of privileged access to the centre (ibid., pp. 74-5). Access was considered more important in a centralized regime and the "main significance" of the Scottish Office role was in lobbying to secure material benefits for Scotland (Jones and Keating 1985, p. 107).

This leaves open the question as to whether the postwar welfare state contributed to sustaining among Scots a sense of belonging to Britain. It certainly weakened enthusiasm for home rule within the Labour Party, which as a state-wide party had itself served to cement working-class Scots to the union. Labour's devolution commitment was eventually abandoned in 1958, on the grounds that "Scotland's problems can best be solved by socialist planning on a United Kingdom scale" (Labour Party [Scottish Council] 1958, p. 1). This remained the position until political expediency forced a reluctant change in 1974, in response to the rise of the Scottish National Party (Wood 1989). The postwar welfare state tied the interests of the working class to the centralized state structure promoted by Labour. Although an appeal to working-class unity was often a justification for upholding the centralized state structure and resisting concessions to sub-state territorial claims (ibid.), the welfare state drew upon a "one nation" rhetoric which correlated the interests of the working class with the interests of the nation. Election studies also confirm that Scots exhibited a stronger sense of British identity in the 1970s than in later years and reveal that the Scottish working class in particular demonstrated a greater degree of solidarity with English people of the same class than with their fellow Scots (Bennie, Bland and Mitchell 1997; Brown, *et al.* 1999; McEwen 2000, Tables 1-3).

## Nation-Building and the Development of a Pan-Canadian Welfare State

The federal system has rendered at once more explicit and more limited the Canadian state strategy of reinforcing nationality through welfare-state development. Social policy falls largely within provincial jurisdiction and new initiatives in social insurance required constitutional amendment, necessitating agreement with the provinces. Although this hindered the development of a pan-Canadian welfare state, federal governments have acquired a role in social welfare in three respects (Banting 1998, pp. 41-47). First, a pan-Canadian welfare state was fostered by unconditional equalization payments to poorer provinces which increased their fiscal capacity to deliver social programs comparable to those offered in wealthier provinces (ibid., p. 45). Second, many social programs were developed on a shared-cost basis, including social assistance, health care, and postsecondary education. By attaching conditions to its financial support, the federal government was in a position to promote national standards. Third and most controversially, the federal government, by virtue of its spending power, has provided direct benefits to individual citizens, including Unemployment Insurance, Family Allowances, and Old Age Security. Although some regional variation remained, these policies were largely national in scope and Banting suggested they "represented social rights of the type described by Marshall and other students of the social dimension of citizenship" (ibid., p. 42).

The increased role of the federal government in the social policy field, particularly under the postwar Liberal governments, appeared to be explicitly tied to a "national policy" of strengthening a common Canadian identity and reinforcing the sense of belonging to the Canadian state. Linteau *et al.* insisted that the federal role in delivering direct welfare benefits was intended to enhance the legitimacy of the federal state and bring it closer to Canadians. "These (welfare) cheques represented direct, tangible contact with citizens, shoring up Ottawa's legitimacy and creating stronger identification among Canadians with their 'national government'" (1991, p. 283).

However, the extent to which the welfare state served to integrate Quebecers into the Canadian state is open to question. The Union Nationale, which dominated postwar Quebec politics until 1960, criticized Ottawa's welfare initiatives as centralist and against the spirit of the *British North America Act.* Its resistance was in the name of provincial autonomy but this masked a commitment to economic liberalism and a belief that meeting welfare needs should remain a matter for private charity and the church (Vaillancourt 1988, pp. 128-33). The ideas emanating from the federal government certainly informed growing opposition within Quebec to the Duplessis regime and the conception of Quebec national identity it promoted. This gave rise to demands for modernization and increased government intervention to enhance the living standards and prospects of francophone Quebecers. While for some like Pierre Trudeau, opposition to the regime combined with an outright repudiation of Quebec nationalism, for others, it gave rise to a new version of nationalism which regarded the Quebec state as the vehicle of Quebec's modernization (Balthazar 1986, pp. 111-22; Linteau *et al.* 1991, pp. 252-60). The latter was the most influential during the years of the Quiet Revolution. Responsibility over education and health care was gradually removed from the church to come within the ambit of the Quebec government and Quebec governments increasingly demanded opt-outs from federal social programs. During negotiations to secure agreement on a constitutional amendment in 1964, the Quebec government secured the right, offered to all provinces but accepted only by Quebec, to opt-out of a wide range of federal and shared-cost programs in exchange for fiscal compensation and increased tax points (Courchene 1994, p. 114). It also won the right to introduce its own pension plan, closely tied to but distinct from the plan offered to Canadians outside Quebec (Simeon 1972, pp. 58-59). These opt-outs ensured enhanced autonomy and flexibility and facilitated the development of a recognizably Québécois welfare state, constraining the extent to which federal governments could draw upon the provision of state welfare to reinforce belonging among Quebecers to the Canadian national state.

Whereas the federal government under Pearson had demonstrated a willingness to accommodate Quebec's demands for increased autonomy, control over social policies became more explicitly tied to the competing nation-building agendas of Ottawa and Quebec following Trudeau's emergence in federal politics (Banting 1995, pp. 284-87). Trudeau was determined to reinforce the idea of Canada as one national community and recognition of Quebec's distinctiveness through asymmetrical federalism was anathema to that vision (McRoberts 1997, pp. 55-73). As McRoberts observed, "not only was Trudeau opposed to particular status for Quebec in principle but his strategy for transforming the political allegiances of Québécois made it important for them to receive direct services and benefits from the federal government" (ibid., p. 144). While the Trudeau vision was most obviously challenged with the rise to power of the Parti Québécois, even committed federalists within Quebec found its interpretation of the federal government's role unacceptable. During the 1971 Victoria Conference, convened to agree on an amending formula for patriating the constitution, Quebec Premier Robert Bourassa sought legislative primacy for Quebec over all aspects of social policy (Canada. Constitutional Conference 1971). A failure to reach agreement on the division of powers led Bourassa, in response to political pressure in Quebec, to reject the Charter (Bourassa 1995, pp. 90-95; Gagnon 1993, p. 100; McRoberts and Postgate 1980, pp. 168-70).

Thus, although the development of the welfare state in Canada was more closely related to a territorial nation-building strategy than in the UK case, the federal division of powers and of political parties meant it was more constrained in its capacity to reinforce state nationality.

## THE TERRITORIAL IMPACT OF WELFARE RETRENCHMENT

The capacity of the state to draw upon social policy in nation-building was impeded in the 1980s by the increasing predominance of a neo-liberal agenda in public policy making and a reduction in the scope of state welfare. The consequences for the strength and the nature of support for constitutional change in Scotland and Quebec are considered below.

## Thatcherism and the Scottish Response

From the perspective of the New Right, the welfare state had stifled free enterprise and encouraged a culture of dependency. Its scope had to be diminished to encourage individual responsibility and facilitate tax cuts. To this end, government imposed cuts in local authority budgets and social expenditure, reasserted the family's duty to care for dependent children and adults, and introduced market discipline to promote "efficiency" and choice in public services (Hay 1996; Kavanagh 1990). The extent to which the welfare state could be rolled back was modified by the needs of an aging population and the mass unemployment which was in part a consequence of Thatcherite economic policy. Ideological objectives were further constrained by an awareness of the continued popularity of the welfare state, particularly in health care and education (Crewe 1988). Nevertheless, Hall suggested that Thatcherism gave neo-liberal ideology a populist appeal in its reconstruction of British national identity. Rather than drawing upon the achievements of the postwar welfare state to reinforce Britishness, postwar social democracy was regarded as a symbol and cause of British decline. The essence of Britishness was instead "identified with self-reliance and personal responsibility, as against the image of the over-taxed individual, enervated by welfare state 'coddling'" (Hall 1983, p. 29). The conception of social citizenship associated with the postwar welfare state was replaced by a concept of citizenship achieved through property ownership and participation in the free market and the promotion, especially under the Major governments, of the rights of the "consumer citizen" (Gamble 1988; Pierson 1996).

Conservative social policies affected Scotland as much as England (Midwinter, Keating and Mitchell 1991). Welfare retrenchment, however, met with greater resistance in Scotland, where in contrast to England, a greater proportion of people either worked in the public sector or relied upon social security benefits. Though often exaggerated and over-simplified in notions of a north-south divide, survey evidence also suggested a slight Scottish bias in favour of collectivist policies and values which could not be explained by socio-cultural factors alone (Curtice 1988; McCrone 1992). The scope for the Scottish Office to act autonomously was severely constrained and the decline in the Conservative vote in Scotland gave rise to a feeling that policies were being imposed on Scots by a government that had no electoral mandate (Jones and Keating 1988). Consistent failure of the electoral system to reflect Scottish voting preferences undermined the legitimacy of the state structure. Successive general election defeats also weakened the integrative function of the Labour Party in Scotland, exposing the contingency of the quid pro quo exchange of autonomy for access (ibid.).

Labour's expedient support for home rule in the 1970s was transformed into enthusiastic endorsement in the 1980s (Mitchell 1998a). Thatcherism also transformed the nature of the home-rule debate. It engendered greater demands for a parliament with economic powers which could resist the cuts to social services imposed by central government (see, for example, Labour Party [Scottish Council] 1981). Opposition to government policies was also harnessed to reinforce support for home rule. Robin Cook, an anti-devolutionist in the 1970s, insisted that support for constitutional change should be mobilized around "the question of jobs, of industry, and of the welfare state which will have a more immediate resonance amongst the mass of the Scottish electorate" (1983, p. 11). Mitchell and Bennie suggested that the Scottish response to Thatcherism provoked a "chain of equivalences" whereby continued support for state intervention and welfare combined with perceptions that the Conservatives had become an anti-Scottish party reinforced Scottish distinctiveness and support for home rule (Mitchell and Bennie 1996). For those committed to constitutional change, a Scottish Parliament came to be considered a prerequisite for the protection and improvement of public services. An analysis of the 1997 referendum vote suggested that support for a Scottish Parliament, especially one with tax-raising powers, was based upon the expectation that it would produce improvements in the NHS, education, welfare services, and the economy (Brown et al. 1999).

## Welfare Retrenchment in Canada: Weakening the Bonds of Nationhood?

The welfare state in Canada was also challenged by neo-liberalism, yet debates over the future of federal and provincial social programs were eclipsed by constitutional upheaval throughout much of the 1980s. The Trudeau vision of Canada as one bilingual, multicultural nation was enshrined in the patriated constitution of 1982 and especially in the Canadian Charter of Rights and Freedoms which accompanied it. Neither had the consent of the Government of Quebec and the following decade was dominated by ill-fated attempts to reintegrate Quebec into the constitution.

Welfare retrenchment may nevertheless have had a cumulative impact upon national unity. Fiscal restraint evident since the late 1970s was reinforced by an ideological shift toward the New Right after the election of the Progressive Conservatives in 1984. By the end of its second term, the Mulroney government had cut back a number of social security programs, but the most severe cuts were in transfer payments to the provinces (Rice and Prince 1993; Guest 1997). Rice and Prince believed that social programs helped to strengthen Canadian citizenship and encouraged a sense of identification with federal institutions. Consequently, the "restraints in federal social transfers will produce a weakening of the bonds of nationhood" (ibid., p. 399).

The election of the federal Liberals in 1993 did not mark a significant ideological change. Indeed, Phillips claimed that their second budget in February 1995 heralded "much deeper cuts to social programmes than the Tories ever attempted" (1995, p. 75). The overhaul of the system of federal transfers saw the introduction of a single block-transfer program, the Canada Health and Social Transfer (CHST). Although promoted, especially in Quebec, as offering greater flexibility to the provinces over social policy, critics suggested that the CHST was conceived as an easy way to reduce federal spending and thereby reduce the deficit (Phillips 1995; Cohn 1996). Over the two fiscal years from 1996-98, transfers were reduced by some 33 percent and Maslove (1996) argued that this effectively downloaded a portion of the federal debt to the provinces.

The governments of Quebec during the same period certainly exhibited a similar tendency toward reducing the scope of the welfare state and promoting the virtues of a free-market economy. Following its re-election in 1981, the Parti Québécois government retreated from many of the social democratic measures it had introduced in its first term and adopted a more favourable stance toward the business community (Tanguay 1993). The Quebec Liberal government which followed embraced neo-liberalism in its support of deregulation, individual responsibility and a downsizing of the provincial state, though as Tanguay noted, its neo-liberal rhetoric far exceeded its public policies (ibid.).

Nevertheless, cumulative cuts imposed by the federal government altered the nature of the debate during the 1995 referendum campaign and may have contributed to increased support for Quebec sovereignty. Whereas during the 1980 campaign, the federalists were in a position to raise doubts over the viability of old age pensions and other social programs in the event of a "yes" vote, by 1995 the "yes" side used campaign publicity and debates to highlight federal budget cuts. Then Bloc Québécois leader, Lucien Bouchard, also raised the spectre of "drastic cuts" to pensions and social programs in the event of a "no" vote (*Le Devoir* 1995: 18 September; 29 September; 14-15 October). By contrast, the sovereignists' manifesto, *Le coeur à l'ouvrage*, presented among its pledges social democratic ideals of full employment, greater equality, and a stronger safety net, with the promise of a *seconde revolution tranquille* (Conseil de la Souveraineté du Québec 1995, p. 14). In a subsequent analysis of the referendum, Gagnon and Lachapelle (1996) argued that each side proffered distinctive and competing visions of society. The sovereignist option promoted social democracy while the federalists favoured a neo-liberal agenda. As such, although the linguistic divide remained the most important cleavage, the "yes" side benefited from increased support among the working class and among those with economic and social concerns (ibid.). The contingency of the sovereignists' social democratic conception of society in the run-up to the referendum may be evident in the Parti Québécois government's subsequent promotion of deficit reduction and welfare reform. It may be argued that the elimination of government deficits at state or sub-state level is a prerequisite to the preservation of systems of state welfare. Yet, cutbacks in social programs are often a consequence of a preoccupation with deficit reduction. In the 1995 referendum campaign, cuts in federal government expenditure and transfer payments may have undermined the credibility of federal arguments concerning the economic risks of secession and may have rendered Canada less attractive to undecided voters (Lemieux 1996).

As was noted in the theoretical discussion above, promoting solidarity through the delivery of social programs and the recognition of the social rights of citizenship may be of greater importance to the nation-building strategies of states, particularly where they face strong sub-state challenges to their territorial integrity. Welfare retrenchment in the UK and Canada may have weakened the rationale and emotional resonance formerly associated with membership of the state. It certainly informed the rationale for constitutional change, with reform presented by its advocates as a prerequisite to safeguarding public services. Where the social and economic security of citizens is undermined by the state while those advocating constitutional change bring the promise of enhanced security, increased support for sovereignty may partly rest on an assumption that there is "nothing to lose."

## RE-INVOKING THE WELFARE STATE IN NATION-BUILDING

The postwar welfare state raised living standards among the working class and embodied a shared national project and national institutions with which the citizens of sub-state nations could identify. As a nation-building strategy, the welfare state has been more important to the liberal-left and there is some evidence to suggest that the current Labour and Liberal governments in the UK and Canada have reverted to its symbolism in an attempt to reinforce national unity. The effectiveness of such efforts is considered below.

### The Welfare State and Scottish Devolution

Devolution has transformed the constitutional debate in Scotland into a choice between the new status quo of a parliament within the UK and the nationalist option of independence. In this context, the New Labour government has sought to emphasize the continued relevance of dual (i.e., Scottish *and* British) national identity among Scots with reference to the achievements of the postwar welfare state. In a pamphlet published in the run-up to the first Scottish Parliament election, Chancellor Gordon Brown and fellow Scottish Labour MP Douglas Alexander spoke of a Britishness borne of the shared suffering of war and "cemented further by the common endeavour of thereafter building the welfare state" (1999, p. 19). Free health care and social protection under the NHS and National Insurance were embraced as symbols of British citizenship and national unity. Survey evidence was presented to demonstrate that Scots identified the NHS well above the army, the monarchy, the BBC or Parliament as the institution which best represented Britain (*Herald*, 15 April 1999). As a means of sustaining Britishness and a continued commitment to the union among Scots, this discourse is problematic. The extent to which it may find substance in public policy is constrained in two respects.

For New Labour, social and economic change rendered the "old" welfare state unsustainable and Keynesian social democracy and a citizenship founded upon social rights belong to a bygone era. Thus, they accepted their predecessor's restructuring and partial retrenchment of the welfare state and moved closer to Conservative social policies, reflected in a refusal to restore the earnings link to state pensions, the embrace of private pensions, and the tightening of eligibility criteria in relation to benefit entitlement (Hay 1999). New Labour has also shown a commitment to transforming the welfare state, embarking upon a series of welfare reforms aimed at promoting work as the route out of poverty and social exclusion (Hills 1998, p. 26; Annesley 2000). The prevalent conception of citizenship to emerge has shifted the emphasis from welfare entitlements to social obligations and according to Plant (1998), contribution and reciprocity have become the central conditions of citizenship status. As suggested in the theoretical discussion above, such a definition of citizenship is less likely to reinforce a sense of national community.

The second constraint is a consequence of devolution. The establishment of the Scottish Parliament entailed the devolution of legislative authority over much of the welfare state, including health, education, and housing, areas for which the Scottish Office previously had administrative responsibility. This further restricts the scope of the state to draw upon social policy in nation-building and opens up the possibility that a rather different vision of the welfare state may be pursued in Scotland. The Scottish Parliament provides an institutional framework within which Scottish distinctiveness can be nurtured and expressed, not just by adding a Scottish dimension to central government legislation but by developing distinctive public policies and honouring distinctive rights.

In the short term, such policy divergence is unlikely. The current Scottish Executive remains closely allied to central government and shares its social policy objectives. Moreover, Joint Ministerial Committees have been established, bringing together representatives from the devolved administrations and the UK government under the chairmanship of Gordon Brown, to discuss and coordinate policy on child poverty, pensioner poverty, and on preparing the economy for the "new information revolution" (Brown 1999). The precise terms of reference of these JMCs remains unclear but their establishment suggests the continued influence of a UK agenda, in particular a Treasury agenda, on the direction of welfare policy in Scotland. In part, this reflects the fact that while the Scottish Parliament enjoys distributive and regulatory power, the power to redistribute rests firmly with Westminster, save the less than progressive power to vary the basic rate of income tax by three pence in the pound (Mitchell 1998b). Thus, although the Scottish Executive has placed the objective of tackling poverty at the heart of its own "Programme for Government" (United Kingdom. Scottish Executive 1999a), its targets and policy priorities reveal a continued dependence upon central government (see United Kingdom. Scottish Executive 1999b, c).

It is not unforeseeable, however, that the Scottish Executive and the Scottish Parliament will face pressure to pursue a distinctive approach in welfare in the longer term. Inasmuch as New Labour policy at a UK level is motivated by a desire to remain electable in "middle England," three distinctive electoral factors influence Scottish politics. First, the system governing elections to the Scottish Parliament virtually ensures coalition government. The furore and subsequent compromise over tuition fees for higher education underlined that in areas of the welfare state within its jurisdiction, the Scottish Executive may go its own way, albeit with a little pushing.[5] Second, the Scottish electorate is strongly committed to the welfare state and this limits the scope of the Scottish Executive to endorse its fundamental reform. A third and related factor is that Labour's main challenger in Scotland is not the Tories but the Nationalists, who have placed themselves to the left of New Labour in a bid to capture the votes of disenchanted supporters of "old" Labour and convert these votes into support for independence. The longer term impact of devolution may thus enhance the distinctiveness of Scottish social policy and political debate, further circumscribing the capacity of UK governments to re-invoke welfare solidarity in nation-building.

## Social Solidarity and the Renewal of the Canadian "Social Union"

In the aftermath of the Quebec referendum, the Liberal government viewed the welfare state, embodied in the notion of the "social union," as a non-constitutional path toward renewal of the federation (Noël 1998, p. 27). Intergovernmental Affairs Minister Stéphane Dion noted:

> One of Mr Bouchard's arguments during last year's referendum campaign was that Canada had abandoned its traditions of promoting social justice and generosity towards those in need ... Now that the federal government ... has made tremendous progress towards putting Canada's economy back on a sound basis, the government, in cooperation with the provincial governments, will increasingly focus on the renewal of Canada's social union ... strong social union is crucial for the preservation of the Canadian political union (1996, pp. 1, 8).

The provincial premiers produced their own proposal for a renewed social union. This offered to any province the right to opt-out, with full compensation, of all new or modified Canada-wide social programs that fall within provincial jurisdiction, on the understanding that it would offer a similar program which shared the same pan-Canadian objective (Conférence annuelle des premiers ministres provinciaux 1998). However, the final agreement signed with the federal government envisaged a rather different social union (Canada 1999). In recognizing the federal spending power, the Framework Agreement on the Social Union permitted the federal government the right to establish new shared-cost initiatives with the support of a simple majority of provinces. At the extreme, this could represent just 15 percent of the population (Gagnon 1999). A right to opt-out remained but was limited to provinces that had already introduced a similar program and carried the somewhat absurd commitment that the federal monies not required be reinvested in the same or a related program. Moreover, most recent innovative federal social policy initiatives have bypassed the shared-cost route in favour of direct transfers to individuals or organizations, from which no opting-out provision is permitted and no consent required (Noël 1999). These policies, such as the Millennium Scholarship program and the National Child Benefit, have provoked fierce debates between Ottawa and Quebec over policy jurisdiction.

The imposition of the federal government's vision of "the social union" reflected a deliberate attempt to strengthen the federal government's role in the social policy arena and to reinforce a pan-Canadian dimension to social programs. It committed the signatory provinces to eliminate, within three years, all residency-based policies and practices "that constrain access to post-secondary education, training, health and social services and social assistance unless they can be demonstrated to be reasonable and consistent with the principles of the Social Union Framework" (Canada 1999, clause 2). In building support for a stronger social union, the federal government made frequent appeals to Canadian national identity and citizenship. Anne McLellan, minister of justice and attorney general of Canada and chair of the Cabinet's Social Union Committee insisted that "Canada's social programmes reflect and give expression to our fundamental beliefs and values and help define us as a country ... The notion of social union captures our solidarity with one another, our understanding that we are stronger together" (McLellan 1998, pp. 6-7).

The renewal of the social union did not imply an enthusiastic return to a social rights conception of citizenship. As Gagnon (1999) noted, the politics of distribution took the place of a politics of redistribution. Ostensibly, the purpose of the agreement was to facilitate mobility and ensure that Canadians across Canada would have access to comparable social programs. Mobility was even elevated to the status of "an essential element of citizenship" (Canada 1999, clause 2) reflecting a determination that "Canadians be considered as Canadians everywhere in Canada" (Dion 1999, p. 2).

Within this discourse of equal access and equitable treatment, several Quebec-based politicians and academic commentators detected a clear attempt on the part of the federal government to build a unitary national state at the expense of provincial autonomy (Facal 1999; Gagnon 1999; Noël 1999; Ryan 1999). However, the Government of Quebec did not endorse the agreement of 4 February 1999 on the grounds that Quebec has the right to set its own priorities and develop its own social programs without federal interference (Facal 1999). Quebec is therefore neither bound by the commitment to eliminate residency requirements nor to any new shared-cost initiatives which the federal government may propose. The consequences of its exclusion may depend on the extent to which the federal government uses its enhanced authority in the provision of direct social services and the conflict this engenders. There is, however, a distinct possibility that this particular nation-building strategy may serve to strengthen the bonds of nationhood among Canadians outside Quebec, while accentuating the difference between Quebec and the rest of Canada.

## CONCLUSION

There is some evidence, then, to suggest that social citizenship and the welfare state have played a role in nation-building in the UK and in Canada. If the postwar UK welfare state was conceived as a nation-building strategy, it was to integrate the working class rather than wayward territories into a one-nation Britain. Yet it contributed to reinforcing a commitment among Scots to the UK state and thus served to sustain the state's territorial integrity and legitimacy. To this end, its role in nation-building was probably more effective than in the Canadian case, where the federal division of powers and the fragmentation of the party system impeded the development of a national agenda in social policy and a pan-Canadian welfare system. Both case studies suggest that the rise of neo-liberalism and the contraction of the state influenced demands for home rule/sovereignty in Scotland

and Quebec and may have contributed to increased support for change. In both cases, recent efforts to reinforce a common nationality by invoking the rhetoric of the welfare state and social solidarity are circumscribed by a continued predominance of neo-liberal economic assumptions and sub-state autonomy in social policy making.

Nation-building at different levels of the state does not occur in isolation and the predominant conceptions of nationhood and national identity at each level need not be incompatible. Indeed, the welfare state may have helped to reinforce a "social nation" which could rest alongside and stretch beyond the territory and boundaries of the sub-state cultural-historical nation. For those with a dual national identity, however, the sense of belonging to the national state may be more contingent and the welfare state may have helped to strengthen it. The extent to which it can continue to serve this purpose in the current political climate remains an open question. In the ongoing nation-building process, national states may need to search for alternative symbols of nationhood to maintain consent throughout their territory and sustain the integrity of existing state boundaries.

## NOTES

1.  Tilly described national states as "relatively centralized, differentiated organisations, the officials of which more or less successfully claim control over the chief concentrated means of violence within a population inhabiting a large, contiguous territory" (1985, p. 170). The term is used here, in preference to the more traditional term "nation-state," as a more appropriate description of states facing sub-state challenges from national minorities.
2.  The chapter considers only the Scottish and Quebec challenge to their respective states. It is acknowledged at the outset that the state faces other significant territorial challenges, from the First Nations in Canada and from Wales and Northern Ireland in the UK, but they are beyond the scope of this chapter.
3.  Free secondary education for all children had already been provided for under the *Education Act* (1944) and the *Education (Scotland) Act* (1945) enacted under the National government.
4.  Although such legislation specifically related to Scotland, MPs from throughout the UK were eligible to participate in the legislative process leading to their enactment.
5.  As a result of the proportional representation system of elections to the Scottish Parliament, the Labour Party had to form a governing partnership with the Liberal Democrats. The Liberal Democrats along with the opposition parties opposed tuition fees and secured a concession to replace tuition fees for Scottish students with a graduate endowment scheme payable after graduation. Consequently, the system of financial support for Scottish students is now markedly different from the system elsewhere in the UK.

REFERENCES

Annesley, C. 2000. "New Labour and Welfare," in *New Labour in Power: Ideology, Party and Policy*, ed. M.J. Smith and S. Ludlam. London: Macmillan.

Balthazar, L. 1986. *Bilan du nationalisme au Québec*. Montréal: l'Hexagone.

Banting, K.G. 1995. "The Welfare State as Statecraft: Territorial Politics and Canadian Social Policy," in *European Social Policy – Between Fragmentation and Integration*, ed. S. Leibfried and P. Pierson. Washington: The Brookings Institute.

_____ 1998. "The Past Speaks to the Future – Lessons from the Postwar Social Union," in *Canada: The State of the Federation 1997: Non-Constitutional Renewal*, ed. H. Lazar. Kingston: Institute of Intergovernmental Relations, Queen's University.

Bennie, L., J. Brand and J. Mitchell. 1997. *How Scotland Votes*. Manchester: Manchester University Press.

Bourassa, R. 1995. *Gouverner le Québec*. Montréal: Fides.

Brown, A., D. McCrone, L. Paterson and P. Surridge. 1999. *The Scottish Electorate: The 1997 General Election and Beyond*. London: Macmillan.

Brown, G. (Chancellor of the Exchequer) 1999. *Speech Delivered in Edinburgh City Chambers*, 1 December.

Brown, G. and D. Alexander. 1999. *New Scotland, New Britain*. London: The Smith Institute.

Canada. 1999. "A Framework to Improve the Social Union for Canadians," 4 February. Available at <socialunion.gc.ca>.

Canada. Constitutional Conference. 1971. "Constitutional Conference, Proceedings, Victoria, British Columbia, June 14, 1971." Ottawa: Information Canada.

Cohn, D. 1996. "The Canada Health and Social Transfer: Transferring Resources or Moral Authority Between Levels of Government?" in *Canada: The State of the Federation 1996*, ed. P.C. Fafard and D.M. Brown. Kingston: Institute of Intergovernmental Relations, Queen's University.

Conférence annuelle de premiers ministres provinciaux. 1998. "Entente-cadre sur l'union sociale canadienne," le texte du communique, 6 August.

Conseil de la Souveraineté du Québec. 1995. Le coeur á l'ouvrage, manifesto of the "oui" during the Quebec referendum.

Cook, R. 1983. "Interview: Devolution," *Radical Scotland,* 4 (Aug./Sept.):9-11.

Courchene, T. 1994. *Social Canada in the Millennium: Reform Imperatives and Restructuring Principles*. Toronto: C. D. Howe Institute.

Crewe, I. 1988. "Has the Electorate Become Thatcherite?" in *Thatcherism*, ed. R. Skidelsky. London: Chatto and Windus.

Curtice, J. 1988. "One Nation?" in *British Social Attitudes*, the 5th Report, ed. R.S. Jowell, S. Witherspoon and L. Brook. Aldershot: Gower.

Deutsch, K. 1966. *Nationalism and Social Communication*. Cambridge, MA: MIT Press.

Dion, S. 1996. "History and Prospects of the Canadian Social Union," Notes for an address to the Canadian Club. Ottawa, 18 November.

_____ 1999. "Statement by the Honourable Stéphane Dion to the House of Commons, Ottawa, 10 February.

Facal, J. 1999. "Pourquoi le Québec a dit non à l'union sociale," *La Presse*, 18 February.

Fraser, D. 1984. *The Evolution of the British Welfare State*, 2d ed. London: Macmillan.

Gagnon, A.-G. 1993. "Quebec-Canada: Constitutional Developments," in *Quebec, State and Society*, 2d ed., ed. A.-G. Gagnon. Scarborough, ON: Nelson Canada.

_____ 1999. *Etude sur le chapitre 4 de l'Entente-cadre*. Report commissioned by the Government of Quebec.

Gagnon, A.-G. and G. Lachapelle. 1996. "Quebec Confronts Canada: Two Competing Societal Projects Searching for Legitimacy," *Publius, The Journal of Federalism*, 26(3):177-91.

Gamble, A. 1988. *The Free Economy and the Strong State: The Politics of Thatcherism*. London: Macmillan.

Gellner, E. 1983. *Nations and Nationalism*. Oxford: Blackwell.

Glennerster, H. 1995. *British Social Policy since 1945*. Oxford: Blackwell.

Guest, D. 1997. *The Emergence of Social Security in Canada*, 3rd ed. Vancouver: University of British Columbia Press.

Hall, S. 1983. "The Great Moving Right Show," in *The Politics of Thatcherism*, ed. S. Hall and M. Jacques. London: Lawrence and Wishart.

Hay, C. 1996. *Restating Social and Political Change*. Buckingham: Open University Press.

_____ 1999. *The Political Economy of New Labour*. Manchester: Manchester University Press.

Heater, D. 1990. *Citizenship: The Civic Ideal in World History, Politics and Education*. London: Longman.

Hills, J. 1998. "Thatcherism, New Labour and the Welfare State," Centre for the Analysis of Social Exclusion Paper No. 13. London School of Economics, Centre for the Analysis of Social Exclusion.

Jones, B. and M. Keating. 1985. *Labour and the British State*. Oxford: Clarendon Press.

_____ 1988. "Beyond the Doomsday Scenario: Governing Scotland and Wales in the 1980s," Strathclyde Papers on Government and Politics, No. 58. Glasgow: University of Strathclyde, Department of Politics.

Kavanagh, D. 1990. *Thatcherism and British Politics: The End of Consensus?* 2d ed. Oxford: Oxford University Press.

Keating, M. 1988. *State and Regional Nationalism*. Hemel Hempstead: Harvester Wheatsheaf.

_____ 1996. *Nations Against the State*. London: Macmillan.

Labour Party (Great Britain 1945) 1975. "Let Us Face the Future," *General Election Manifestos 1900-1974,* ed. F.W.S. Craig. London: Macmillan.

Labour Party (Scottish Council). 1958. "Let Scotland Prosper: Labour Plans for Scotland's Progress," presented by the Scottish Executive to the Special Scottish Conference of the Labour Party, Glasgow.

_____ 1981. Interim Policy Statement on Devolution, presented by the Scottish Executive to the 66th Scottish Conference of the Labour Party, Perth 1981.

Lemieux, V. 1996. "Quelques explications du référendum" in *Québec-Canada: Nouveaux sentiers vers l'avenir*, ed. J. Trent, R. Young and G. Lachapelle. Ottawa: University of Ottawa Press.

Linteau, P.-A. *et al.* 1986. *Quebec Since 1930*, translated by R. Chodos and E Garmaise. Toronto: J. Lorimer.

Macdonald, M. and A. Redpath. 1980. "The Scottish Office 1954-79," in *Scottish Government Yearbook*, ed. H. Drucker and D. Denver. Edinburgh: Unit for the Study of Government in Scotland.

McCrone, D. 1992. *Understanding Scotland: The Sociology of a Stateless Nation.* London: Routledge.

McEwen, N. 2000. "Devolution and the End of the British Welfare State?" paper presented to the Annual Conference of the Political Studies Association, London School of Economics, 11 April.

McLellan, A. 1998. "Modernising Canada's Social Union," *Policy Options/Options Politiques,* 19 (Nov.):6-8.

McRoberts, K. 1997. *Misconceiving Canada: The Struggle for National Unity.* Toronto: Oxford University Press.

McRoberts, K. and D. Postgate. 1980. *Quebec: Social Change and Political Crisis.* Toronto: McClelland & Stewart.

Marshall, T.H. 1963. "Citizenship and Social Class," in *Sociology at the Crossroads and Other Essays.* London: Heinemann Educational Books Ltd.

Maslove, A.M. 1996. "The Canada Health and Social Transfer: Forcing Issues," in *How Ottawa Spends 1996-97*, ed. G. Swimmer. Ottawa: Carleton University Press.

Midwinter, A., M. Keating and J. Mitchell. 1991. *Politics and Public Policy in Scotland.* London: Macmillan.

Miller, D. 1995. *On Nationality.* Oxford: Clarendon.

Mitchell, J. 1998*a*. "The Evolution of Devolution: Labour's Home Rule Strategy in Opposition," *Government and Opposition*, 33(4):479-96.

_____ 1998*b*. "What Could a Scottish Parliament Do?" in *Remaking the Union: Devolution and British Politics in the 1990s*, ed. H. Elcock and M. Keating. London: Frank Cass.

Mitchell, J. and L. Bennie. 1996. "Thatcherism and the Scottish Question," in *British Elections and Parties Yearbook 1995.* London: Frank Cass.

Morgan, K. O. 1990. *The People's Peace.* Oxford: Oxford University Press.

Noël, A. 1998. "Les trois unions sociales," *Policy Options/Options Politiques*, 19 (Nov.):26-29.

_____ 1999. *Etude générale sur l'Entente.* Report Commissioned by the Government of Quebec.

Paterson, L. 1994. *The Autonomy of Modern Scotland.* Edinburgh: Edinburgh University Press.

Pierson, C. 1996. "Social Policy under Thatcher and Major," in *Contemporary British Conservatism*, ed. S. Ludlam and M.J. Smith. London: Macmillan.

Phillips, S. 1995. "The Canada Health and Social Transfer: Fiscal Federalism in Search of a Vision," in *Canada: The State of the Federation 1995*, ed. D.M. Brown and J.W. Rose. Kingston: Institute of Intergovernmental Relations, Queen's University.

Plant, R. 1998. "So You Want to Be a Citizen?" *New Statesman*, 6 February.

Renan, E. [1882] 1990. "What is a Nation?" reprinted in *Nation and Narration*, ed. H.K. Bhabha. London: Routledge.

Rice, J. and M. Prince. 1993. "Lowering the Safety Net and Weakening the Bonds of Nationhood: Social Policy in the Mulroney Years," in *How Ottawa Spends 1993-94: A More Democratic Canada?* ed. S.D. Phillips. Ottawa: Carleton University Press.

Rokkan, S. and D. Urwin. 1983. *Economy, Territory, Identity*. London: Sage.

Ryan, C. 1999. "The Agreement on the Canadian Social Union," *Inroads*, 8.

Simeon, R. 1972. *Federal-Provincial Diplomacy: The Making of Recent Policy in Canada*. Toronto: University of Toronto Press.

Soysal, Y.N. 1996. "Changing Citizenship in Europe," in *Citizenship, Nationality and Migration in Europe*, ed. D. Cesarni and M. Fulbrook. London: Routledge.

Strain, F. and D. Hum. 1987. "Canadian Federalism and the Welfare State: Shifting Responsibilities and Sharing Costs," in *The Canadian Welfare State: Evolution and Transition*, ed. J.S. Ismael. Edmonton: University of Alberta Press.

Tanguay, A.B. 1993. "Québec's Political System in the 1990s: From Polarization to Convergence," in *Québec: State and Society*, 2d ed., ed. A.-G. Gagnon. Scarborough, ON: Nelson Canada.

Tilly, C. 1985. "War Making and State Making as Organised Crime," in *Bringing the State Back In*, ed. P. Evans, D. Rueschmeyer and T. Skocpol. Cambridge: Cambridge University Press, pp. 169-91.

United Kingdom. Scottish Executive. 1999a. "Making it Work Together: A Programme for Government." Available at <www.scotland.gov.uk/library2/doc037>.

_____ 1999b. "Social Justice ... a Scotland Where Everyone Matters." Available at <www.scotland.gov.uk/library2/doc07>.

_____ 1999c. "Social Justice ... a Scotland Where Everyone Matters: Milestone Sources and Definitions." Available at <www.scotland.gov.uk/library2/doc07>.

United Kingdom. Scottish Office. 1943. "Department of Health for Scotland 1943," *Statement to Reconstruction Committee*, 21 July, SRO HH50/154.

Vaillancourt, Y. 1988. *L'Évolution des Politiques Sociales au Québec, 1940-1960*. Montréal: Les Presses de l'Université de Montréal.

Williams, F. 1989. *Social Policy: A Critical Introduction*. Cambridge: Polity.

Wood, F. 1989. "Scottish Labour in Government and Opposition, 1964-1979," in *Forward! Labour Politics in Scotland 1888-1988*, ed. I. Donnachie, C. Harvie and I.S. Wood. Edinburgh: Polygon.

# 7

# Canada's Shifting Citizenship Regime: Investing in Children

*Jane Jenson*

Notions of the "model citizen" are political constructions. Definitions vary across countries, in time, and from one philosophical family to another. They are also an important component of any citizenship regime, this being defined as the institutional arrangements, rules, and understandings that guide concurrent policy decisions and expenditures of states; problem definitions by states and citizens; and claims-making by citizens.[1] Each regime is rooted in its own place and time, an historical product of actors' strategies in specific times and places.[2] It may alter as economic and social conditions restructure and as the balance of political forces shifts. The direction of change is never given in advance, however; it is the result of choices among alternatives. Each path taken will have consequences for relations of equality and inequality, as well as outcomes in terms of fairness and justice.

This chapter focuses on ongoing adjustments to the citizenship regime in Canada outside Quebec. As Canadians, citizens of Quebec receive many programs designed in Ottawa. In addition, the provincial government does participate to a varying extent in intergovernmental politics. Therefore, there are significant overlaps in the two citizenship regimes. Nonetheless, there are also important differences. While some patterns do apply to Quebec, it is also the case that there are two separate citizenship regimes taking form, one that encompasses Ottawa and nine provinces, and another in Quebec (Jenson 1997).

The story this chapter tells is one of change. As one observes the currently ongoing redesign of the post-1945 Canadian welfare state, one might ask how the citizenship regime is changing in light of new visions of governing, of the role of the state, and of the division of responsibilities among the state, markets, and families?

I will consider three types of changes in this chapter, observable in the goals underpinning social and employment policies and programs, as well as in political discourse. They are reflected in the ways in which institutions, particularly intergovernmental ones, are being changed. All these new modalities imply a new way of thinking about and addressing the needs of children and the families within which they live, so as to promote social cohesion. They are altering the geometry of the welfare triangle of state, families, and markets.

First, in terms of institutions, intergovernmental relations (most often without the participation of Quebec), have been altered by the creation of the Social Union Framework Agreement (SUFA). The development of the National Child Benefit (NCB) was the "proving ground" for the SUFA, and efforts to establish new early childhood initiatives as well as a National Children's Agenda continue to be its testing ground.

Second, patterns of redistribution are affected. Governments have moved away from the notion that social cohesion results from common circumstances and therefore is best promoted by universal programs. Instead, they view social policy as primarily an anti-poverty measure targeting programs to low-income families (Myles and Pierson 1999). This is a perspective based on the creation of "social safety nets" rather than universal programs. Accompanying these are a range of programs focused on the "early years" [*la petite enfance*], intended to promote healthy child development and give all children an "equal start."

Finally, in ideological terms, social policies reflect a redefinition of the responsibilities of the state and of individuals. They put greater emphasis on adults' responsibility for their own well-being, their own life chances, their own income. In turn, the state concentrates its attention on "investments" in children and focuses on equality of opportunity. Because this change is the most general, the chapter begins with it.

## AN IDEOLOGICAL SHIFT: FROM PARENTAL CHOICE TO INVESTING IN CHILDREN

Changes to the Canadian citizenship regime are evidenced in ongoing redefinitions of collective responsibility and social justice. Abandoning any attention to equality of outcome, political discourse now promotes only a liberal version of equality of opportunity, while at the same time, and somewhat ironically, reducing some areas of family autonomy for "private" choices about child-rearing and the gender division of labour.

## *Recognizing Citizens as Adults and Parents –*
## *The Previous Regime*

At the end of the Second World War the Canadian government undertook the first stage of the construction of the postwar citizenship regime. The social policy decisions made in the 1940s and through the 1960s derived from particular understandings of equality. Values were basically liberal, but principles of equity were strong. In particular, the federal government assigned itself the responsibility for public policies that would foster a pan-Canadian identity and give broadly similar access to income security and social protection across the country. This meant, in concrete terms, that the federal government took the lead in employment and social policy, inducing provincial governments to follow its initiatives by making funding conditional on following its direction in program design.

At the same time, key programs were intended to reduce the inequalities and inequities associated with life-cycle risks. Core programs of the 1940s were a pan-Canadian Unemployment Insurance system and family allowances, followed in the 1960s by the Canada Assistance Plan (CAP), Canada and Quebec Pension Plans, universal health care, and so on. These programs were of two types. Some, such as health care, old age pensions, and family allowances, sought a certain socio-economic equality, being available to all Canadians as a right of citizenship. They were designed to smooth over the unequal risks of sickness, of old age, or of child-rearing. Others, and here the CAP is the classic example, were designed to provide for the "needy" or those "at-risk of dependence," who had fallen out of the other structures that were supposed to maintain income security, such as the labour market or the family (Guest 1985, p. 116). Social assistance was for the lone parents who had "fallen out" of the protection of marriage, or the long-term unemployed who had "fallen out" of Unemployment Insurance and so on. These were anti-poverty programs, designed to protect against poverty, but not to equalize conditions.

In all cases, however, whether the regime was designed to provide equality or equity, the citizen represented as typical in this regime was the adult worker. All other statuses were defined in relationship to this ideal-typical figure. Access to social citizenship rights depended on being a worker, or the wife of a worker, a retired worker, a school-age worker "in training," and so on. The norm was self-sufficiency, and it included the capacity to contribute to the general well-being by paying taxes as well as supporting oneself and one's family. Nonetheless, in the extraordinary situations where self-sufficiency was not possible, social programs filled the gap. Unemployment Insurance (UI) was available for those workers who were laid off temporarily while social assistance supported adults who were "unavailable" for employment. While disabled adults were in the latter category, the largest number was single parents (read mothers) caring for young children.[3]

Indeed, as a legacy of Mothers' Allowances (the first program offering support to adult women living without a male breadwinner), social assistance payments in several provinces supplanted labour force participation for certain people. Traditionally, governments which exempted the single mother from seeking employment did so because they regarded "her function in the home of greater social importance than her economic earnings" (Boychuk 1998, p. 37). It was only in 1996, for example, that lone mothers with children younger than 16 were not automatically exempted from all employability programs in Ontario; now they must participate in Ontario Works (the workfare program) if their children are six or older.

Policies explicitly designed around children in the postwar citizenship regime were of two types. There were those recognizing the extra costs of raising children by transferring income to parents. Family Allowances created in 1945 provide one example, and tax deductions for dependent children a second. In 1919, the first year that income tax was instituted in Canada, a tax deduction for dependants, including dependent children, was included in the tax code, in recognition of the extra costs parents faced because they had children. There was also a deduction for non-earning spouses.

Secondly, as it finally became clear to policymakers not only that women's labour force participation was rising, but that young women with children were among the most likely to be in the paid labour force, governments moved to facilitate balancing work and family responsibility, when both parents "chose" employment. In 1971, the federal government instituted paid maternity leaves within the Unemployment Insurance regime.[4] The tax code was also modified at the same time to provide a Child Care Expense Deduction (CCED), in order to reduce the costs to parents of engaging in paid work.

This regime focused on adults; children were dependants. Adults who received UI or social assistance did so because they had insufficient income from employment. Despite there being extra benefits to households with children, *access* to the regime always depended on the adults' relationship to the labour market. Even Family Allowances, which were intended to help meet some of the extra costs of child-rearing faced by adults with children, went to parents because they were heads of families, with the adult responsibility of providing for their dependants. As will be documented below, both the access point and the representation of *who* is the deserving recipient of any social transfers has changed in recent years.

In this postwar citizenship regime parents were *free to choose* between employment or child-rearing, as well as among forms of child care. The state was relatively neutral about parents' decisions about whether to participate in the labour force or not. The CCED and child-care subsidies for low-income families helped cover some of the costs parents incurred in order to work, but the choice was obviously the adults' to make.[5] Tax deductions for dependent spouses also recognized that some couples might choose full-time parenting by one of them rather than two incomes. In most provinces, as well, single parents on social assistance were allowed to substitute full-time parenting for labour force participation.

Parents also had full responsibility for ensuring that their preschool children were thriving and prepared to enter school. Good quality child care was available, but expensive. Therefore, parents were "free" to choose how much to spend on care, and whether to accept the least expensive alternatives. Choices among types of services were exclusively the parents' responsibility.[6] The role of the state was to regulate for health and safety in situations of collective care, but it took very little interest in the educational quality of care that parents chose or its effects on early childhood development. They could choose to entrust their children to neighbours, relatives, or anyone else. The state's main interest, expressed through the rules governing the CCED, was in ensuring that payments were duly receipted by babysitters and other caregivers, and therefore taxable.

## Promoting Gender Equality

The postwar citizenship regime was also committed, eventually, to providing a measure of gender equality. By the late 1960s the second wave of the women's movement was making equality claims, including in the world of work. In addition to attention to combating discrimination and promoting equality in hiring and the workplace, feminists agitated for child care and parental leaves. Publicly funded child care was high on the list of demands of the Fédération des femmes du Québec in its founding documents of 1965. For its part, the Royal Commission on the Status of Women argued for "choice." This was interpreted to mean having child care available so that the option of employment for mothers of young children was a real one. Movement organizations and their allies were sufficiently strong to extract the equal rights guarantees embedded in the 1982 constitution and eventually prompted pay equity laws in several jurisdictions, as well as legislation on equal treatment for Aboriginal women and other civil rights victories. But they were also the force behind claims for parental leaves and the CCED, again in the name of promoting choice for families and equality within them.

To say that gender equality was a dimension of the citizenship regime does not imply that gender inequalities were eliminated, of course, any more than antipoverty social policies eliminated the risk of being poor. However, it did become meaningful and, most importantly, legitimate in political discourse to make claims in the name of equal rights for women, and thereby to expose the structures of discrimination and other blockages to achieving equality.[7]

If these principles and programs are examined more closely, it can be observed that *an adult* was the central figure of the citizenship regime, the "citizen" who was imagined as the object of state action as well as the bearer of political and social rights. This citizen was a voter and also either a worker (and, therefore, usually but not always male), a retired person, or a parent. Social programs and social rights protected against the risks of adult life — old age via pensions, unemployment with UI, lack of sufficient earning power via social assistance, and so on.

In recent years this imagined "model citizen" has altered in the face of a rising tide of neo-liberalism, with its preferences for privileging market relations, reducing the role of the state, and thrusting more responsibility onto communities and families. Such a shift involves both a redefinition of the model citizen and altered citizenship rights. Social rights still exist, to be sure; welfare state retrenchment has not eliminated social spending by any means. "Post-deficit" politics are dominated both by debates about *where* to reinvest public monies as much as about whether to do so.

The direction of spending has two important characteristics. First, virtually every adult is assumed to be employable. There is no longer a choice about whether to participate in the labour force. Only those who can earn enough to support a family on one income are able to choose full-time parenting. Other than a tax deduction, there is no financial support for full-time parenting. This situation both explains the outrage of almost-always middle-income families about the supposed lack of support for their life-style "choice" and the fact that Alberta, influenced by right-wing family values ideologies, will provide a very generous deduction for dependent spouses in its new flat tax (Jenson with Thompson 1999).

Low-income parents are induced, if not compelled, to seek a job, schooling, or training. As is shown below, the principal goal of the National Child Benefit is to encourage low-income parents to stay in the labour force. "Employability" is the watchword of social and labour market policy, while unemployment benefits have been significantly reduced.

Second, the state has reconfigured its role, presenting it as managing "investments."[8] Social assistance and unemployment insurance, the two key programs of social citizenship of the post-1945 decades, have shed any dimensions of "decommodification" that they might have had.[9] Social spending has been redefined as an investment, rather than service provision. While some of these investments are in training and other employability programs, there is a gamut of new programs reflecting the appearance of a new target, that is children.

In this shift, children, particularly the youngest, have become the preferred investment opportunity. They are the "good investments" for the future, while those categories of the population that are labelled "poor risks" (including many of the parents of such children) are increasingly treated as a pool of inexpensive labour to be shifted from social assistance into the labour force, often via a form of workfare (Boismenu and Jenson 1996).

This shift is expressed in the several elements of the "children's agenda" now shaping many policy discussions in Ottawa and provincial capitals, an agenda which is key to the notion of the social investment state and the emergence of the child as the "model citizen."

## REDESIGNING SOCIAL ASSISTANCE: PROGRAMMATIC SUPPORT FOR REPRESENTATIONS OF THE CHILD AS MODEL CITIZEN

Increasingly, manifestations of social solidarity — in the form of income transfers and social services — come to adults *because* they have dependent children. Rather than receiving income because of a relationship to the labour force truncated by unemployment or parenting responsibilities, they receive income transfer payments and access to enriched labour market programs because they live with children under the age of 18.

There is, therefore, a shift in the purpose of such programs and the contours of the citizenship regime. Social policies are meant to provide equality of opportunity for citizens-in-becoming, that is children, via investments in them. All this has involved a major institutional redesign, including the invention of the Social Union Framework Agreement. The SUFA has brought a fundamental change to intergovernmental relations within Canada. It recognizes formally for the first time that Ottawa may legitimately act in areas of provincial jurisdiction. Thus, Quebec refuses to participate in the SUFA, preferring to insist on adherence to the federal principle, and to non-interference by Ottawa in areas constitutionally assigned to the provinces (Boismenu and Jenson 1998). Therefore, there now exists a form of intergovernmental relations best described as "asterisk federalism."[10]

The development of policies for children, which eventually fed into the SUFA, is a long story. They are the result of several decades of movement toward targeted benefits. Without going into detail on all the twists and turns, it can be said that postwar universal benefits, such as Family Allowances and tax exemptions, have disappeared. By 1993 the Working Income Supplement (WIS) provided a "top-up" to families whose earned income was low, while the Child Tax Benefit (CTB) went to low- and middle-income adults with children under 18.

This was the state of play in 1995, when Paul Martin brought in his infamous budget, unilaterally abolishing CAP, the shared-cost program that had shaped income security since the 1960s. In its place, Ottawa provided the Canada Health and Social Transfer (CHST) as the mechanism for transferring funds to the provinces. Without going into all the financing details, suffice it to say that the trade-off offered provincial governments more independence in spending decisions against a reduction of several billion of dollars of transfers.

This exchange did not please the provinces. Therefore, when the premiers met in the summers of 1995 and 1996 to craft their demands to Ottawa about federalism and social policy, social assistance reform was already on the agenda. The Provincial/Territorial Council on Social Policy Renewal was the arena in which ideas about reform of social assistance were debated and policies designed. To borrow only a portion of a well-known slogan, Canada has also eliminated "social assistance as we know it."

The National Child Benefit (NCB) was one important initiative, designated as a tool for fighting child poverty. A double-barrel strategy was adopted to achieve this: income transfers and employability measures. The NCB, in effect since July 1998, was designed to serve two purposes: to reduce the depth of child poverty and to promote parents' attachment to the workforce by ensuring that families will always be better off as the result of working.[11] It seeks to create a more stable base of income for low-income families that face frequent job changes or who move on and off social assistance. It also treats all poor children the same way, no matter the source of their parents' income.[12] Finally, the program is meant to foster federal-provincial collaboration. Hence the attention to negotiations, compromise, and the solidification of basic principles of governance and accountability.

## THE NCB AS A MODEL FOR THE SUFA AND A POST-SUFA CANADA

A comparison of the benefits paid before and after the NCB shows that the initial monetary effect of the shift from the Child Tax Benefit and Working Income Supplement, in place since 1993, to the NCB was not enormous (Table 1).

The similarities between the two moments in time follow from two aspects of the CCTB. Originally, the amount of money in the system was more or less the same.[13] The cut-off points and the principles of targeting were the same, as were the amounts paid. In addition, the design of the policy allowed provinces to reduce social assistance benefits by the same amount, so that the effect of the new CCTB would be "income neutral" for social assistance clients. Only two provinces, New Brunswick and Newfoundland and Labrador, choose not to avail

TABLE 1:  A Comparison of Family Benefits, Federal Government
Eligibility and Payment Amounts

| Child Tax Benefit and Working Income Supplement (1997 rates) | Canada Child Tax Benefit – CCTB (1998 rates) |
| --- | --- |
| **Child Tax Benefit** received by 80% of families<br>• maximum received by families with income less than $25,921<br>• CTB disappeared at $66,721 (1 or 2 children) | **Basic Child Tax Benefit** received by 80% of families<br>• maximum received by families with income less than $25,921<br>• CTB disappeared at $66,721 (1 or 2 children) |
| **Working Income Supplement** received by families with earned income between $3,750 and $25,921<br>• maximum to a family with income less than $20,921 but earned income over $3,750 | **National Child Benefit Supplement** received by low-income families<br>• maximum to families with incomes under $ $20,921; disappears at $25,921<br>• an additional amount to families with income less than $20,921, a child under 7 and no Child Care Expense Deduction |
| **CTB plus the WIS:**<br>$1,020 + $605 = $1,625 | **Basic CTB plus the Supplement :**<br>$1,020 + $605 = $1,625 |

Source: Clark (1998, ch. 1).

themselves of this option; the other eight as well as the Territories reduced their social assistance benefits.

However, behind what might seem to have been only a minor adjustment was actually a very important shift in principle. First, the NCB marked a new commitment on the part of Ottawa to post-deficit social spending that would "pay off." The NCB clearly allows the federal government to use its spending power so as to enter directly into contact with Canadians, rather than via the cost-sharing style of CAP. It has done so enthusiastically, announcing frequent increases to the NCB.[14] The payment schedule and other details of the NCB, as of July 2000, are provided in Tables 2 and 3.

As part of a redesign of social assistance in the post-CAP era, the NCB "relieved" provinces of some of their social assistance costs, thereby creating what have been termed "reinvestment funds." They are to be used according to provincial preference, for income transfer or for services. While there are requirements for reporting and transparency (requirements that have reappeared in SUFA), there is

TABLE 2:   Structure of Child Benefits, Federal Government, July 2000

|  | Basic Child Tax Benefit | + | National Child Benefit Supplement | = | Canada Child Tax Benefit |
|---|---|---|---|---|---|
| 1 child | $1,104 | | $ 977 | | $2,081 |
| 2 children | $2,208 | | $1,748 | | $3,956 |
| 3 children | $3,389 | | $2,442 | | $5,831 |
| 4 children | $4,570 | | $3,136 | | $7,706 |

Source: Compiled based on information from Appendix 3 of the 1999 National Child Benefit Progress Report available at <www.socialunion.gc.ca/ncb>.

TABLE 3:   Cut-off Points for the Canadian Child Tax Benefit

|  | Family Income |
|---|---|
| Maximum Child Tax Benefit | Under $30,004 |
| Maximum supplement | Under $21,214 |
| Partial supplement | Between $21,214 and $30,004 |
| Family income above which no basic CTB is received | $74,000 (1 and 2 children) |

Source: Compiled based on information on the National Child Benefit available at <www.socialunion.gc.ca/ncb>.

no effort to shape spending; cross-provincial variation is even more the norm than before.[15]

The provinces and territories have spread their money over a range of program areas, as described in Table 4. Fully $347 million of their $500 million expenditures have gone to services and transfers useful for employed parents, however (the first three categories of Table 4).

The design of the NCB has broad consequences for the citizenship regime. First, there is much less emphasis on pan-Canadian nation-building than there was in earlier programs. Variety and provincial choice is valued over symmetry. Second, the NCB marks a profound change in the ways income support is structured. Families with children and *equal amounts of income* — whether from earnings, child maintenance payments, Employment Insurance, or social assistance — receive exactly the same benefits from Ottawa. The CCTB eliminates the distinction between "unavailable" and available for work that structured so much of postwar income security. Third, and coupled with other reforms by provinces,

TABLE 4:   Provincial and Territorial Reinvestment Expenditures, 1998-1999

| | |
|---|---|
| Child benefits and earned income supplements | $154.4 million |
| Child care | $172.4 million |
| Supplementary health benefits | $ 20.5 million |
| Early childhood services and children-at-risk services | $ 49.6 million |
| Other | $103.6 million |
| Total | $500.5 million |

Source: See Table 2.

almost everyone must now seek to enter the labour force, and has a responsibility to do so. There is no more "choice" about the matter, unless families can afford out of their own earned incomes the luxury of a stay-at-home parent. All governments are quite clear that "the National Child Benefit aims to prevent and reduce the depth of child poverty and help low income parents stay in jobs by ensuring that when parents leave welfare for work, they keep benefits and services for their children."[16] The "welfare wall" has become the target, while the responsibilities of parenting alone are no "excuse" for not earning income. It is important to note that these changes to social assistance programs and child benefits were preceded by an important reform in Unemployment Insurance. It is the complement to the reforms in the social assistance programs.

In 1994, the Liberal government redesigned one of the most important programs of the postwar citizenship regime. Employment Insurance (EI) replaced Unemployment Insurance, signalling a new emphasis on fostering "market readiness," via training and so on.[17] Subsequently, the Labour Market Agreements negotiated between Ottawa and most of the provinces consolidated responsibility for training and other "employability" measures at the provincial level. In doing so they blurred the boundaries between employed, unemployed, long-term unemployed, and social assistance clients. All four were classic categories of the postwar citizenship regime, two of which identified people as "in" the labour force and two which treated them as "out" of it. Now these categories are less meaningful, as the newly unemployed line up with the single mother seeking training in order to maintain her benefits.

In both EI and the Labour Market Agreements the emphasis is clearly on labour force participation, no matter how low the wage. While not all provinces have instituted workfare with the enthusiasm of Ontario, they have all undertaken to facilitate movement into the labour force, and to remove barriers to participation, such as loss of benefits associated with taking a low-paying job. These allow parents with low-paying or precarious jobs to retain some of the benefits they had while on social assistance, sometimes only for their children and sometimes for the whole family. Health cards and drug coverage, and sometimes dental care, are the classic choices here; as Table 4 shows they are an important component of the reinvestment funds. These employment-related benefits, it must be again noted, are provided through the NCB — that is, only to those who are parents of children under 18.

Equality of opportunity is now for children, who receive services such as educational and developmental child care through the NCB, as well as raising their parents' income through child benefits and income supplements. They can, by opening access to the NCB and to "enriched" employability programs, lead the low-income adults who are their parents toward benefits. Many adults now gain *access* to the social rights of citizenship because they have dependent children, rather than as a direct result of their individual relationship to the labour market.

With the NCB's emphasis on "taking children off welfare," social assistance for youth or families without dependent children, becomes truly a program of last resort, with the consequences for future exclusion that might imply.

The companion piece to the NCB, the National Children's Agenda (NCA) and its emphasis on school readiness and early childhood interventions sends a similar message. It too put the accent on investments in children. The goal of this initiative is to develop a shared vision and common understanding of children's changing circumstances and needs. The process began in 1997, with an agreement by first ministers of Canada, the provinces, and territories to develop an agenda, including a public engagement process.[18] The need for such a common agenda was justified by "strong evidence, including scientific research, that what happens to children when they are very young shapes their health and well-being throughout their lifetime. Science has proven what we have intrinsically known all along — healthy children grow into healthy, successful adults, who will shape our future." [19]

In June 1999 the consultation document, *A National Children's Agenda – Developing a Shared Vision* was published, setting out six actions to achieve the four goals of good health, safety and security, success at learning, and social engagement and responsibility. It included a description of processes for coordinating government and non-government efforts, or how the policy actors would work together. The actions listed were:

- support the role of parents and strengthen families
- enhance early childhood development
- improve income security for families
- provide early and continuous learning experiences

- foster strong adolescent development

- create supportive, safe and violence-free communities.[20]

Year-long consultations involved individuals and groups across the country, except in Quebec, and including the main five Aboriginal organizations.

The NCA has since then become caught up in the tangles of intergovernmental relations, however. Whereas the consultation document mentioned six specific areas of specific policy, the *Public Report* on year-long consultations is much vaguer about what governments might do. It mentions that governments currently, that is in June 2000, "are exploring opportunities for further collaboration on early childhood development" (2000, p. 12).

The press release by Manitoba's minister of family services and housing, who co-chaired the Federal/Provincial/Territorial Council on Social Policy Renewal that has responsibility for the NCA, helps to explain this reduction in precision; the issue is again a matter of intergovernmental relations. After noting the premiers' reminder that children's issues are "primarily an area of provincial/territorial responsibility," the minister went on to report that "Premiers and Territorial Leaders have also unanimously advocated the need for the full and immediate restoration of $4.2 B to the Canada Health and Social Transfer to return it to 1994-95 levels, plus an appropriate escalator."[21] In other words, for the moment, agreement on new early years initiatives remains caught up in the familiar conflicts between Ottawa and the provinces.

It is interesting to note, however, that the language of investment in children is not universally popular. The consultations of 1999-2000 produced significant changes in the wording of the vision statement, as parents and other advocates argued for a greater appreciation of children and childhood, and less emphasis on their contributions for the future.

## CONSEQUENCES?

What are the consequences of the "juvenilization" of the "model citizen"? The emphasis on measures to ensure equality of opportunity via investments in children has its downsides, as does any choice of social policy. Clear benefits to some children and their parents have come with some costs or at least risks. Other dimensions of citizenship, such as equal access to democratic institutions, or fostering gender equality in the economy, the society, and the family are now somewhat more difficult to pursue.

Increasingly, neo-liberalism's preference for equality of opportunity has come to influence policymakers and social reformers, even those speaking the language of social justice. The latter recognize, of course, that equality of opportunity must be fostered; some form of redistribution is often necessary if the promise is to be more than formal. Social policy in Canada has returned to a theme already present in classic texts of social liberals such as Lord Beveridge in Britain or Leonard Marsh and others in Canada. This is the recognition that many jobs do not generate sufficient income to raise children (Battle 1998).

This problem was understood before, but it has become exceedingly pressing in recent years. Labour market restructuring has eliminated more and more full-time, well-paid, permanent jobs, while creating more and more part-time, temporary and/or low-paid jobs. Four of ten poor working-age families have 40 or more weeks annually of employment. In 1996, 60 percent of couples with children living below the poverty line *earned* half their income in the labour market, while 22 percent of female-headed, lone-parent families did the same. Yet they were poor; they could not earn enough in the market to raise their family above Statistics Canada's Low Income Cut-Off (LICO) (Vanier Institute 2000, pp. 116-23).

Faced with these labour market structures and market incomes, Canadian governments have invented what the Caledon Institute calls the first truly national social policy since medicare and the Canada Pension Plan in the 1960s (Battle 1998). This is the National Child Benefit, and in particular the federal government's portion, which is the Canada Child Tax Benefit. It is the major success of the social union process (Boismenu and Jenson 1998).

The NCB and the NCA are the flagships of the new era. Why? Because equality defined as equality of opportunity really makes most sense when one is thinking of children. All of the notions associated with equality of opportunity, such as investments in human capital, social investment, training, and the like are most relevant for the young. Surveys reveal that the most popular and politically legitimate social spending in Canada is that most associated with a children's agenda. The "new" policy thinking focuses on schools, on population health and the importance of the "early years," on child care, child development and healthy starts, on enforcing the financial responsibilities of "deadbeat dads." Even employment policy focuses on the youngest of the workers — unemployed youth. It seeks to manage their transition to labour force participation. The goal in all this is to prepare the next generation to take its place as responsible adults. The role of the state is to make sure that children are not made to suffer for the conditions that their parents' lives — their choices and their actions — impose on them.

The most general point is, then, that the redesign of Canada's citizenship regime is doing more than cutting some social programs and redesigning others. Canada emerges from the dark years of pure neo-liberalism and seeks new ways to re-knit the bonds of social cohesion, new values of social justice and equality are being constructed. The debates about the social union are the place that this is happening. These are constructed around the figure of the child. He or she is the focus of collective as well as private responsibility. Moreover, the equality promoted is confined to equality of opportunity for future life chances.

In the meantime, however, adults and their needs are pushed into the background. The political consequences are that some lament the lack of support for full-time parenting. Others, however, struggle to get their concerns about the overwhelming stress of balancing work and family life onto anybody's agenda, whether employers or governments.

This chapter's point is not to argue against the National Child Benefit. It is rather simply to point out that restricting the definition of equality to one of equality of opportunity, and then making children the primary focus, may reinforce or foster other forms of inequality. A citizenship regime that could simultaneously focus on the needs of adults and children would be a more balanced regime. In the current situation, however, real risks are present.

The first is the issue of outcomes. Promoting equality of opportunity is perhaps the most limited definition of social justice. The language of substantive equality and of social and economic rights has been toned down significantly.

The second issue is that of adults. Such a redesign of welfare and income redistribution does nothing to address the income security needs of adults whose children are grown or have no children. In particular, employment policies focused on the youngest cohorts render virtually invisible the needs of older workers, whether women returning to the workforce or male workers who have lost their employment in traditional industries.

Third, there is the issue of gender equality. It is true that much of the focus on children has had the happy consequence of bringing the need for child care to the fore. However, Canada is actually experiencing declining attention being paid to matters of gender equality. Even the importance of "balancing work and family" is taking second place in many jurisdictions. It is simply invisible once adults and their needs fade into the background. In particular, questions of gender power in the workplace, in politics, and even in everyday life are more and more difficult to raise, as adults are left to take responsibility for their own lives.

Finally, there is the matter of democracy. Children may be symbolic citizens in this analysis, but they are never full citizens in fact. They remain minors. Therefore, they cannot, as real citizens must, employ the force of democratic politics to insist on social reform in the name of equality. A child-centred definition of equality is, then, also one that renders less visible the need for collective action by citizens mobilized to make claims and thereby use the state against all forms of unequal power.

NOTES

1. The concept was developed in Jenson and Phillips (1996), in particular to address the issues of access to political institutions and processes of intermediation. It has also been applied to social policy restructuring in Boismenu and Jenson (1996, 1998).
2. For a classic analysis in historical terms of citizenship and equality, see Bendix (1964).
3. It is important to note that able-bodied adults who were not caring for children had few rights of social citizenship in most provinces. They tended to be eligible for the most controlled and limited types of assistance, in which they had to "prove" need (Boychuk 1998).
4. These became parental leaves in 1991.
5. All provinces developed subsidies for child care, available to low- and sometimes middle-income parents, paid to service providers, and financed through the Canada Assistance Plan (CAP). They were paid in the name of the working poor, in order to reduce their chance of becoming "dependent" on social assistance (Guest 1985).
6. The one exception was the program of child-care subsidies which could only go to non-profit providers. However, given that family daycare (in which the carer has no training and regulations focus only on health and safety) was included as well as centre-based care, the concern was less with quality than with the notion that the state should not be subsidizing commercial and profit-making companies.
7. This same shift toward a commitment to gender equality was visible in many European countries such as France, Sweden, or Belgium in the 1970s, as well as in the developing European Community (Jenson and Sineau 1997).
8. For a review of the notion of social investment state and its links to Britain's New Labour, see Saint-Martin (2000, pp. 37ff).
9. For the concept of decommodification and its role in welfare state regimes, see the classic statement in Esping-Andersen (1990).
10. The practice is the following. On the first page of each major document setting out the terms of an agreement among the federal, provincial, and territorial governments for a "national" program, there is an asterisk and a note which says something like, the Government of Quebec agrees with the objectives of the program. However, the Government of Quebec has chosen not to participate because it wishes to assume full control over programs in its territory. This asterisk exists for the National Child Benefit and the National Children's Agenda, as well as in other areas of social policy such as policies designed for the disabled.
11. See the numerous documents, dating since 1997, at <www.socialunion.gc.ca/ncb>.
12. It is, therefore, substantially different from the strategy of the US government, which has systematically widened the distinction between "deserving" and "undeserving" by investing more and more in the earned income tax credit while eliminating "welfare as we know it." The Canadian strategy of income-testing seeks a middle way between totally targeted and universal programs.
13. In the 1997 Throne Speech, Ottawa announced an increase of $850 million per year in additional federal support for low-income families with children, $250 million of which had been already allocated in the 1996 Budget.
14. Most of these increases have gone to the Supplement, although there has also been an increase in the basic benefit. In 1997 when the process first started, the federal government promised to increase its contribution by an additional $850 million "in this mandate." See the *Backgrounder* to the NCB prepared in conjunction with the 1997

Speech from the Throne at <www.socialunion.gc.ca>. In July 2000 the increases were slightly ahead of the targeted number, having reached $1.7 billion, and this before the end of the mandate. In 2000 as well, a further commitment was made to an increase of $2.5 billion by 2004, including indexing for inflation.

15. Boychuk (1998) argues convincingly that cross-provincial variation has always been the hallmark of social policy in Canada.

16. See <www.socialunion.gc.ca/ncb>.

17. In the process eligibility rules were significantly tightened, such that the numbers of claimants able to receive benefits fell dramatically.

18. The Government of Quebec does not participate in the development of the NCA or the SUFA.

19. This is from the *Backgrounder* on the NCA, available at <www.unionsociale.gc.ca/nca>. It is virtually the same language used to justify the NCB. See *Seeing Possibilities* as well as the *Backgrounder* prepared after the 1997 federal Throne Speech.

20. These goals are reproduced in *Public Report* (2000, p. 6) on consultations on *A National Children's Agenda – Developing a Shared Vision*. Available at <www.socialunion.gc.ca>.

21. Press release dated 21 June 2000.

REFERENCES

Battle, K. 1998. "The National Child Benefit: Another Hiccup or Fundamental Structural Reform?" presented to the Conference on the State of Living Standards, CSLS, 30-31 October. Available at <www.caledoninst.org>.

Bendix, R. 1964. *Nation Building and Citizenship*. New York: John Wiley.

Boismenu G. and J. Jenson. 1996. "La réforme de la sécurité du revenu pour les sans-emploi et la dislocation du régime de citoyenneté canadien," *Politique et Sociétés*, 30.

_____ 1998. "A Social Union or a Federal State? Intergovernmental Relations in the New Liberal Era," in *How Ottawa Spends 1998-99. Balancing Act: The Post-Deficit Mandate*, ed. L. A. Pal. Ottawa: Carleton University Press.

Boychuk, G. 1998. *Patchworks of Purpose: The Development of Provincial Social Assistance Regimes in Canada*. Montreal and Kingston: McGill-Queen's University Press.

Clark, C. 1998. *Canada's Income Security Programs*. Ottawa: Canadian Council on Social Development.

Esping-Andersen, G. 1990. *The Three Worlds of Welfare Capitalism*. Princeton, NJ: Princeton University Press.

Guest, D. 1985. *The Emergence of Social Security*, 2d ed. Vancouver: University of British Columbia Press.

Jenson, J. 1997. "Fated to Live in Interesting Times: Canada's Changing Citizenship Regimes," *Canadian Journal of Political Science,* 30(4):627-44.

Jenson, J. and S. Phillips. 1996. "Regime Shift: New Citizenship Practices in Canada," *International Review of Canadian Studies*, 14(Fall):111-35.

Jenson, J. with S. Thompson. 1999. *Comparative Family Policy. Six Provincial Stories*. Ottawa: Canadian Policy Research Networks.

Jenson, J. and M. Sineau. 1997. *Qui doit garder le jeune enfant?* Paris: LGDJ.

Myles, J. and P. Pierson. 1999. "La réforme des États-providences "libéraux" au Canada et aux États-Unis, ou la revanche de Friedman," *Lien social et Politiques-RIAC*, 42:25-37.

Public Report. 2000. *Public Dialogue on the National Children's Agenda: Developing a Shared Vision.* Available at <www.socialunion.gc.ca/menu_e.html>.

Saint-Martin, D. 2000. "De l'État-providence à l'État d'investissement social: Un nouveau paradigme pour *enfant-er* l'économie du savoir?" in *How Ottawa Spends 2000-2001. Past Imperfect, Future Tense*, ed. L.A. Pal. Toronto: Oxford University Press.

Vanier Institute of the Family. 2000. *Profiling Canada's Families II.* Nepean, ON: Vanier Institute.

# 8

# Success, Omissions and Challenges in Harmonizing Canada's Social Programs

*Claude E. Forget*

This chapter attempts to assess the degree of success achieved in Canada in combining decentralization and harmonization in the area of social policy. The first section is descriptive and shows that Canada has effectively, if haphazardly, combined diversity with unity. In the second section, the argument is made that success in harmonizing social policies is perhaps more fragile than it seems, for a variety of reasons, which are briefly discussed. The most important of these reasons lies in the over-reliance on financial incentives and the apparent inability to develop an institutional framework to provide stability and offset political fatigue in the central government's role. The third and concluding section contains suggestions to correct the balance between financial and institutional means to foster harmonization — and incidentally — comments on the social union proposal that constitutes the current attempt to achieve that objective. It also argues for changing the focus of harmonization from health to labour market regulation. Finally, it recommends that "national standards" in social programs could be enforced by treating them (or those that can be) as entitlements to be administered by the courts rather than by any cumbersome intergovernmental mechanism: a process that is, in any case, already under way.

## UNITY WITHIN DIVERSITY

Canadian provinces play a very significant role in setting the direction for, and in supervising the management of, social policies. For instance, they determine and from time to time, amend the legislative framework governing labour relations as well as working conditions through minimum-wage legislation, legislation on store openings, overtime, and working hours that apply to all but a few industries such as banking, transportation, and telecommunications.

With regard to social expenditures, provinces determine the benefits structure under social assistance programs, and with regard to health services, they set the legal framework within which health institutions and professional groups operate. For all practical purposes, provincial governments are the ultimate employers guaranteeing job security, and negotiating and signing collective agreements for all health and social services personnel. Naturally, they also set budgets for health services, and determine, for example, hospital openings and shutdowns as they do for other public services.

The very substantial decentralization that one can observe in Canada in the field of health and social services and social policies generally, reflects the decentralization of political power in the country as defined by the Canadian constitution which allows the provinces to legislate freely and to spend their own financial resources as they see fit, in their own right and not as agents of the central government. Decentralization, of course, is an ambiguous concept since it may refer both to political decentralization and to administrative decentralization two concepts that may well coexist as they do in Canada. For instance, Ontario and Quebec respectively with populations in excess of 10 and 7 million are as populated as some European states such as Sweden and Switzerland. As a result, administrative decentralization is also an issue within each of those provinces and indeed several more. Quebec in particular has regional health and social services boards analogous in many ways to the English District Health Authorities with many of the same problems.

A paramount illustration of this political decentralization is provided also in the field of social policy by the use of provincial taxing powers. Although all provinces except Quebec have their provincial income taxes administered by Ottawa, they have discretion in the use of tax credits as well as tax rates, to implement social policy goals in this way.

Despite the very high degree of decentralization of social programs and policies, there is also in Canada significant convergence, but not identity, of those policies and programs. The concept of a national social policy is not an oxymoron. That convergence is particularly marked in the area of health services. A national health service program was introduced in two different steps that took place respectively in the late 1950s and the late 1960s. Federal hospital insurance legislation was introduced offering to pay more or less 50 percent of the cost, in each province, of providing a free, comprehensive, and portable program of hospital care. Over a four-year period all provinces implemented their own part in this bargain. A similar formula for medical services was introduced in the late sixties with the same rapid take-up rate by all provinces. In parallel, in the field of social services and income support programs, the central government also introduced in the mid-sixties a general cost-sharing formula with basically no design feature requirement that provinces were expected to comply with, except the absence of any residence requirement for beneficiaries.

Simultaneously, a contributory earnings-related public pension plan was put in place. Quebec insisted, as it was entitled to because of national constitutional provisions, on designing and administering its own system, whereas all the other provinces were happy to have their pension system administered by the central government. Through a successful negotiation, the resulting plans have been closely related and administered in a seamless way; this is a particularly important attribute for people who move between Quebec and other provinces.

These instances of federal-provincial cooperation in the setting up of social policies and programs were imitated in other less pre-eminent areas. Concurrently, and contributing equally strongly to the overall picture of a convergent set of national social programs, there are such totally and exclusively federal programs such as Unemployment Insurance (recently rather coyly renamed Employment Insurance) and Old Age Security, a non-contributory, non-earnings-related pension scheme. It is noteworthy that these last two programs were introduced following a change in the Canadian constitution giving the central government power to legislate in those areas. Given the inherent difficulty of amending any constitution, this certainly illustrates the strength of the support for a national social policy felt at the time. In parallel, yet a third national social program was put in place, family allowances, which not only did not require any constitutional amendment but which triggered, because of a court challenge, a Supreme Court decision that has played an important role in intergovernmental debates ever since, namely that Ottawa may spend at will in any field of activity over which provincial governments alone may legislate.

Canada therefore seems to have enjoyed tremendous success in combining decentralization with harmonization in its social policy. While this judgement is true, this self-congratulation should be tempered with an acknowledgement that there is a lot of fuzziness in the extent of harmonization of provincial policies, a surprisingly narrow focus in the scope of the harmonization effort and a number of emerging issues for which no solution is in sight.

The fuzziness statement applies mostly to health insurance. If private insurers provided coverage, the fine print of the respective provincial policies would read very differently. Harmonization in this area has been applied very pragmatically. This is not necessarily a criticism. Provincial variations have to do with services that may be considered of secondary importance such as chiropractic services, dispensing opticians' services, and drugs, etc.

The narrow focus of convergence reflects the fact that the debate about policy harmonization in Canada has consistently ignored labour-market policies and regulation. This is a vast area that is managed in a totally incoherent way. Provincial labour-market regulation on minimum wage for instance can create unemployment, which then triggers federal expenditure. Unemployment benefits can be modified because of stricter eligibility rules for instance, in a way that increases provincial outlays for social assistance. Perhaps most perverse of all, the design of the completely centrally administered Unemployment Insurance program has been deliberately distorted to fit the special requirements of certain regions of the country in a way that has produced incentives for labour mobility in a direction opposite to what would be economically sound. For instance, in periods of high unemployment, the program offered more generous benefits in areas of highest unemployment thereby creating an incentive for the unemployed to move toward those areas where by definition their chances of finding a job were bleakest! This is an amazing demonstration of a national policy that fails the test of national objectives.

The success of Canada's harmonization in the field of social policy has been obtained in the context of strong economic growth and a frenzy of social expenditure expansion. The political dynamics of harmonization through shared-cost programs might be found to work very differently if at all, in the different context of expenditure restraint and of scaling down of social programs. It is uncertain whether the implications of this new context are understood by politicians.

In February 1999, the central government and nine of ten provinces concluded an agreement on the social union that they hope might help them cope with tomorrow's problems in harmonizing social policies. It basically creates a process of mutual consultations at the policy formulation stage and envisions a dispute settlement mechanism. Before venturing an analysis of these matters, it is useful to describe the various sources of tension that are at work within decision-making circles concerned with social policy and social programs.

## TENSIONS THAT ARE THREATENING CURRENT POLICY HARMONIZATION

### Asymmetrical Political Impact

In a study I did for the McDonald Commission 15 years ago, I attempted to show that conditional federal grants to the provinces where the best, and indeed even probably the only, instrument for harmonizing social policies that Canadians were ever likely to get. Indeed, they have proven to be incredibly effective. When health services programs were introduced, Ottawa effectively twisted the provincial governments' arms. When in the 1990s the mood turned to deficit reduction and

Ottawa sharply curtailed its funding, the provincial governments had no choice but to squeeze hospital budgets.

However, use of this instrument impacts federal and provincial politics in a very asymmetrical way at various stages in a program's evolution. At the inception of the program, the central government occupies the centre of the stage, and gets all the visibility and the political credit. Once the program is in place and is generally taken for granted, the focus of attention shifts to the provincial governments that have to take management-type decisions while federal politicians who continue to provide a significant portion of the funding, crave visibility. Over time, central government funding therefore gradually shrinks or even suddenly melts down. From a position, about 25 years ago, where the central government contributed almost half of total funding for so-called shared-cost programs, federal funding has now been eroded down to a mere 15 percent share. In a process of budget cutbacks, it is not very difficult for the central government to write a somewhat reduced cheque to provincial governments. For the latter, stuck with the ultimate responsibility of making hospitals work, it is politically distressing to reduce their commitments with the attendant huge loss of goodwill. Thus, at various times, at least one of the two orders of government involved in a shared-cost program has reasons to dislike its political implications.

Federal-provincial programs are also a very blunt instrument for harmonizing the design features of given programs. Imagine for instance that the central government decides that palliative care ought to be included in the definition of insured services in each province. How can it enforce this wish except through the offer of 100 percent financing of the marginal cost of such a service? Even then, the mechanism to identify and share the cost of a very specific element within the health services disappeared as long as 20 years ago. More to the point, if a province decided not to avail itself of this offer, what kind of penalty would the central government define to obtain leverage? This is the reason why many of the so-called basic characteristics of health-service programs such as public (as opposed to private) administration, comprehensiveness, and portability have been interpreted differently in different provinces and with no corresponding effort by the central government to enforce uniformity. It is also probable that the central government's eventual attempts to enforce those fundamental characteristics would be struck down by the courts as a non-permissible form of regulation in a field of provincial jurisdiction.

It is not a very significant criticism of federal-provincial grants to say that provincial politicians do not very much relish their use, for after all if an instrument of harmonization is to work it has to imply from time to time a degree of coercion. What is more significant is that once the good-news decision has been made, federal-provincial grants offer very little gratification for federal politicians.

Their lack of visibility in funding and their ineffectiveness in shaping managerial decisions and details of program design mean that funding inevitably declines to a point where its survival may be in question.

## Governance Issues

The preceding remarks were based on very pragmatic, down-to-earth considerations mostly of interest to politicians. There are also issues of principle that tend to detract from the practicalities of social policy and social program harmonization.

On more than one occasion Canada's auditor general has remarked that a lot of federal social expenditure is done without any regard for principles of accountability. For instance, it is now impossible to state with any precision or even within a wide range of approximations, how much Ottawa spends on health services. This is due to a trade-off negotiated between the central government and the governments of the provinces whereby a reduced federal commitment to a variety of federal-provincial programs in the field of health, higher education, and social assistance, would somehow be compensated by a much greater discretion given to the provinces in allocating federal funds according to their own priorities. To this first breach of the principles of accountability, must be added the fact already mentioned that the basic characteristics of the Canadian health-care system, with one exception relating to the prohibition of extra-billing, are in effect not enforced. On the provincial side, but as can be expected especially from Quebec, the issue of accountability has also been raised to object to the very notion of federal spending in areas of provincial legislative jurisdiction.

There is little doubt that the Canadian federal system of government, particularly with extensive use of joint central-provincial financing of many programs, lacks in transparency and is a source of extensive confusion for the general public. Its only defence is the pragmatic one that the system has worked and has probably encouraged a more vigorous development of social programs than would otherwise have been the case. It has also encouraged a fairly flexible interpretation of the system's so-called basic principles, a form of accommodation to regional differences in the perceived importance of various secondary services.

However, upon reflection criticisms of the present system based on a principled interpretation of accountability and parliamentary sovereignty (at either the central or the provincial level), may be misguided. First, although governments can bind themselves through international treaties by virtue of the royal prerogative they cannot do so vis-à-vis each other within a federation because this would be an encroachment on Parliament's sovereignty. This has paved the way for much instability in intergovernmental arrangements inside the federation with unilateral amendments decreed by the central government sometimes only months after a painstakingly arrived at consensus. Indeed, in Canada, there is no such thing as an intergovernmental "agreement" in any legally enforceable sense beyond the press release that announces that an agreement has been reached! Second, it may not be very useful to uphold accountability to Parliament at a time when parliamentary control has become an empty concept. Party leaders emerging successfully from a general election control both the executive power and the legislature. As a result, meaningful checks and balances are virtually non-existent and the general public by and large ignores parliamentary debates. By contrast, federal-provincial debates receive a lot of attention and provide, in fact, if not the only, at least the most important existing check on the use of power at either level of government. The confusion in responsibilities often seen as the negative implication of federalism might come to be perceived, if this is right, as the twenty-first century version of political equilibrium!

## Distributional Issues

Central government initiatives, whether they consist in the introduction of new social programs or in substantial changes in funding levels, impact differently on different provinces. The respective revenue-raising potentials of provinces as well as social preferences diverge widely in a country where average income levels differ by a magnitude of two between the poorest and the richest provinces. Canada has a program of equalization of the revenue potentials of individual provincial governments up to a five-province "national" average. However, differences in spending needs are not compensated for. Beyond the sometimes acrimonious debates this opens up, lies the substantive question as to how far should social policies and programs be harmonized as long as such large disparities endure?

In any case, when the central government decides to alter the level of its financial contribution, it has the discretion to do so in a way that falls unevenly on different provinces. For instance, when Ottawa cut back its grants under the Canada Assistance Plan in the early 1990s, it did so by freezing at their existing levels its otherwise rising contributions to the richest provinces. When it recently restored some of its financing for health services it did so in a way to allow of the richest provinces to catch up to a uniform national per-capita figure. On both occasions, these choices attracted protest.

## National Identity Issues

With regard to some important social programs, the federal government has set the tone for policy development, yet it is by definition divorced from managerial pressures in the day-to-day operations of those programs. This has led federal

politicians to indulge in a lot of *a priori* reasoning and grandstanding and to foster in federal provincial debates about such programs a relatively high degree of
rigidity in contemplating any required adjustment process.

What is even worse is that the Canadian health-services program has gradually
emerged over the last ten years as a national icon, a defining characteristic of
national identity. It is of course nothing of the sort, since the Canadian system is
not materially different from the systems in existence in most other western countries except the United States. This sole exception naturally gives the health-services
programs their salience! The resulting symbolism lends to any debate about health-
care reform a quasi-religious fervour. This is not a very promising starting point
to approach the inescapable reassessment of the role of government in financing
health services in the coming century.

The only fundamental characteristic of the Canadian health system that has
been enforced by Ottawa is the "universality" criterion or what Americans would
call "first dollar insurance coverage." User charges introduced by provincial governments were effectively reversed by the central government using in effect what
were fines. This issue will not go away but may turn out to be impossible to
resolve because of an already evident intergovernmental gridlock.

## THE SOCIAL UNION MIRAGE

It is Clausewitz who said: "War is nothing but a continuation of political inter-
course with a mixture of other means." Similarly, the administrative agreement
concluded in February 1999 on the social union is basically the Canadian constitutional debate pursued through other means. The arguments of participants and
commentators, pro and con, are entirely borrowed from the country's inconclu-
sive and long-lasting constitutional debate and have almost nothing to do with the
realities of social policy harmonization. Whereas such "administrative agreements"
had been seen by some as a way to bypass unproductive constitutional concerns,
unfortunately the "escape velocity" was never attained and the debate has remained stuck in its familiar orbit.

The social union concept had arisen in the context created by the escalating
cutbacks in central government financing of social programs, particularly in the
1995 budget. Provincial governments wanted to impose a discipline of sorts upon
the central government to give early warning of intended changes in financing
levels or of new initiatives, to consult them, and even to subordinate central initiatives to the existence of a consensus among provinces.

It is anyone's opinion whether the social union concept will prove to be fruit-
ful. Leaving aside the objections of the Quebec government, the atmosphere of an
emerging consensus was somewhat troubled by the central government's initiative,

taken simultaneously, to bypass the spirit of this agreement by setting up a Millennium Scholarship Fund which escapes the spirit of the social union consensus by virtue of its being funded 100 percent by Ottawa and by making substantial changes in social transfers in this year's budget with no prior consultations.

The breadth of vision and leadership from the centre that would seem to be required ingredients for success, are not yet visibly present.

Finally, at the insistence of Quebec, much energy was expended in dealing with potential so-called "opting out" by provinces from central government programs. This is a made-in-Canada concept that has never had any substance even when historically Quebec, of all provinces, opted out of federal cost-shared health programs and received in lieu of central government cash transfers, a central tax abatement that allowed it to increase its own income tax revenues. In reality, Quebec then played exactly by the same rules as all the other provinces. The social union agreement similarly provides for a totally vacuous opting-out option.

The only meaningful opting-out that has ever taken place in Canada is the gradual and sometimes precipitous erosion of financial involvement of the central government in social expenditure, a pressing problem that the social union document does not really address.

## Concluding Wish List

Canada has so far been successful in combining unity and diversity in its social policies and programs. However, after having expressed so many misgivings about the perceived weaknesses of present arrangements in the foregoing, it is necessary to indicate the direction in which efforts at bringing remedies for those deficiencies should go. Conceivably such suggestions could be of interest even outside Canada in emerging situations that in many ways resemble the federal-provincial context familiar to Canadians.

## Harmonization Is Best Effected Through a Combination of Financial and Institutional Instruments

Financial incentives offered by the central government to the provinces have more than proven their effectiveness in bringing about significant changes in policy. In all probability, they will continue to be used with significant impact. However, the strictly financial framework that Canada has used to achieve harmonization is less than optimal. There is also a need for an institutional framework allowing the two orders of government to enter into legally binding accords that would retain their full strength and validity for a predetermined period.

Crucially, those agreements should provide an exit strategy for the grant-giving central government for the time when it is believed the new policy will be in place and the political motivation and enthusiasm of the central government will predictably fall to very low levels. As is known from private-sector financing, an investment option without an exit strategy offers very poor prospects indeed.

The European Union has tackled the harmonization challenge through an entirely institutional framework that allows the Commission and Council to issue directives, which become templates to be used in national legislation. There is, at present, no element of financial transfer from the union to national governments to stimulate policy harmonization. This was not so important as long as national governments adopted directives through a rule of unanimity. The generalization of majority voting will open a totally new vista with respect to the ability of the European Union to adopt and modify such directives. In order to lubricate the mechanism of that majority voting, financial transfers might well come into play.

## Harmonization Should Only Occur Where it Matters Most

Political union, because it is achieved through political means, carries all the vices of public sector thinking, namely an inordinate taste for uniformity. The promise of federalism, and its most difficult challenge, is to marry unity with diversity. Before embarking on harmonization efforts, the first question to ask is "why"?

Canada would benefit from refocusing its policy harmonization effort so as to give greater importance to policies and programs that impact the labour market and move away from its harmonization attempts in other fields and, in particular, with regard to health services. In this field, given the emerging technological and demographic context, governments will require a great deal of flexibility to shape program design and entitlements. The current desire held in some quarters to define Canada in terms of its health programs would be misguided at any time but is particularly wrong-headed now and for the foreseeable future.

## Define Legally Enforceable Entitlements

Instead of attempting to manage the detailed features of social programs through the cumbersome machinery of federal-provincial relations, decisionmakers should consider giving the courts jurisdiction to enforce policy principles that can and should be translated into entitlements for intended beneficiaries. It is interesting to observe that in the context created by budget cutbacks and deficit-reduction over the past five years, the courts have begun to look at the high level principles found in federal and provincial health-services legislation as well as in the Canadian

Charter of Rights and Freedoms and to censure some glaring discrepancies be-tween promise and performance. The ripple effect from a few recent decisions and those that are expected to follow, have not made themselves felt as of now. If they induce politicians to be less ambitious in stating the purposes and expected effects of new programs and thereby diminish the rather large dose of hypocrisy now surrounding many public policies, this would be welcome.

# 9

## Canadian Labour Market Policies: The Changing Role of Government and the Extent of Decentralization

*Harvey Lazar with Peter Stoyko*

### INTRODUCTION

This book is concerned with several questions relating to public policy trends in the United Kingdom and Canada. In what ways has the role of the state been changing in the two countries? Has there been a shift in authoritative decision making away from governments to markets and civil society? Within the government sector, has there been a trend for powers to be transferred from central governments to regional and local governments? In short, is governance changing in content and style and, if so, what can be said about these changes and their efficacy?

This chapter tackles these questions in relation to Canadian labour market policies. Specifically, three sets of questions are posed about governance since the late 1980s. First, is the role of government changing in Canada with respect to labour market policies and what explains those changes that have occurred? Second, has there been a trend toward decentralization of program responsibilities from the federal to provincial or local orders of government? And what is the driving force behind any such reallocation? Finally, can anything be said about the effectiveness of what has been happening? How is the public interest being affected?

Over the past decade, the Organization for Economic Cooperation and Development (OECD) has devoted considerable attention to issues related to employment, public management, and welfare state governance. The extensive OECD Jobs Study called for a move away from passive support to the unemployed and toward active measures that improve employability and the efficient allocation of labour (OECD 1994). The growing global integration of trade and investment was said to necessitate a transition toward governance structures and policies that promote international competitiveness. This included specific recommendations calling for the decentralization of decision-making authority in labour market programs in order to make programs more responsive to users. Indeed, the public management arm of the OECD (PUMA) has also made a series of recommendations calling for the use of less coercive, top-down policy instruments for the sake of making government organizations more flexible and adaptive (OECD 1995).

Recent OECD reports about the implementation of the Jobs Study claim that Canada has implemented recommendations to decentralize labour market governance structures in order to improve economic and administrative efficiency (OECD 1997). This is mostly a reference to the reallocation of certain labour market responsibilities from the federal government to provincial governments. This study will shed new light on these findings by providing a more detailed account of the extent to which a jurisdictional reallocation of responsibilities has taken place and the reasons that prompted them. It will also look more closely at the prime motivators of any centralization or decentralization trends, for such trends may take place for reasons completely unrelated to economic and administrative efficiency considerations underscored by the OECD.

## Canadian Labour Market and Employment Policy Themes

Four broad themes have characterized Canadian labour market policy over the last decade. First, governments have reduced their role in the labour market. This has been reflected in federal government policies and has generally been the case for provincial governments. This has been especially true of spending and regulatory policies. The motivation underlying these trends may have been linked, in part, to concerns about the need to enhance economic efficiency in the face of low rates of productivity growth and the increasingly competitive nature of international markets. However, this concern was not the principal influence propelling these changes. On the whole, the principal influence has been the pressure to improve Canada's public finances.

Second, there has been a trend to decentralization, but only a modest trend. There is one prominent case of administrative devolution, but the detailed analysis below will show that the overall direction is not unambiguously decentralist in its general thrust. Taken as a whole, the trends hint at a new approach to federal-provincial relations that goes beyond rudimentary questions about centralization and decentralization. The approach involves closer collaboration between federal and provincial governments in establishing objectives and policy frameworks while, at the same time, leaving each order of government free to design and deliver its own programs within that collaborative framework. While it is much too soon to be sure that this trend will have staying power, at least for the moment it is an interesting experiment in combining collaborative and classical models of federalism.

Third, the cause of these intergovernmental trends is, for the most part, unrelated to the changes in the role of government. They are motivated primarily by domestic political considerations, particularly those relating to relations between the federal government and the Province of Quebec.

Finally, while it is too soon to evaluate the efficacy of the policy trends of the last decade, a preliminary analysis suggests that they may have contributed modestly to stronger employment growth and less tension in the federation. On the down side, however, these trends may have also played a role in widening economic disparities among Canadians.

## Organization

This chapter is divided into five parts. Part two sets out the broad context required for understanding Canadian labour market policy over the 1990s. Part three outlines the scope of inquiry, including the selection of the labour market policies studied. The fourth part describes and analyzes each of these four policy areas in relation to the three sets of questions posed at the outset of the chapter. Conclusions are stated in the final section.

## CONTEXT

Putting Canadian labour market policy trends in context requires an understanding of developments within six broad areas: public finance, international competitiveness, domestic political pressures, new theories of governance, trends in employment and unemployment, and the constitutional distribution of labour market powers.

## Government Fiscal Conditions

During the 1990s, Canadian governments at both the federal and provincial level were confronted with the necessity of reversing their long-standing practice of deficit financing. By the mid-1990s, over two decades of deficits had left the federal and provincial governments with combined accumulated debts of close to 100 percent of annual gross domestic product (GDP) (with the federal government the larger culprit). When the Mexican currency crisis hit in December 1994, there was a widespread recognition of the need to reduce vulnerability to world financial markets. Deficit reduction had in fact been one of two key priorities when Jean Chrétien's Liberal government came to power in 1993 (the other priority being employment creation) and it had become the top priority by the time of the 1995 federal budget. The effect of his government's restrictive budgets allowed the federal government to balance its books within a few years. These budgets also affected provincial government finances as well, however, as federal transfer payments to provinces were cut sharply as a part of the federal cost-cutting package. In turn, this added to the need for the provinces to further cut their spending. The overall result was to restore the fiscal integrity of governments in Canada. At the same time, direct employment creation through traditional pump-priming activities became much less acceptable as an approach to improving employment levels. As the 1990s progressed, employment creation also lost much of its urgency as unemployment rates dropped slowly to a ten-year low of 7.5 percent in 1999 and to under 7 percent in 2000.

## Concerns about International Competitiveness

Sluggish productivity growth since the 1970s has raised concerns about the ability of Canadians to maintain their standard of living and the ability of governments to finance the welfare state. During the late 1980s and early 1990s, the Progressive Conservative government of Brian Mulroney attempted to solve the problem by implementing an economic agenda that featured ambitious free trade agreements and a heavy emphasis on enhancing economic efficiency. By the mid-1990s, public debate began to centre on Canada's productivity growth relative to the United States with widespread fears, not always substantiated with evidence, that Canada was falling behind its largest trading partner. The resulting preoccupation with competitiveness and "globalization" has created what Harry Arthurs (1996) refers to as a "conditioning framework" for labour market policy. New trade rules, and attempts to ensure that labour market policies do not interfere with competitiveness, reduced the range of policy options considered to be viable within government circles.

## Domestic Political Pressures

Since the failed constitutional round known as the Meech Lake Accord (1990), there has been considerable pressure within Canada to further decentralize the federation. This had its most visible manifestation in changes to the complexion of party politics. The secessionist Bloc Québécois (BQ) became the official opposition in Ottawa after the 1993 federal election and the separatist Parti Québécois (PQ) came to power within the Province of Quebec in 1994. The Reform Party, which succeeded the BQ as official opposition after the 1997 federal election, also maintained a staunchly decentralist policy stance. In 1995, the Quebec government held a referendum to obtain a mandate to negotiate for greater sovereignty. Although the Quebec government did not receive such a mandate, it obtained more than 49 percent of the vote, thus adding to the pressure to provide a further measure of decentralization in the federation. In the aftermath of the referendum, the provincial premiers outside Quebec endorsed the Calgary Declaration calling for a large-scale rebalancing of the federation that would provide provinces with greater powers. Divestiture of many labour market policies to the provinces had long been a top priority among those advocating decentralization, particularly in Quebec. This led the Chrétien government to make a series of non-constitutional changes that broadened the Government of Quebec's effective authority, including one initiative that gave all provinces greater authority over some labour market programs. This devolution will be discussed in some detail below.

## New Theories of Governance

By the late 1980s and early 1990s, there was considerable acceptance within Canada of the new approaches to effective governance. Neoclassical economic thought and new private sector management theories had eradicated in some cases and weakened in others the conventional wisdom about governments' appropriate role in the economy. For example, Keynesian style counter-cyclical, macroeconomic policies were no longer considered to be effective in stabilizing the economy. Economic efficiency and responsiveness to citizens were by then seen as better served by deregulation, greater use of inducements (instead of restrictions), flatter and more transparent taxation, and the decentralization of administrative structures. Since many labour market policies were rooted in traditional instruments — progressive taxation, income redistribution, and regulation of labour relations — it is evident that the intellectual climate was not by then as supportive of the basics of Canadian labour market policy as it had been in earlier decades.

## Trends in Employment and Unemployment

Unemployment rose in every decade from the 1940s to the 1980s. By the 1990s, there was a widespread concern about a shortage of employment and career opportunities. Although around 7.5 percent in 1999, for much of the previous 15 years the unemployment rate had been at or above 10 percent. There was also a growing consensus that much of this unemployment was structural in nature. In turn, this contributed to a belief that labour market policies should encourage more flexibility in the labour market (a viewpoint consistent with the changing intellectual climate referred to above) and more effective investments in skill development (not necessarily consistent with this changed intellectual context) but in keeping with the OECD emphasis on active measures referred to at the outset of this chapter.

## Constitutional Distribution of Powers

Under widely accepted interpretations of the constitution, the regulation of labour (including such items as collective bargaining legislation, law in relation to occupational health and safety, and minimum wage) are seen as assigned to the provinces except in industrial sectors that are explicitly assigned to the federal government (such as banking, interprovincial transportation, the federal public service, and communications). The result is that about 90 percent of the labour force falls within provincial jurisdiction for the regulatory purposes just mentioned. Owing to an amendment to the constitution almost 60 years ago, the federal government has authority to legislate unemployment compensation schemes. The constitutional authority to legislate or regulate in respect of other labour market matters is ambiguous. Training, for example, has links to provincial constitutional powers over education. But it also is connected to federal powers related to economic policy and to federal powers related to a specific population group (namely Aboriginal people living on reserve and thus to training of this group). Some relatively new areas of policy, such as policies directed toward youth, are targeted to a segment of the population rather than a program area. No order of government has a monopoly of constitutional authority to legislate in relation to them. This complexity has made the distribution of labour market powers a contentious issue that governments have spent the mid-to-late 1990s attempting to resolve.

### SCOPE AND METHOD

Much of the focus of this chapter will be placed on policy trends since the late 1980s. This time frame was selected based on the supposition that the pressure to decentralize, reduce expenditures, and reform the incentive structure of programs had gained considerable momentum by that time.

The types of labour market program under consideration were selected based on two overriding criteria. First, in order to control for selection bias, a broad cross-section of policy instruments was selected. For this reason, taxation, regulation, and spending programs are included. Although they do not constitute an exhaustive list, they do represent the three largest "families" of traditional policy instruments available to governments. Second, in order to determine if interjurisdictional decentralization had occurred, the policy types studied were ones in which the federal government had maintained an active role historically. In sum, the breadth of examples used is large enough and sufficiently well distributed to justify some broad generalizations about the recent experience in Canada.

The five labour market programs analyzed are as follows. First, unemployment compensation programs are studied, in part because they are the largest labour market programs in terms of expenditures, and in part because some critics see them as harmful to economic (i.e., allocative) efficiency. They were a major target of reform proposals during the 1980s and 1990s because of their cost to the public purse and the adverse incentives many claim they create with respect to the supply of labour (creating a presumed disincentive to work and search for jobs).

The second set of programs are so-called "active labour market programs," including training, employment creation schemes, employment agencies, and other initiatives designed to mobilize labour supply. This also includes a relatively new and high profile set of active programs targeted toward youth. Active measures grew in political prominence in the 1980s and early 1990s as a set of responses intended to improve the employability of labour market participants in the face of growing structural unemployment. Many active programs are seen as a lasting investment in human capital and, as such, possess a strong appeal in a political climate extolling the virtues of self-reliance and self-determination.

The third area is labour relations policies. As already noted, the federal government is responsible for labour relations policies only in those sectors of the economy that most obviously transcend provincial jurisdictional boundaries. These are also sectors of the economy of strategic importance to the international competitiveness of Canada's economic infrastructure. Given the pressures created by global and continental integration, one would assume that the pressure toward deregulation would be particularly strong here.

Fourth, many economists have claimed that the direct taxation of payrolls is an impediment to employment growth. Taxation of labour is claimed to be a "tax on jobs." As such, taxation has figured prominently in reform proposals, including proposals surfacing within the intergovernmental arena.

Finally, standards and certification for many professions and occupations are set by governments or by professional/occupational self-regulating bodies authorized by governments to do this. The authority in this area rests largely with provincial governments. One effect of this arrangement is that individuals who wish to move from one province to another have to re-qualify in order to be certified to practise their profession/occupation. Whatever the merits of these provisions, they have long been thought to be barriers to mobility by the federal government and also a kind of dilution of the rights of citizenship. This has led to calls for a reduction in these barriers to mobility.[1]

## POLICY AND PROGRAM TRENDS

Policy trends in these five program areas are considered next. A comparison will be made between the state of a program area in the late 1980s and its state at the turn of the century. The examination will focus on the three sets of questions stipulated at the beginning. To recap, these questions are: (i) *role of government* — has it changed and, if so, in what direction and for what reasons? (ii) *allocation of responsibilities between orders of government within the federation* — has decentralization taken place and, if so, what is the magnitude of changes and what are the reasons for the changes? (iii) *result of the policy trends* — what is known about the impacts of the changes that have occurred?

## *Unemployment Compensation*

Unemployment compensation in Canada consists of two distinct programs: a compulsory social insurance program designed to provide short-term financial assistance to the unemployed who qualify for benefits; and, social welfare programs designed to provide financial assistance to the unemployed and non-employed as a matter of last resort. The two are administered by different orders of government, with Employment Insurance (EI; formerly Unemployment Insurance, or UI) administered by the federal government and social welfare programs administered by provincial governments. The division of powers governing authority over the two sets of programs is entrenched within Canada's written constitution. The *Constitutional Act of 1867* provides provincial governments with exclusive jurisdiction over welfare programming. A 1940 revision to the same Act provided the federal government with exclusive jurisdiction over unemployment insurance. This clear-cut division of powers has led both orders of government to maintain separate delivery systems. The federal government operates roughly 500 local offices, and provinces maintain networks of local offices in numbers that differ considerably from province to province. Given the discreteness of the jurisdictional boundaries, one would expect that intergovernmental tension would be low within the area of unemployment compensation. There are at least two broad reasons why this has not been so.

One is that there is overlap between the federal-provincial programs. Unemployed individuals receiving benefits from the federal government under EI/UI may move on to provincial social assistance when their federal benefits have been exhausted. They may even be drawing provincial social assistance payments when they are receiving EI/UI if the EI/UI entitlements are very low. Therefore, when Ottawa tightens or loosens its EI/UI benefits system, it may affect provincial social assistance programs and expenditures. There is also overlap because the federal government has transferred money to the provinces to help them finance social assistance. These transfers date back to the early post-Second World War years. To the extent that Ottawa has altered the terms of these intergovernmental transfers from time to time, this has also affected provincial programs and finances and, at times, led to significant tensions in federal-provincial relations.

The second reason that intergovernmental tension grew was that the EI/UI program became a matter of interregional controversy after the federal government enriched benefits substantially in a major 1971 reform package. As a part of that reform, the federal government began incorporating regional unemployment rates into the calculation of UI benefits. With unemployed individuals in particularly depressed regions enjoying generous extended benefits, governments of less affluent provinces acquired a greater stake in the federal EI program. Subsequent efforts by the federal government to reduce program generosity encountered fierce opposition from these regions. The flip side of this large interregional transfer from rich to poor regions has been opposition from more affluent provinces. In summary, reforms that have made the EI/UI program more sensitive to regional differences have created a political climate in which provincial premiers are more emboldened to lobby for their regional interests.

Calls for the reform of Canada's unemployment compensation system gained considerable momentum during the 1980s. Some expressed concern with the size of the system and its growing cost. Between two recessionary spells, 1982-83 and 1991-92, the cost of UI benefit payments almost doubled, from $9.3 billion to $18.5 billion. This increase in cost was not in proportion to increases in the number of recipients, which was only 12.3 percent (Green 1994, pp. 5-6). A similar trend can be found in provincial social assistance programs, with the number of recipients climbing steadily through the 1980s before nearly doubling in the period between 1990 and 1994. The proportion of social assistance recipients who may be classified as unemployed, it should be noted, differs a great deal across the provinces, from a low of 28.2 percent to a high of 76.7 percent in 1992 (McIntosh and Boychuk 2000, p. 6). At a time when deficit reduction became a growing concern, unemployment compensation programs were seen as a major cause of governments' financial woes.

The 1980s also witnessed renewed concern about the economic incentives created by unemployment compensation. Unemployment Insurance benefit payments were 60 percent of insurable earnings up to a maximum. In general, the number of weeks of work that were required to qualify for benefits was low in comparison to unemployment insurance schemes in most countries and benefits could run for up to a year. The increases in the generosity of the UI program in 1971, in conjunction with growing levels of unemployment during the 1970s and 1980s, had led to worries that the program itself had created a disincentive to work among certain classes of worker.[2] Concerns were raised about how the duration and generosity of benefits discouraged job searches, thus prolonging the duration of unemployment spells and encouraging workers to leave poorly paid jobs. A Royal Commission (the Macdonald Royal Commission) and a Commission of Inquiry (the Forget Commission) were established in the early to mid-1980s in part, to look at these incentive effects and the future of unemployment insurance. Similar fears were expressed about provincial social welfare schemes, particularly the disincentives to work caused by benefit schedules that reduced benefit payments sharply as recipients obtained small amounts of income from elsewhere. While the evidence about disincentive effects proved to be mixed and somewhat exaggerated (Corak 1994), a debate about the dysfunctions and cost of unemployment compensation was well underway by the beginning of the 1990s. The stage was set for an overhaul of the system.

Reforms in the 1990s involved three principal trends: (i) the UI program (renamed EI) was made much smaller; (ii) social assistance was made less generous and more restrictive; and, (iii) federal transfers to the provinces, including those aimed at helping the provinces to pay for their social assistance programs, were reduced and made less conditional. Each of these trends is discussed further below.

Unemployment Insurance became a more modest program during several waves of reform that included program changes in 1990, 1994, and 1997. The overall effect was to make the program significantly less generous, with replacement rates lowered, entrance requirements toughened, and benefit durations shortened. However, efforts to reduce substantially the interregional differences in benefit entitlements were largely unsuccessful.

At the same time that the federal government was reducing compensation to the unemployed, provincial governments were making social assistance entrance requirements more restrictive and benefit levels less generous. Entrance requirements in many provinces were changed in a way that reduced the portion of "undeserving" recipients, or the employable unemployed, eligible for benefits. Thus, social assistance has moved away from supporting labour market participants. There has also been a tendency toward more onerous fraud verification measures and an increased reliance on incentives designed to promote a welfare-to-work transition. These incentives range from reductions in benefit eligibility and generosity, to more positive supports that help individuals make the transition.

Turning to the federal transfers to the provinces, during the late 1970s and 1980s the federal government cut its payments for postsecondary education and health several times. The aim was to slow the growth rate of such payments to growth rates in the economy and thus allow the federal government to gain more control over its finances. Transfers for social assistance (the Canada Assistance Plan or CAP), on the other hand, remained largely unchanged during this period and were based on a 50:50 cost-sharing formula under which Ottawa contributed one-half of provincial welfare outlays. In 1990, however, for deficit reduction reasons, the federal government imposed a limit on CAP transfer payments to the three wealthiest provinces (Ottawa covered one-half of the welfare costs of these provinces but only up to an arbitrary ceiling), a change the three affected provinces considered unfair. In 1995, the federal government decided to reduce sharply the amount of money it was providing to the provinces for social assistance, health, and postsecondary education and in so doing it consolidated the monies into a single bloc-transfer program, the Canada Health and Social Transfer (CHST). Ottawa argued that the enhanced flexibility to reallocate funding between these large program areas would enable provinces to be more efficient in working with the reduced amounts. As a further concession for the reduction in the amount of its transfers, the federal government also eliminated several conditions it had placed on the design of provincial social assistance programs. During the period under review here, this change in restrictions constitutes the only case of devolution within the area of income support for the unemployed.

As this overview suggests, changes to unemployment compensation programming resulted from the interplay of several factors. First, although successive Conservative governments between 1984 and 1993 showed concern for deficit reduction, it was not until the first Chrétien government took office that successful deficit reduction efforts took place. The EI/UI program and provincial transfers were among the first to sustain heavy cuts by virtue of their sheer size within the federal budget. Provincial governments, looking to balance their own budgets as federal transfers declined, looked to tighten up social welfare programs to help obtain much needed savings. Since many of the recipients of the program were economically marginalized and lacked electoral power, political resistance to the changes was not difficult for governments to overcome. In brief, the main reason for reducing the generosity of these programs, at both the federal and provincial levels of government, was to improve public finances. A secondary factor was no doubt the changed intellectual environment. As Neil Bradford points out, the post-Keynesian, neoclassical critique of interventionist government had become commonplace after the Macdonald Royal Commission (1985) and set the terms of reference for labour market policy reforms of the 1990s (Bradford 1998, p. 121). Without the impetus to improve public finances the changes in the intellectual paradigm might not have been sufficient. In this case, however, these two factors were mutually reinforcing.

The reason Employment Insurance was not decentralized is relatively straight-forward. The formal division of powers, as stipulated within Canada's written constitution, provides the federal government with unambiguous jurisdiction over the program. Some provincial governments had proposed that the federal government turn over the administration of the program to the provinces. However, in the absence of a compelling rationale and a concerted campaign on the part of the provinces, pressure to devolve the program was negligible. The implementation of the CHST involved some very modest further decentralization. Some federal conditions that had been imbedded in the previous CAP program were dropped by Ottawa, leaving the provinces with modestly greater discretion over social welfare programming. The federal government removed these conditions recognizing that, since it would be paying less to the provinces, it had to give up some of its influence over their programs.

The end result of reforms in unemployment compensation is far from clear. However, a number of things can be said with some confidence. First, the portion of labour market participants eligible for unemployment insurance declined considerably during the 1990s. Benefit/Unemployment Ratios (B/U ratio), which is the number of individuals receiving unemployment benefits relative to the total number of unemployed, remained steady during the 1980s (between 70 and 80 percent) before dropping in the 1990s (to just over 40 percent by 1997). Although the B/U ratio does not provide a full picture of the program's role, it does show that fewer people are able to take advantage of an important program in Canada's "social safety net," not to mention a less generous one. Second, given that provincial governments have also been making access to social assistance more restrictive, there is a worry that a group of the unemployed (of unknown size) has become eligible for neither unemployment insurance nor social assistance — effectively falling through the cracks in the system. Third, it seems intuitive that the amount of dependence on unemployment compensation has declined, as the programs were made more restrictive. In any case, unemployment rates in Canada have dropped significantly in recent years, although they remain higher than UK rates. Overall, however, there is evidence of the beginnings of some polarization in the disposable incomes of Canadians, after a prolonged period in which Canada was one of the few countries in the OECD world where after-tax, after-transfer incomes had remained relatively stable.

## Active Labour Market Programs

The question of which order of government has constitutional jurisdiction over active labour market programs does not have a clear-cut answer. As a result, control over active measures has been a source of tension within the federation as the role of active measures as grown since the late 1960s. The constitution gives provincial governments responsibility for education and many provinces have consequently long maintained that measures such as training fall within their jurisdiction. The federal government plays an active role in economic policy and, accordingly, this order of government has maintained that measures such as employment supplements, wage subsidies, and direct job-creation schemes fall within its jurisdiction. Such ambiguity is made worse by the development of new active measures, such as programs targeted toward youth, which transcend traditional departmental structures, not to mention jurisdictional boundaries. By the late 1980s, both orders of government maintained sets of active programs with considerable overlap (although not duplication), a few cases of partnership, and a general lack of coordination.

At the federal level, there were two distinct sources of funding for active labour market measures, the Employment/Unemployment Insurance Account and the Consolidated Revenue Fund (CRF). More than half of spending was financed through that part of the EI/UI program known as "developmental uses," which by law was not to exceed a maximum of 10 percent of the total EI/UI budget. The portion of the EI/UI budget devoted to developmental programs went from 4 to 5 percent in the 1970s to a little over 9 percent by the early 1990s (Riddell 1995, p. 156). Most federal programming for persons with disabilities, youth, Aboriginal peoples, and certain other groups was financed out of the CRF, as many people in these groups did not have EI/UI entitlements. At the end of the 1980s, active measures included work-sharing schemes, direct job-creation schemes, self-employment assistance, employment services, various training-related measures, and a few measures related to youth. From the mid-1980s to the mid-1990s, controlling for the business cycle, federal expenditures on active measures did not increase as a share of GDP. Indeed, they may have declined a little.

As for provincial programs, their active measures have traditionally been handled within departmental structures devoted to training, education, and/or labour. The variety of active measures offered, and the amount of resources devoted to each, differs enormously from province to province.

During the 1993 election campaign, Chrétien's Liberal Party had placed considerable emphasis on active measures, characterizing them as an important "investment in people" in their campaign manifesto. In conjunction with the OECD call to emphasize active measures, the federal Liberal's election pledge to invest in people might have been expected to lead to a heavier financial commitment to active measures by Ottawa. This was not, however, the case. After the 1997 Quebec referendum, the profile of active measures was downgraded in part because of fiscal austerity measures and in part because of a new wariness about encroaching on turf to which some provinces, and especially Quebec, had laid claim. The intellectual commitment to active measures remained, at least as indicated by the rhetoric of politicians in the 1990s, but it did not remain at the forefront of federal policy making or budgetary priorities.

Thus, in the 1995 federal budget, for reasons related to deficit reduction, Ottawa reduced its financial commitments to active measures through the CRF by more than half. It offset these large reductions in part by diverting more EI/UI funds into developmental uses. But in the aggregate, expenditures on active measures were cut significantly. Not long thereafter, the federal government announced these changes, Prime Minister Chrétien promised a divestiture of active measures to the provinces, and a formal offer of devolution was made in 1996. Although the federal government also offered funding to the provinces, the net amount of the federal government's financial commitment to active measures had dropped as a result of the budget changes. This constituted an abrupt change in direction. The federal government retained a modest operational role in this policy area, including gathering and distributing national labour information and support for select groups of labour market participants (youth, the disabled, Aboriginals, and immigrants) and support for Canada-wide industry sector councils. But most of its programming activity was available to be transferred to any province that wished to take up that role.

The devolution of active labour market programs took place during the rest of the 1990s in the form of Labour Market Development Agreements (LMDAs) between the federal government and individual provinces. The enabling legislation involved the new two-part federal EI Act. The first part of the statute set out the new rules for EI eligibility and entitlements. The second part set out the five kinds of active measures that the federal government would be authorized to finance and provided the federal government with the authority to enter into administrative agreements with provincial governments to design and deliver these measures.

It is important to consider a few features of the LMDAs in order to understand the nature of the change in roles that took place. First, although these agreements allow the provinces to design and deliver these measures with funds transferred to them from Ottawa, the agreements are subject to accountability frameworks set out in the agreements that were established by the federal government alone.[3] Second, the LMDAs are five-year agreements, and although they are very likely to be renewed after they expire, there is no constitutional requirement to do so. Third, LMDAs were struck with each province on a bilateral basis and include an "equality of treatment clause" (like a most-favoured-nation provision in an international trade agreement) that allows all provinces to obtain favourable provisions that have been negotiated by other provinces. Fourth, because of the bilateral nature of the agreements, there is considerable variation in devolution across the federation. Some provinces did not opt for full devolution and, instead, agreed to partnerships and co-management with the federal government. Finally, it is important to note that Ontario, Canada's largest province, is the only province that has yet to sign an agreement. This is partly because of resistance by the federal Liberal Party's Ontario caucus about transferring programs to a Conservative provincial government that it appears to detest and partly because Ottawa and Queen's Park disagree on the amount of money the federal government should be transferring to Ontario for this purpose.

In brief, while a significant devolution of active labour market programs has taken place, it is not necessarily a permanent change in jurisdiction, nor is it a wholesale devolution to the provinces. In this regard, it is worth re-emphasizing that it was the federal Parliament that passed the enabling law that created the broad policy framework for the LMDAs. And the absence of a bilateral deal with Ontario (at least at the time this chapter was being completed) serves to underline the point that Ottawa has not abandoned fully its role in this program area.

As to motivation, this was driven overwhelmingly by domestic political considerations, much more so than by new ideas about the merits of a more decentralized state. Indeed, given that the federal government has had local offices for program delivery for a long time, it is not even evident that this change brings the programs closer to the communities it serves.

The federal government's approach to youth employment programs stands in some contrast to its approach to other active measures and serves to further emphasize that Ottawa retains considerable discretionary authority in relation to such measures. Federal programs directed at youth had existed since the 1970s and many new proposals for youth-centred initiatives were made in the 1980s, but it was not until the 1990s that youth programming had been given any coherence. Part of the reason for this was the political appeal of such programs (youth being an attractive target group). But this change in direction was also inspired by worries about generational equity given the demographic structure of the economy and concerns that today's young generation would ultimately bear an unfair share of the accumulating debt of the country and related public pension obligations. Youth programs were rebundled under the auspices of a *Youth Employment & Learning Strategy* (1994) and included a program for at-risk youth and school dropouts (Youth Services Canada and the Stay-In-School Program), internship and summer employment programs, student loans, and learning initiatives. In addition, pilot projects had been established with a few provinces to improve intergovernmental cooperation with respect to youth. Along with this change in organization came an infusion of new money, less than originally planned, but as the federal government gained control of its deficit, more money followed. The 1990s witnessed a large expansion of the federal government's involvement in this field. At the same time, many provincial governments were also focusing on youth programs, particularly in more affluent provinces, which experienced a net in-flow of youth from other parts of the country. British Columbia and Ontario became leaders in the field, as did New Brunswick (owing to federal pilot project money) and Quebec (for reasons of maximizing autonomy), while other provinces (such as Newfoundland and Prince Edward Island) lagged far behind. Overall, this new emphasis on youth programming involved a change in emphasis in welfare state design toward segments of the labour market less able to exercise self-sufficiency and self-determination. It also marked an emphasis on making early investments in the intellectual development of youth in order to better prepare them for a labour market that places a new premium on knowledge, given advances in technology.

A number of developments took place to change the direction of this expansion in youth programming. First, pressure to include youth programs in the LMDAs, particularly by Quebec, and hence to devolve them to the provinces, caused the federal government to adjust its strategy to avoid any obvious intrusion into provincial jurisdiction but by no means to move out of this area. A new *Youth Employment Strategy* (1997) was implemented that downplayed the federal government's role in any programs that directly touched educational institutions, educational curricula, or teaching certification. This more cautious posture did not extend, however, to limiting Ottawa's effort to improve opportunities for post-secondary students through scholarships and loans. And indeed a new program in the late 1990s with increased direct federal funding for such students (the Millennium Scholarship Fund) served to reinforce this point. Second, provincial governments expressed concerns that the federal expansion of youth programming had taken place too quickly and was not designed in a way that complemented existing provincial programs. Conversely, the federal government expressed concern about the unevenness of youth programming across the country, particularly the dearth of programs in less affluent provinces. This led the federal government and the provinces (except Quebec) to engage in a formal dialogue about developing a *National Youth Strategy*. Although it is too early to tell whether this cooperation will be a success, an attempt is being made to better coordinate policies between the two orders of government. Third, during the late 1990s a set of "social union" intergovernmental negotiations took place to set down ground rules and a new vision regarding the way in which federal and provincial governments would work together in relation to social policy (including labour markets). The Social Union Framework Agreement (1999) is a political document, not a legal one. On the face of it, it implies neither centralization nor decentralization but rather establishes a framework for intergovernmental cooperation. However, it does place certain procedural restrictions on the federal government, including restrictions that effect youth programming that did not previously exist. But at the same time, it legitimizes the federal role in social policy. In summary, while there are now a few new (self-imposed and intergovernmental) restrictions placed on the federal government, these restrictions do not constitute decentralization. On the contrary, the federal government throughout the decade has expanded its role considerably in the field of youth, with and without consideration of the provinces.

It is also important to note that, during the late 1980s and early-to-mid-1990s, the federal government and several provinces flirted briefly with the use of corporatist governance structures to design active labour market programs. The federal government established a Canadian Labour Force Development Board in 1991 to obtain private sector input into developmental programs. Several provinces followed suit. These experiments did not last long, for governments proved reluctant to divest significant powers to a separate governance structure. Canada's Westminster model of government, by its very design, is not conducive to the creation of governance models premised on divided authority (Haddow 1998).

The decentralization that took place under the LMDAs was caused by federal government attempts to diffuse nationalist tensions within Quebec by giving in to long-standing provincial demands for control over training and other active programs. This was accompanied by sustained pressure on the part of other provinces, particularly Alberta, for a greater role in this area. It is worth noting that the decentralization that took place was praised by the OECD, although it is not clear that the reforms were exactly what the international organization had in mind in its Job Study recommendations. First, exclusively domestic political pressures, not considerations of administrative efficiency, caused the decentralization. Second, in many instances it is not clear whether the enhanced provincial role actually amounts to a decentralization of administrative structures. As already noted, the federal government had serviced active measures out of an extensive network of local offices that had been given a certain amount of operational discretion, at least compared to some provincial systems. Third, the most persuasive rationale for decentralizing active measures can be made for programs targeted toward youth (as this group is only a few years removed from the provincially run secondary and post-secondary system educational systems), yet the federal government maintains a strong role in this area. Thus, in the one area in which one would expect the greatest synergies from decentralization, no such decentralization exists. Nonetheless, taken as a whole, the story around active labour market measures points to a significant decentralization. The balance in the relative roles of federal and provincial governments has changed in favour of the provinces. When the five-year agreements come to be renewed, it will be clearer whether the devolution that has occurred is just a first step or whether the federal government will withdraw further from this field.

It is unclear what the overall impact of these reforms to active measures has been on the public interest. Part of the problem is that short-term program evaluations provide very little insight into the results of the program, the effects of which are likely to be spread out over a long period. There are worries that the provinces will substitute federal transfers for existing provincial funding and, in so doing, reduce the total amount of funds devoted to active measures. Regardless, the federal government has also devoted fewer funds to active measures, a trend of considerable importance since, prior to the LMDAs, the federal government was responsible for a larger portion of active measures than the provinces. While the government has increased funding for youth and students, much of this is offset by declines in federal transfers to postsecondary education that caused tuition fees (and student debt) to rise dramatically.

## Labour Relations

It has already been observed that around 90 percent of employees in Canada are subject to provincial legislation in relation to labour relations matters. Although the constitution, as such, does not lay out an explicit division of powers in respect of these issues, a 1926 Supreme Court decision placed several limitations on federal government involvement in this area. Thus, the federal government's Canada Labour Code (CLC) relates only to federal government employees and sectors that either transcend provincial boundaries or relate to other federal responsibilities. As a result, the federal government regulates only its own employees and private sector workers in industries such as banking, interprovincial transportation, defence, grain handling, and telecommunications. Although a small segment of the economy, it should be noted that many of these industries are integral to Canada's infrastructure and, as such, play a particularly important role in international competition. A great deal of restructuring that has taken place since the mid-to-late 1980s — such as privatization of Crown Corporations (airports, port authorities, airlines, and railways), reductions in transportation subsidies for farmers, and airline deregulation — have placed strong pressures on workplaces that fall within CLC jurisdiction to be more competitive.

Provincial governments' labour relations acts (LRAs) are administered by government-appointed labour boards, except in Quebec where a labour court operates. The content of provincial LRAs vary considerably, depending on the industrial composition of the province and the political strength of organized labour. In addition to labour relations acts, each jurisdiction maintains employment standards legislation (governing minimum wages, maximum hours, and layoff procedures) and health and safety legislation. The federal government and several provinces also maintain employment equity legislation. All told, there is relatively little intergovernmental tension with respect to labour relations, with the federal government and progressive provincial governments occasionally taking a lead role in legislative reform. The main exceptions to this lack of intergovern-mental tension occur during strikes or lockouts at major ports which create prob-lems for regional economies dependent on the transportation of goods. Since these employees are generally subject to federal labour law, provincial governments have historically lobbied Ottawa for a quick resolution of such labour conflicts.

Prior to the late 1980s, the general trend in labour legislation was to expand the rights of workers to organize and implement policies that increased the bargain-ing power of their unions. Employment standards and health and safety legisla tion were also broadened in scope and coverage. After the late 1980s, the picture changed considerably. Although reforms during the 1990s contain concessions to both labour and management in many jurisdictions (including large-scale changes to the CLC), the overall effect of legislative changes across all jurisdictions has been to weaken organized labour. Although Canada's largest provincial jurisdic-tion, Ontario, made several sweeping union-friendly reforms in the early 1990s (particularly with respect to labour disputes and employment equity), they were repealed with the change of government in that province. More recent reforms have reduced the likelihood of industrial conflict and shutdowns and have pro-vided employers with greater flexibility over the workplace. Minimum wages became less important to ameliorating earnings inequality as minimum wages declined markedly relative to average wage levels. Although public sector unioni-zation has grown since the mid-1960s, from the 1980s onwards there has seen a weakening of wage bargaining in the public sector.

Most of these changes were the result of pressures from the business commu-nity and its concerns about the international competitiveness of the Canadian economy, especially in the aftermath of the recession of the early 1990s. There has been a shift toward recognition that enterprise requires a greater flexibility in order to adapt to international changes. However, it should be noted that changes in government's role (such as in cases of privatization and deregulation in key industries) have also placed new pressures on workplaces to change. Weakening of public union wage bargaining was also related to public sector deficit reduc-tion efforts and governments' ability to exercise sovereign power to impose wage and collective bargaining restrictions. Attempts to "reinvent" the way govern-ment operates in order to better service citizens has led many governments (par-ticularly the federal government) to weaken union restrictions placed on person-nel policy.

There has not been any significant reallocation of responsibilities between fed-eral and provincial orders of government in this area. The only change that can be reported has been the federal government ceding its political leadership role in setting minimum wage levels. Where it was once the leader in setting minimum wages for all jurisdictions, the federal government now tends to set its minimum wages at the level of the provincial average. The cause of this change appears to be twofold. Since the federal government is responsible for labour law in relation to industries (particularly those related to the nation's infrastructure) that play a strategically important role in international competition, Ottawa came to believe that it was appropriate to set minimum wages that reflected this new level of competition. Second, and perhaps more important, the federal government simply ceded the leadership role to the order of government (the provinces) for which labour relations policy is more important. This changed political attitude was linked directly to tensions about Quebec's future in the federation.

Several observations can be made about this sector and developments within it. First, this area of labour law has long been mainly the responsibility of the provinces so that there has been relatively little scope for decentralization toward the provinces. Indeed, Canada's labour relations system has historically been one of the most decentralized among advanced capitalist nations. Second, however, a decentralization of collective bargaining has taken place within Canadian workplaces (from firm to plant-level bargaining) that has been facilitated by changes to legislation that have increased employer flexibility. Third, unlike many other countries (including the United Kingdom), unionization levels have remained stable in the aggregate. A more detailed look at this trend reveals that public sector unionization has propped up unionization levels, while highly competitive industries have faced an erosion of labour organization. As well, there has been little in the way of unionization of the growing low-wage service sector. Finally, many of the changes that have taken place have promoted labour market flexibility. The corollary of this is that they have also contributed a growth of inequality in labour force earnings.

## Taxation of Labour

The taxation of labour is the fourth area of policy that remains to be considered here. In the main, this refers to the kinds of premiums and contributions that federal and provincial governments levy to help finance various social insurance programs. In Canada, the federal government charges a premium of all employers and employees to help finance both EI/UI and the Canada Pension Plan. This levy is a percentage of earnings up to a legislated ceiling. Provincial governments impose similar taxes to help finance workers' compensation and, in a few provinces, public health care.

The political charge against these kinds of levies is that they discourage employment by making it more expensive for employers to hire or retain employees than would otherwise be the case. Indeed, in his first federal budget (1994), federal

Finance Minister Paul Martin described these types of taxes as "silent killers of jobs."

Historically, Canada has in fact had one of the lowest levels of payroll taxes among the OECD countries. During the 1990s, however, Ottawa gave priority to other objectives rather than to keeping these taxes very low. Two examples illustrate this point. First, notwithstanding his 1994 comment about the adverse effects of high payroll taxes, the federal finance minister maintained much higher EI/UI premiums in the second half of the 1990s than was required to finance EI/UI benefits. This was a break with past practice in managing of the EI/UI account. By the year 2000, there was a cumulative surplus approaching $30 billion in the account. Since surpluses and deficits in the EI/UI account are, under Canadian government accounting conventions, folded in with the Consolidated Revenue Account, they help to determine the size of the government's overall budgetary surplus or deficit. In effect, EI/UI premiums have been kept higher than necessary in order to help balance the books of the Government of Canada.

This decision to maintain high UI premiums has been resisted strongly by the governments of the provinces whose residents make the largest net contributions into the EI/UI account. In particular, the Government of Ontario has attempted to mount political pressure to have these taxes lowered, both because they impact in a disproportionately adverse way on Ontario and also because they run against the Ontario government's low tax philosophy. Ottawa has largely ignored these calls for premium reductions.

The second important change during the 1990s was a decision to raise the contribution rate significantly for the Canada Pension Plan (and a similar decision taken by the Government of Quebec in respect of the parallel Quebec Pension Plan). Under Canadian law, changes to the contribution rate for the Canada Pension Plan (CPP) require the approval of the federal government and at least two-thirds of the provinces representing two-thirds of the population. As a result of the concern that the CPP fund was too small, and that this would adversely affect the well-being of future generations, federal and provincial governments (over the objection of two provincial governments) agreed to raise CPP rates in 1997. Quebec made a similar decision in respect of the Quebec Pension Plan. Raising contribution rates was probably the appropriate program decision in the context of the situation that faced the CPP in the 1990s. The main point to note here is that Ottawa was willing to raise rates when program circumstances required it, as in the case of the CPP. But when program requirements would have allowed a substantial reduction in premiums, as in EI/UI situations, rates were kept much higher than required to help reduce the federal budgetary deficit. In short, improving public finances was given a much higher priority than lower taxes or employment growth through a reduction of payroll taxes.

While provincial governments retain a large interest in the federal payroll taxes, Ottawa for the most part stays out of debates about provincial taxes relating to workers' compensation or health care. In any case, there were no changes in provincial payroll taxes in the 1990s that are germane to this chapter.

The allocation of responsibilities relating to federal and provincial payroll taxes has not been a subject of public debate in recent decades. Thus, there has been no discussion of further decentralization although, under the constitution, provinces have paramountcy in relation to old-age pensions. Thus, it is open to any province to withdraw from the CPP, as Quebec effectively did by never participating in it. But no other province seems inclined to do so.

The taxation of labour thus serves as an excellent example of how public finance came to dominate the policy agenda in much of the 1990s. Consideration relating to devolution, reduced taxation, and competitiveness were all subordinated to improving the public purse.

## Barriers to Labour Mobility

The last area to be examined relates to the role of government, either directly or by authorizing others, in establishing standards for various professions and occupations and in certifying individuals who have satisfied these standards to practise in these professions or occupations. In a large majority of these cases, associations representing these professions/occupations establish the standards and allocate the certificates. These associations often also play an active role in defining the curriculum that enables an individual to achieve the appropriate standard and become certified.

The federal government has long argued that these certification processes create an inappropriate barrier to people who wish to move from one province of Canada to another, believing they impede the efficient allocation of resources and also detract from the rights of citizens to move freely within the country. Some provinces shared this view but by no means all of them. In any case, on two occasions during the 1990s, multilateral agreements were signed between the federal government and the provinces that included commitments to eliminate these barriers. In the 1994 Agreement on Internal Trade, measures relating to occupational standards, licensing, certification, registration, and residency requirements for workers that created barriers to mobility were to be eliminated over a period of time. The agreement provided for voluntary compliance where this could be obtained but when this was not forthcoming, governments were to ensure such compliance. In 1999, the Social Union Framework Agreement reiterated and extended the mobility provisions of the Agreement on Internal Trade. (Quebec signed the first of these agreements but not the second.) In the negotiation for the Social

Union Framework Agreement, the federal government made these mobility provisions a high priority.

While it may take a number of years for all of the existing restrictions on labour mobility to be effectively removed, a process has been launched which, over time, will make it easier for Canadians to practise their professions and occupations wherever in Canada they live. The details of how this is to be achieved will vary from one occupation to the other, with, in some cases, the various provincial associations perhaps agreeing to harmonize their standards and, in other cases, we may see some form of mutual recognition (as is the case in the European Union).

In the context of this chapter, there are a few points of interest. The first is that this policy initiative will, over time, remove barriers to mobility and make the labour market more efficient. This is thus consistent with a more market friendly approach to economic management. Second, in some sense this involves a weakening of the regulatory process of individual provinces and replaces it with an interprovincial regulatory process. The result is not to shift power to Ottawa but it is to move effective decision-making authority from the provincial level to this broader national interprovincial level. In any case, this is an exception to the other case studies where there is either no shift in effective power between orders of government or a modest shift toward the provinces. In this case, the shift is away from the individual provinces.

## CONCLUSIONS

The first question posed in this chapter had to do with whether the role of government was changing in Canada in respect of labour market policies. A related question had to do with the reasons for those changes. The evidence above confirms that changes in government policy helped to make Canadian labour markets more flexible during the 1990s. The generosity of unemployment insurance and social assistance programs was reduced very significantly. Legislation regulating labour relations was relaxed to enhance the freedom of employers and this has tended to move collective bargaining to the establishment level. A process was launched that will remove provincial barriers to interprovincial mobility. The result is that there are fewer constraints on the operations of the labour market than there were a decade ago.

As to the reasons for these changes, wherever matters related to public finance were at issue, they trumped all other considerations. The reduction in benefits for EI/UI and social assistance were overwhelmingly driven by the desire of federal and provincial governments to get their deficits under control. The same factor also helps to explain the maintenance of much higher than necessary EI/UI premiums and the spending restraints on active labour market programs. The fact that changes in policy might help with international competitiveness and were consistent with a changing intellectual setting reinforced these decisions, but it was the need to slay the deficit that dominated. As for the regulatory changes in cases where public finances were not directly affected, the growth of support for more market friendly governance was an important consideration.

A shift toward more decentralized decision making was associated with these changes but only a modest shift. The main example of such a change was the federal government's partial devolution of labour market training and development programs to the provinces. This was an administrative change, not a constitutional one, and still leaves the federal government with some role in this area. Nonetheless, it is a change that Quebec and several other provinces had clamoured for and their political pressures, in the aftermath of the Quebec referendum, led to this change. As noted earlier, the events here reflect domestic political considerations more than anything else.

This chapter has also provided a few other examples of decentralization. The removal of some conditions on transfers to the provinces for social assistance was noted. And the federal government's position to back off from its political leadership role in the setting of minimum wages is another illustration. Both of these cases, however, are very small items in terms of how the Canadian federation operates. And the gradual removal of barriers to labour mobility is operating in the opposite direction.

Equally of interest is that the labour market provides an illustration, though far from the best illustration, of what may become a trend in Canadian federalism. This is the tendency for the federal and provincial governments to establish a broad framework for a policy area, or for Ottawa to do so alone, and then devolve responsibility for program design and delivery to the provinces subject to an accountability framework. The devolution of labour market training fits into this category. The reduction in conditions associated with the change in federal transfers to the provinces for social assistance may appear, at first glance, inconsistent in the sense that it lacks an accountability framework. But it is similar in that it illustrates a continued federal government interest in a provincial policy area but without the desire to become involved in the program details.

Finally, it is worth saying a word about the overall impact of these changes. The first is clearly a smaller government role in labour markets. These more flexible labour markets may have also played a role in helping to reduce unemployment but this is hard to pin down. The second is a reduction in social protection for employees. The 1990s trend in labour market policies affected adversely both the distribution of earnings, for example, due to weaker collective bargaining legislation, and the distribution of after-tax and after-transfer income, for example, due to reduced generosity of EI/UI and social assistance. These changes have contributed to a growth of inequality in Canadian society.

## NOTES

1. The present study does not address the role of macroeconomic policy levers as an employment stabilizer. As with other advanced capitalist economies, Canada abandoned the idea of using macro-policies to stabilize the business cycle in the early 1990s. Employment goals are no longer attached to macroeconomic policy, which is instead focused mainly on price stability and prudent and stable public finances.
2. This was especially a concern for workers in seasonal industries in Atlantic Canada and eastern Quebec. They could work as little as two to three months every year in their industry (say, the fishery or the forests) and receive UI benefits the rest of the year, without looking seriously for off-season work.
3. It is likely that the provinces will have some say in the accountability framework when these agreements come up for renewal.

## REFERENCES

Arthurs, H.W. 1996. "Labour Law Without the State?" *University of Toronto Law Journal*, 46(1):1-45.

Bradford, N. 1998. *Commissioning Ideas: Canadian National Policy Innovation in Comparative Perspective.* Toronto: Oxford University Press.

Corak, M. 1994. "Unemployment Insurance, Work Disincentives, and the Canadian Labour Market: An Overview," Analytical Studies Branch, Research Paper 62, Ottawa: Statistics Canada.

Green, C. 1994. "What Should We Do with the UI System?" in *Unemployment Insurance: How to Make it Work,* ed. C. Green, F. Lazar, M. Corak and D.M. Gross. Toronto: C.D. Howe Institute.

Haddow, R. 1998. "Reforming Labour-Market Policy Governance: The Quebec Experience," *Canadian Public Administration*, 41(3):343-68.

McIntosh, T. and G. Boychuk. 2000. "Dis-Covered: EI, Social Assistance and the Growing Gap in Income Support for Unemployed Canadians," in *Federalism, Democracy and Labour Market Policy in Canada*, ed. T. McIntosh. Montreal and Kingston: McGill-Queen's University Press for Institute of Intergovernmental Relations, Queen's University.

Organization for Economic Cooperation and Development. 1994. *The OECD Jobs Study: Evidence and Explanations, Part I: Labour Market Trends and Underlying Forces of Change.* Paris: OECD.

_____ 1995. *Governance in Transition: Public Management Reforms in OECD Countries.* Paris: OECD.

_____ 1997. *Implementing the OECD Jobs Strategy: Member Countries' Experience.* Paris: OECD.

Riddell, C.W. 1995. "Human Capital Formation in Canada: Recent Developments and Policy Responses," in *Labour Market Polarization and Social Policy Reform,* ed. K.G. Banting and C.M. Beach. Kingston: School of Policy Studies, Queen's University.

# 10

# Perspectives on Regional Inequalities and Regional Growth

*Sir George Quigley*

They say that, whatever you forecast, you should never forecast the future. The great historian, essayist, and public figure, Thomas Babington Macaulay, was therefore appropriately diffident when in 1830 he wrote:

> If we were to prophesy that in the year 1930 a population of fifty million, better fed, clad and lodged than the English of our time will cover these islands, that Sussex and Huntingdonshire will be wealthier than the wealthiest parts of the West Riding of Yorkshire now are ... that machines constructed on principles yet undiscovered will be in every house ... many people would think us insane (Lord Macaulay 1830).

And yet he was of course right, even though his time arrow did land in the midst of the Great Depression. And he shrewdly foresaw the reversal of the north-south regional divide of his day. The widening of this north-south gap during the past decade, to the detriment of the north, has resurrected a debate about regional policy in the United Kingdom that had fallen largely silent. The apparently dead horse has refused to lie down.

At the postwar zenith of active regional policy, the then prime minister, Harold Macmillan, to appease the regional lobbies, split a steel strip mill between Scotland and South Wales, thereby, it could be argued, sacrificing national economic advantage. That is a far cry from the advice contained in a report prepared in 1999 for government by inspectors appointed to examine plans prepared for housing and transport in the southeast of England. It urged that economic growth, even in the most buoyant areas such as the Thames Valley, should be unconstrained and that "sufficient housing should be available for all who wish to live in the region." The southeast, they said, should be "an engine of growth in the national economy." "The effect of reducing development pressures would have little or no beneficial effect on the economies of other regions of the UK" (Crow and Whittaker 1999). The inspectors said that any problems of road congestion and labour shortage should be overcome by improving public transport and building houses within sustainable travelling distance.

What is at issue here is a typical example of an agglomeration of economic activity, fuelled by the externalities from which its economic players benefit. Does one accommodate and even encourage its capacity for self-reinforcement? This is the inspectors' solution, reflecting a refusal to allow physical planning to become a backstop for weak regional policy. They could argue that to do so would simply lead to disjointed development and escalating house prices.

Such escalation in the southeast was a key element in the decision by the Bank of England's Monetary Policy Committee to tighten monetary policy in recent years. And it has been precisely the occasions when interest rates have risen over that period which have stimulated most debate about the north-south divide. It is argued that higher interest rates sustain an uncompetitive exchange rate, which appreciated by as much as 30 percent in four years. This may contain inflationary pressures but is very damaging for exporters (and also hits agriculture severely). Since manufacturing is strongest in the north, and agriculture is a disproportionate contributor to gross domestic product (GDP) in regions like Northern Ireland, Wales, and Scotland, a strong pound has a differential regional impact and produces a two-speed economy. It is argued that, even within manufacturing — say, in engineering — the north is worse hit than the south, because it has high volume, low margin basic metals and commodities firms that are more exposed to competition from low-cost economies.

Some exporters have recovered their confidence, perhaps through a process of adjustment to the perception (probably correct) that a strong pound is no temporary phenomenon. This would entail aggressive strategies for profitable growth which reverse the worsening trend in the UK, both absolutely and relatively, in productivity performance and in unit labour costs. Manufacturing has already shed 150,000 jobs in the past 12 months. Any radical restructuring would impact differentially on the north.

There is therefore acute criticism of a "one size fits all" monetary policy. That is also, of course, the criticism which is mounted of the Economic and Monetary Union (EMU) which, atypically as regards most of postwar history, has in the run-up to EMU had a cool core and a hot periphery (which includes the Republic of Ireland). When it would take an extra 11 percentage points on Ireland's inflation rate to raise the Eurozone's inflation rate by 0.1 percent, the chances of the European Central Bank running a monetary policy to suit a small member state must be judged to be poor.

The issue at the heart of the debate, in whatever context, is the degree of convergence required in order to ensure that one size *does* fit all. Convergence, whether of national or regional economies, is clearly not simply a matter of a single crossing point between economies with different cycles and different characteristics. Correlation between growth rates, for example, is not enough. Convergence is better regarded as a similarity of shocks and structures sufficient to achieve similar growth in spite of sharing the same interest rate.

In a monetary union, some of the ability of the nation or region to respond to asymmetric shocks is lost. The labour market is the only effective safety valve and if wages do not adjust and labour is immobile, a shock that damages one region more than others will lead to higher unemployment in the affected region.

It is interesting that, given the potentially damaging consequences of a "one size fits all" monetary instrument, voices have been raised in the UK in favour of diversifying the weaponry to deal with inflation and the excesses of metropolitan consumers, by, for example, greater use of targeted fiscal policy or by encouraging savings by means of tax breaks. Fiscal policy, unless carefully targeted, can of course have adverse differential impacts on the poorer regions. Studies of UK budgets showed such impacts in respect of Northern Ireland for the earlier part of the 1990s.

There are various ways of measuring the north-south regional divide. On the traditionally favoured measure — unemployment rates — the gap in the UK is in fact narrower (at around six percentage points) than it has been in previous periods, with the southeast at under 4 percent and the northeast over 9 percent. The proportion of people of working age in work ranges from 80 percent in the southeast to 66 percent in the northeast. Gross domestic product in the northeast is just 73 percent of that in the southeast (excluding Greater London). Ten years ago it was 77 percent. It has been estimated that economic growth in 1999 is likely to range from virtually nil in the northeast to 2.3 percent in the southeast.

Surrey residents enjoy an average household income that is 71 percent higher than that of Tyne and Wear (in the northeast). Over 4 percent of people in London have personal taxable incomes of more than £50,000, whereas in the northeast and Wales it is only 1 percent. On the other hand, the cost of living is generally lower in the north. Where a middle-class family in Croydon in the southeast would spend £18,000 a year on food and other essentials, the bill for a comparable family in Billingham in the northeast would be 80 percent of that.

It is likely that in the short term the north-south gap will narrow again, as manufacturing recovers and public spending on health and education picks up. The north tends to have about 25 percent more of its jobs in the public sector than the south and Northern Ireland's public sector dependence is higher still.

For the very reason that they are operating in a regionally differentiated context, there are national policy measures in the shape of the tax and social security regimes, for example, which, albeit uniform throughout the country, serve to reduce regional disparity. Inevitably the south pays more taxes, whilst the north receives more benefits. Moreover, the public spending levels in Northern Ireland, Wales, and Scotland (but not in other regions) stem from an assessment of need (done some 20 years ago) and are well above per-capita levels for England as a whole. This enables spending on industrial support in Northern Ireland, for example, to be at a far higher level per-capita than in the rest of the UK. (Public expenditure transfers from the London Treasury to Northern Ireland, Scotland, and Wales are regarded as a bloc within which the devolved institutions have considerable discretion as to spending priorities.)

But over the longer term it would be sanguine to believe that, on current policies, the widening of the north-south gap would not resume. The south is stronger in the fastest growing sectors, such as business and financial services and ICT. The City of London itself is a major factor. The south is closer to the Continent, whilst the north, although not wholly dependent on the Channel Tunnel for access, is distanced from it by inadequate infrastructure. Further drift from the major conurbations in the north, running at a net 40,000 a year, can be expected.

There is a pattern in the evolution of the north-south gap, which has been described as the tortoise and the hare syndrome. In boom times the south speeds away but gets into trouble and the slower tortoise narrows the gap. But at each peak the south's advantage is greater than it was before. Unless there is a repetition of the disastrous housing boom and bust of the late 1980s, which hit the southeast particularly hard, it is difficult in present circumstances to see the tortoise catching up.

The regional problem is not, however, fully described in terms of the north-south divide. There are significant disparities *within* regions both north and south. More than half the most deprived local authorities in England are in London (with unemployment rates as high as 12.5 percent) and London has more unemployed people of working age than Scotland and Wales combined. At 17.5 percent of 16 to 24 year olds, it has the highest youth unemployment rate in the country. In all regions, deprived inner cities coexist with more prosperous suburbs. Cornwall is struggling in comparison with Devon, which is in the same region. Hastings is depressed whilst Brighton, also on the south coast, is booming. In the northwest region, Liverpool lags Manchester. In the north, Leeds, due to buoyant growth in business and financial services, has outperformed every city except London in employment growth since 1981.

The foregoing has focused on the UK but regional disparities between the poorest and richest regions in France, Germany, and Italy are even greater.

The following key points can be extrapolated from the discussion above.

First, regional policy is a matter of achieving balanced regional growth within a national economy which is growing at a sustainable rate rather than lurching between boom and bust. The measures required to deal with a boom can be particularly damaging to the poorer regions, which in any event have probably failed to benefit fully from it. However, whilst the interest rate rises of the past few years have excited the ire of the northern part of the divide, they have ranged within a band of some two percentage points, which compares well with most of the historical precedents.

Second, to achieve balanced regional growth, government has to have a regional policy which addresses the issue of regional success as well as regional failure. The strategy document published in 1999 by the South East Regional Development Agency for the next ten years aims to lift it from being 23rd out of 77 European regions in gross domestic product per head into the ranks of the top ten regions. In the absence of very rapid growth in the lagging regions, this admirable ambition, particularly if it accelerated net outward migration from those regions, would clearly exacerbate regional imbalance. There is a need for nothing less than a change in the core of our political, cultural, and financial structures.

Third, given intra-regional disparities, action needs to be taken at the local level if a rising regional tide is to lift all boats.

Fourth, regional convergence has to be measured on a range of factors. Convergence in incomes has to be achieved by well-structured sustainable growth which creates regional wealth rather than by the ersatz solution of central government transfers which attempt to compensate for inequality but are merely palliative.

Fifth, the latter half of Tolstoy's opening observation in the book, *Anna Karenina* — "each unhappy family is unhappy in its own way" — probably applies to the *less* successful regions. But the first part of the observation that "All happy families resemble one another," is probably inapplicable to the successful regions. All regions have had distinctive histories and each has to develop what, in company terms, could be described as its own business success model. Inclusive opportunism is unlikely to serve. It would savour of Lady Salisbury's practice of mixing all her family's half-used medicines in a jug with an equal measure of port and administering the resultant concoction to elderly tenants on the Hatfield estate. With the advent of devolved institutions in Wales, Scotland, and Northern Ireland and with the creation of nine Regional Development Agencies for England (all or some of which may in due course acquire elected representatives) there is an unprecedented opportunity for distinctive regional therapy.

Sixth, their weaponry, in the shape of their ability to use the levers of monetary and fiscal policy (save for Scotland's ability to vary income tax by 3 p.), is non-existent and they will be even more remote from these levers if the UK joins the

Eurozone, particularly if member states lose their existing measure of fiscal autonomy. The devolved administrations can at least make their own spending decisions within their allowed allocations (and are flexing their muscles in this respect), but the regional development agencies have no control over the setting of spending priorities, although they will no doubt seek to influence them, at least through their ability to propose project expenditure. The need to deal with such proposals should reinforce earlier moves within government to deal more cohesively with the problems of the individual regions. There could be considerable frustration if the devolved institutions and the regions believe themselves to be performing effectively in the areas that are within their control and perceive their efforts to be frustrated or shed by the ineffectiveness of national policy. That policy will increasingly have to subsume regional concerns which can in future be given *institutional* expression, and facilitate and reinforce regional effort.

To deal with such possible situations, regions need growth that is both intensive and extensive. Barry, Hannan, and Strobl (1999) developed the argument in the following way in their contribution to essays seeking to understand Ireland's economic growth. *Intensive* growth is measured by gross domestic product or value added per head of population. However, to understand its significance for policy in any particular context, it must be recognized that it is the product of a number of variables. Vitally important is GDP per worker, which measures regional productivity. It is obviously this that determines the size of the economic cake. But if there are significant numbers unemployed or if, say, the proportion of working women within the population of working age is low or if the population contains disproportionately large numbers of those too young or too old to work, the amount of cake available per capita, however productive the workforce, will be limited. Depending on how these variables move, they can negate the effects of gains in productivity.

Once an economy gets on a roll, one gets a number of the variables moving together to produce a virtuous circle. With regional productivity rates high, growth becomes self-sustaining, unemployment drops, and non-participants are encouraged to come into the labour force. The demographics may also alter so as to reduce the proportion of children in the population. Moreover, by definition, regional economies are very open economies, whose population expands or contracts as economic conditions dictate. Net immigration may therefore also lead to a significant fall in the dependency ratio.

The Republic of Ireland, albeit a sovereign state, has for historical reasons displayed many of the characteristics of a very open regional economy. It is probably the best example of a situation being achieved just recently where all the variables have conspired to boost GDP per head, thereby proving that it can happen. Crudely put, all the ducks are in a row.

But growth within a region could be intensive, in the sense of raising average living standards, without necessarily denoting success in terms of regional economic development. It has been well said that, after the Great Famine in Ireland in the nineteenth century, the living standards of the remaining population improved substantially but it hardly counts as an exercise in successful economic development. Ill-balanced growth or poor distribution of the fruits of growth, leading to emigration from the region, are unacceptable. In the economics of the developing world, emphasis is now placed on the need for active social development, which avoids the creation of insiders and outsiders to the growth process. A similar emphasis is equally crucial in regional economics.

*Extensive* growth, characterized by an increase in the absolute level of GDP, in numbers in work and in the geographical spread of jobs must therefore be a key objective. Balanced growth was a main theme of the economic and spatial strategies published recently for Northern Ireland, as it is in the National Development Plan just produced for the Republic of Ireland. A balanced strategy does not mean a job for all within ten minutes journey time from their home. It does mean taking steps to encourage well-distributed nodes of growth outside the naturally occurring agglomerations of economic activity and having linked policies for settlement and transport which ensure access.

The pivotal figure in developing a strategy for regional economic development is the productivity measure, GDP per worker. Its level is the ineluctable outcome of two characteristics of the region. The first is the sectoral distribution of employment. This will be historically determined by the regions' comparative advantage, in other words by its ability to make more money doing one thing rather than another. Northern Ireland's traditional dependence on textiles and clothing (which still accounts for over 20 percent of manufacturing employment) is a case in point. But the resultant structure of employment is not necessarily skewed toward the high value-added end of the spectrum. In that event, compared with differently structured economies, regional productivity will be low.

The second factor determining GDP per worker is the level of productivity achieved within any given sector, regardless of what its importance within the economy may be.

There is a particular problem with regional economies like Northern Ireland, which have a strong agricultural base. The agriculture sector has experienced strong productivity growth. The consequent displacement of large amounts of labour makes it necessary to run much harder to achieve both intensive and extensive growth.

When all the fancy concepts are stripped away, the key to regional economic development lies in doing whatever is necessary to alter the economic structure so as to achieve higher regional productivity and in benchmarking global best practice and ensuring that, sector by sector, productivity performance matches it. The latter is necessary because the size of a regional economy depends largely on its export base, which in turn depends on its international competitiveness.

Strategy 2010 recently produced by the Department of Economic Development (1999) in Northern Ireland in partnership with the private sector put it neatly. "We must ensure that we develop the growth sectors of the future and at the same time maintain those firms in other sectors which, through innovation and marketing expertise, are capable of moving up the value chain in their sector." That last point, about companies repositioning themselves in the value chain, is important. A feature of Northern Ireland's clothing and textile sector which, wrongly positioned, would be extremely vulnerable to low-cost competition from overseas is that, through a vigorous process of investment, its successful companies have been steadily moving into products that sell on design and quality.

Lagging regions need to engage in a major program of reconstruction, with available resources prioritized in the interests of modernization rather than conservation, building engines of wealth generation dependent on high order jobs. Special transfers for investment of this kind from the national "centre" can be justified, even on the centre's own terms, as far preferable to compensating the region indefinitely for its inability to draw level. In terms of employment, there comes a crossover point where (as has now happened after much effort in the Republic of Ireland) job gains in the newer layers of industry outstrip job losses in the older layers and buoyant consumer spending boosts employment in the service sector.

There is no doubt as to what the theme of such a program of modernization has to be. It is nicely encapsulated by the OECD: "...the emergence of knowledge based economies has profound implications for the determinants of growth, the organisation of production and its effect on employment and skill requirements and may call for new orientations in industry-related policies" (OECD 1998). A region that takes that message seriously will focus sharply on the effective use and exploitation of all types of knowledge in all manner of economic activity. For example, implementing the new e-business model involves a three-part process: building the infrastructure, modifying business processes, and exploiting the data and the feedback loops that the Internet facilitates for business-to-business and customer relationships. Companies in the old economy that ignore the process are at risk of extinction.

But, beyond that, the region will examine all aspects of the regional balance sheet to see where radical change is needed. In the eyes of accountants, companies are quickly reduced to a set of assets and liabilities and the relationship between them. A region can be similarly regarded. It cannot afford unnecessary and debilitating liabilities. Any region, like any company, that shows it has the determination and the ability can access the resources needed for development. The challenge for regions is not to solve all problems locally but to make it possible to solve them by harnessing global resources.

Regions that are serious about restructuring have no option but to tap those global resources by obtaining the largest possible share of foreign direct investment (FDI). The Republic of Ireland has done this brilliantly, capturing 10 percent of all US investment into Europe but, even more spectacularly, attracting some 25 percent of US investment in the electronics, pharmaceutical, and software industries. The Republic's proportion of the total population of the European Union is 1 percent. Northern Ireland has the advantage of being part of the UK, the European country that has gained the largest share of FDI. One of the tragedies of the Troubles has been the region's inability to share nearly as fully in that success as its proven merits as an excellent host location for inward investment warranted.

An important weapon in the Republic's armoury has been its exceptionally favourable corporation tax regime which has acted as a powerful arousal factor. There is a market for FDI and the ability to bid competitively is vital. But of course, as time has gone on, the cluster effect produced by the concentration of investment in key growth sectors in the Republic has in itself acted as a magnet. Success breeds success.

As Young, Hood and Peters point out, an inward investment policy which focuses only on one variable, such as its employment effects, is unlikely to achieve the strategic objectives which should underlie the process of regional restructuring. An integrated policy approach to regional development rather than one in which inward investment per se is the major driver is required. Targeting, coupled with intelligent after-care, holds the key. It is difficult to secure fully integrated units from overseas at the point of entry but it may be possible to encourage them with incentives to enlarge their scope and develop a full range of higher order functions over time, *pari passu* with steps taken within the host environment to upgrade the region as a whole through general supply-side measures. Merely having inward investors as foreign enclaves where linkages with local firms are poor limits their impact enormously. They have to become embedded in the local economy. It is not a matter of simply brokering supply relationships with local firms. What is at issue is knowledge transfer, with knowledge defined (in the terminology of Crone and Roper) as the whole bundle of competencies, know-how, and technological expertise that firms use in the development, production, marketing, and delivery of their products.

Reference was made above to an analogy between regions and companies in regard to the notion of assets and liabilities. Amongst a *company's* key assets are the sheer "fit" of the organization — its internal coherence, the way in which its people work together and combine their efforts to build company learning. Amongst a region's key assets are its quality of community. World-class companies like to be part of world-class communities. That can be the glue that binds them to their host environment.

This is not a "community" merely in quality of life terms, important though that is. Rather, it is the community that reflects a large stock of social capital, which is the quality of the relationships between citizens. High quality interaction and communication create a skein of obligations, expectations, and mutual trust which make for community competence in the widest sense. Social institutions other than the market play a major role in economic development. Innovation is a process of interactive learning: learning between firms (which cooperate as well as compete), between firms and their suppliers and customers, between firms and the basic research and knowledge infrastructure, and between firms and the wider institutional milieu.

Knowledge generated by creative interaction is the most strategic resource and learning and the multiple information channels and feedback loops which underpin it is the most significant process. It is a process that enables the vitally important tacit knowledge, much of it collective in nature, to be mobilized. Interdependency is the name of the game and many of the interdependencies are untraded, not commercial. These and similar themes are explored by Morgan in his study of the notion of the learning region as key to regional economic development.

It is from this learning laboratory that there emerges the distinctive success model which has been referred to earlier. It acquires the brand image — the vocation, the identity, and the values — which give the region its storyline and secure instant and favourable recognition.

It is in the area of community building and branding that locally rooted political structures are going to be able to add most value. A UK commentator said recently, perhaps only half seriously, that London's recent boom started when the Greater London Council was abolished. But he also conceded that one respect in which local politicians could almost certainly help was to try to make their areas nicer places to live in, places with which people who have the choice want to be involved. A region that aspires to become a global player (not least in the world leisure industry) certainly cannot ignore that imperative, which is one reason why peace and political stability in Northern Ireland are so critical.

But the politicians' role can go much wider, into helping to build up the region's institutional capacity and to create the abundance of social capital that has been referred to, bearing in mind that the old categories of government and governed have been overtaken. What we now have is widely diffused governance, a community-wide network of relationships (partly captured under the rubric of a social partnership) through which we can come together to manage matters of collective concern.

And of course, to the extent that politicians are clear-sighted about the dynamic, and more especially the strategy, of regional economic development, they can provide the leadership that is needed if the often tough resource allocation decisions which that dynamic logically imposes are to be taken.

A final analogy can be drawn; that between "company" and "region." Regions like companies, can be viewed as portfolios of competencies which need to be redeployed in a variety of configurations where development or diversification is needed to match fresh opportunities. They must not be trapped by their investment in what is rarely more than obsolescent success. Tides ebb and flow. One surfs the waves as they come along.

Regions can never invest heavily enough in understanding the changes taking place in the business dynamic worldwide — changes in the market, in how business organizes itself, in technology, and in the production process and in how all this impacts on the locational demands of profitable economic activity and on the spatial division of labour worldwide.

In the nineteenth century, regions were differentiated in terms of sectoral specialization of vertically integrated industries, world-class shipbuilding and textile industries, for example, in Northern Ireland. Higher and lower order jobs were all there. The era of the branch factory introduced a radically different spatial division of labour, with lower order jobs predominating in surplus labour, low-cost regions.

The industrial structure of many UK regions consists of what Massey has described as successive geological strata of business formation. The nature of each stratum was dictated by the business logic of the day. It has been fashionable to argue in the past 10 or 15 years that there is a new logic (based on flexible specialization rather than mass production and taking in decentralized multinationals as well as small companies) which is going with the grain of regional economic development. For evidence, we are referred to the rash of area-based production complexes around the world.

This is obviously a welcome development for regional planners but a preferable view is that the new trends are more complex and contradictory than is captured by notions of flexible specialization and a new regionalism. Much more powerful is the integration of global, national, and regional economies. As it has been graphically put, world space is the field in which our epoch is created and it is in that context that regional economies have to be understood. Regions will operate better as networked economies but we also have a globally networked economy. As an interesting survey of the literature by Amin and Robins (1990) makes clear, centripetal and centrifugal forces are both at work. In some but not all cases they will assist the notion of the industrial district and the cluster as the regional paradigm.

Those regions which do best will see themselves as very intelligent nodes within a global economic network. A company that illustrates the point is Bombardier Aerospace Shorts. Through it, Northern Ireland is a very successful node within the global network which now constitutes the aerospace industry. Take the Global

Express, to which Shorts is a key contributor. Mobilized by Bombardier, there are ten major risk-sharing partners in six countries worldwide. Within the UK alone there are 60 suppliers, a number of them in Northern Ireland, and Shorts is linked into precisely the kind of institutional milieu in Northern Ireland (not least through its links with the universities) described earlier. Shorts is involved in more Bombardier Aerospace projects than any other part of the Bombardier Group.

The notion of the regional node within the global network should not induce pessimism as to the scope for local proactivity. Far from it. The more globalism becomes placeless, the more the world becomes what has been called "a space of flows" of capital, trade and investment, the greater our opportunities and the clearer the goal of regional economic development. As it has been neatly put, the future is less determinate and the options wider than ever before.

## REFERENCES

Amin, A. and K. Robins. 1990. "The Re-emergence of Regional Economics? The Mythical Geography of Flexible Accumulation," *Environment and Planning D: Society and Space*, Vol. 8, pp. 7-34.

Barry, F., A. Hannan and E. Strobl. 1999. "The Real Convergence of the Irish Economy, and the Sectoral-Distribution of Employment Growth," in *Understanding Ireland's Economic Growth,* ed. F. Barry. Basingstoke, England: Macmillan

Crone, M. and S. Roper. 1999. "Local Learning from Multinational Plants: Knowledge Transfers in the Supply Chain," Working Paper Series No. 46. Belfast: Northern Ireland Economic Research Centre.

Crow, S. and R. Whittaker. 1999. *Regional Planning Guidance for the South East of England: Report of the Panel.* London: Department of the Environment, Transport and the Regions.

Macaulay, Lord Thomas Babington. 1830. *'Southey's Colloquies on Society' in Macaulay's Essays and Lays of Ancient Rome* (1891). London: Longmans, Green & Co.

Massey, D. 1979. "In What Sense a Regional Problem?" *Regional Studies*, 13:233-43.

_____ 1984. *Spatial Divisions of Labour.* London: Macmillan.

Morgan, K. 1997. "The Learning Region: Institutions, Innovation and Regional Renewal," *Regional Studies,* 31(5):491-503.

Northern Ireland Economic Development Strategy Review Planning Group. 1999. *Strategy 2010.* Belfast: Department of Economic Development.

Organization for Economic Cooperation and Development (OECD). 1998. *Meeting of the Industry Committee at Ministerial Level: Scoreboard of Indicators.* Paris: OECD.

South East England Development Agency. 1999. *Building a World Class Region: Economic Strategy for the South East of England.* London: South East England Development Agency.

United Kingdom. 1999. *Ireland: National Development Plan 2000-2006.* London: Her Majesty's Stationary Office.

Young, S., N. Hood and E. Peters. 1994. "Multinational Enterprises and Regional Economic Development," *Regional Studies*, 28(7):657–77.

# 11

# Toward a New Definition of Citizenship: Beneath and Beyond the Nation-State

*Hugh Segal*

## INTRODUCTION

Legislated rules that have developed over the centuries about the entitlements of citizenship do little to dilute the emotion that surrounds this topic. Historic conflicts around ethnic and linguistic pre-eligibility conditions, battles around rights conferred and hard won, endless debates over the privileges and obligations of citizenship, all conspire to make the definitional challenge one of ongoing and continuous controversy. Rapidly moving economic forces, turbocharged by technological change, often lead politicians and business and labour leaders to lament the lack of debate around many of the sea changes we see around us. A debate about citizenship, its meaning, evolution, and conceptual framework — especially how all these may be changing in a world of both decentralized and supranational decision making around trade, monetary issues, social policy, human and investment capital — may not only be liberating and creative, but also help leverage a broader debate on the changing status and relationships of the nation-state, and the increasingly important subnational units.

In Canada as well as in the United Kingdom, we have no lack of changing dynamics. In Canada, both Quebec on the one hand and our Aboriginal First Nations on the other are clearly in a state of evolution relative to the process of sorting out what national status means to both administrative and constitutional authority, as well as to the terms of adherence to the multinational country we share. This process, in the case of Quebec, both precedes Confederation in 1867 and is likely to continue for some time to come. The Aboriginal issue, while politicized more recently, will also continue in the courts and in our national politics for the foreseeable future. Similarly, with the creation of a parliament in Scotland, an assembly in Wales, and continued efforts toward positive democratic development in Northern Ireland, there is now some convergence between the constitutional reality of the United Kingdom and the historical nationalities that have always been part of the history and development of this part of the world.

The constitutional questions relative to both sides of the Atlantic, the issues around subsidiarity relative to services, social policy, and the rest are addressed by others in this volume. The broad question of how the concept of citizenship should be defined and how it is being changed by the process of decentralization or devolution is this chapter's primary focus.

## A CHANGING CONTEXT FOR THE IDEA OF CITIZENSHIP

It is understandable that the rearrangement of governing instruments, the federalization of unitary states, and the broadening of public jurisdictions to embrace multinational and transnational movements of people and capital should produce definitional challenges. On occasion, some of these changes are portrayed as incontrovertible responses to the ideology of the marketplace. In other circumstances, they are portrayed as responses to this ideology because they reflect ethnic or cultural identities that are energized and made anxious by the overwhelming globalizing force of that same marketplace. The truth is, the limits to the nation-state, itself a rather recent concept, are not new, particularly in the context of any meaningful approach to global issues management. In recent times, ever since the failed League of Nations, states have been trying, more recently with increasing success, to advance broad agendas around peace, international development, reconstruction, economic stability, trade, human rights, and effective deterrent alliances through multinational initiatives. More recently, we have seen the doctrine of justifiable international legal rules on war crimes and multilateral military intervention within sovereign countries both with and without UN sanction.

The obvious questions understate important historical realities. Can one be a citizen of Europe and a British subject at the same time? Are one's interests as a Canadian citizen adequately reflected by decisions approved by the NATO Ministerial Council, where Canada has but one vote? Does a disagreement between the Italian government — duly elected by its citizens — and NATO on strategy or tactics create a more serious democratic deficiency than when that same government faces opposition from its own electorate between elections? And what impact do the elements of this supranational environment, such as from the World

Trade Organization (WTO) for example, have on the democratic rights of citizens within the traditional nation-state and on the definition of citizenship itself?

At the subnational level, those seriously opposed to devolution or decentralization or subsidiarity speak ruefully about the Balkanization of the larger polity; in Canada, proponents of a strong central government who often also oppose enhanced provincial powers ask, "'Who will speak for Canada?" by which they mean, "Canada as a whole" as opposed to any of its provinces or regions. They usually also mean "Canada as a whole" as defined by the central government.

There are, implicit in this sort of lament, some rather fundamental, if questionable, assumptions:

- Citizenship and its benefits derive largely from centrally administered programs that are uniform everywhere within the state.

- Widening pluralism, flexibility, and diversity — in terms of both the nature of programs and their varied applications in different parts of the governed region or country — will weaken both the sinews of citizenship and the common values citizenship reflects.

- Devolution and decentralization somehow denigrate and dilute a more compelling pan-national citizenship in a way that weakens the sense of engagement and mutual commitment important to social cohesion and loyalty.

These questionable but popular assumptions seem to impose a level of structural perversity upon what have become largely unchallenged historical realities in both the United Kingdom, Canada, and elsewhere. These realities may not always be easy to manage, but they are nevertheless a large and ongoing part of our respective multinational citizenship frameworks. Moreover, while their origins are often profoundly cultural, they reflect the changing global context in which as some issues are delegated upward to supra-national bodies, others migrate to subnational jurisdictions. This not only reflects the principle of subsidiarity but also a greater sense of democratic comfort and some measure of cultural homogeneity.

Beyond the issue of service delivery, there is also the question of affinities and passions that run more deeply.

- Scottish, Irish, Québécois, and Aboriginal populations have strong historical loyalties to languages, culture, and territorial sovereignties well beyond issues of public administration, or program design.

- These linguistic, cultural, and historical beliefs are usually more reflective of the underlying premises of citizenship, nationhood, and social cohesion than they are of the debate about the merits of unitary versus federal, or centralized versus devolved, governing instruments.

## THE ISSUE OF DEFINITION

T.H. Marshall's essay, "Citizenship and Social Class," defines citizenship as "a status bestowed on those who are full members of a community. All who possess the status are equal with respect to the rights and duties with which the status is endowed" (Marshall 1950, pp. 28-29). In Canada, this definition has been challenged by Kymlicka and Norman (1994), who argue that eroding cultural homogeneity in most countries and the failure of any passive definition of citizenship to spur active engagement argue for a new definitional path. John F. Kennedy's ringing call for defining one's citizenship in terms of what one could do for one's country, as opposed to what one might expect from that country, sounded a particularly hopeful note for a large and influential generation. The pan-Canadian nationalism of Liberal Prime Minister Pierre Trudeau near the end of that same decade — echoing, ironically, the "One Canada" theme of a previous Conservative prime minister, John Diefenbaker — was aimed at generating similar responses. Sadly, it did so in both cases by displaying systemic insensitivity to legitimate Quebec and Prairie nationalism.

In a sense, the evolution in Canada of Québécois nationalism, and its explicit national citizenship in a majority French-speaking Quebec, is a response to a history of English Canadian politics that seemed, and in some respects remains, ambivalent about pan-Canadian rights and status for the French language in areas where francophones are not in the majority. This is not about an absence of good will or tolerance, although no society is free of these deficits; it is more clearly about a strong linkage among a majority of Québécois between citizenship, language, culture, and the inter-generational survival of French Canadian civilization — something one can never take for granted — on a continent where English and Spanish are markedly dominant or on the rise in key geographic and economic areas.

Critical to understanding what happens to citizenship when devolution, decentralization, and the principle of subsidiarity are on the march is understanding what this process does to language, culture, and the concern for the inter-generational survival of a civilization. These points of impact are not separate from economic reality, as economically robust societies are more able to sustain and advance cultural endeavours than those faced with harsher challenges of economic survival. This cultural/linguistic and civilization-based citizenship — not necessarily hostile to, or disengaged from, broader citizenship relationships — is also challenged by multicultural and multinational migration patterns, by the internationalization of work and commerce, and by the new networks of economic, social, and stateless connections. These connections are classically defined by task or purpose as opposed to nationality or sovereign jurisdiction. It is reasonable to embrace the notion that the networked citizenship, linking the citizen to a series of access points that reflect changing flows of power, authority, and necessity, begins to change the broad context within which citizenship exists. While some supportive parts of citizenship's value — health-care access, overall welfare, community safety, basic socializing education — are not intrinsically portable, other aspects such as economic opportunity, are quite susceptible to a more networked citizenship, not limited by the borders of the province or nation-state.

None of this, it must be recognized, diminishes the cultural dimension of the issue, especially in Quebec. The broad diffusion of "cultural products" out of the United States, the dominant role of English in e-commerce, the ability to form new networks that defy both the jurisdiction and relevance of the traditional nation-state, and the traditional conception of citizenship that has emerged through history have all come together to produce a very new set of ingredients for a post-industrial definition of citizenship. Stephen Castles has argued: "Collectivities which constitute themselves around cultural claims may be based not only on ethnicity, but also on regional location, gender, sexual preferences, and lifestyles" (1997).

It should also be noted that, certainly in the Canadian experience, minority intensity around a citizenship that preserves language and culture is not necessarily reflective of insensitivity to other cultural minorities. In Quebec, for example, if one considers the Quebec Charter of Rights, minority (i.e., English) rights in schools, and public funding of confessional and cultural education that embraces many ethnic and religious minorities outside the francophone majority, the history of inter-cultural relationships is, while not without occasional controversy, largely exemplary. Hence, we have an evolution in Canada of a *de facto* Quebec citizenship that need not denigrate the broader affiliation with Canada or the mutual bonds of duty and entitlement that connect Canadians to each other.

Gordon Brown and Douglas Alexander expressed this overlapping duality in this way:

> this multilayered identity seems entirely compatible with the kind of Scotland emerging in the age of a global economy. Simply put, people feel loyalty to their local community; they feel Scottish; they feel British, and they feel increasingly part of Europe. Loyalty to one need not carry the price of denial of any other (1999, pp. 21-22).

In Canada, our good fortune at not having built a unitary state that denied subnational points of cohesion, and having chosen a confederal union for legitimate linguistic, cultural, and political reasons today affords Canada a measure of pluralist freedom to build a new and dynamic definition of citizenship that better reflects the global economic, social, and technological reality.

## CONSUMERISM, CITIZENSHIP AND GLOBAL CULTURE

The focus of the Citizens' Charter, created almost a decade ago in the United Kingdom as a guide to how government should respond to the legitimate rights and aspirations of the citizen as a consumer of public services, reflects a clear and omnipresent theme in the evolution of democratic notions of citizenship. One's duty to the state, one's responsibility to adhere to duly passed laws is balanced by state obligations in terms of service, respect for rights, and responsiveness to the citizen as consumer and taxpayer. The continued interest in updating that charter speaks to the political salience of the state earning its role again and again in the citizen's galaxy of importance.

In Canada, where a Charter of Rights and Freedoms was incorporated in the constitution in 1982, and where the courts have been activist in defining new rights in response to litigants' arguments, the relationship between the state and the citizen is in constant and controversial evolution. And, as the European Convention on Human Rights is adopted in the United Kingdom, if our experience in Canada is at all indicative, Britons are in for a significant series of changes in this very relationship themselves (Malleson 1999: Hiebert 1999). Citizenship, and the spectrum of rights associated with it — embracing equality of treatment, entitlement, access to certain licensed privileges, historic rights versus contemporary regulatory realities — is a constantly changing framework in Canada, with many of these changes being made regularly by the courts. This has had significant impact upon the jurisdictions of all the provinces, including Quebec, that had been established prior to 1982.

This process of underlying change in Canada and in the UK will also be radically altered, as was suggested earlier, by the degree to which decisions once made nationally or bi-nationally are being made through supranational governance mechanisms. Many of these mechanisms have oblique, indirect or non-existent accountabilities to any ballot box. Yet the impact of their decisions can be profound not just at the macro level but also at the level of individual economic circumstances. It is important here to note that the mere existence of supranational agreements or bodies does not automatically disenfranchise that part of citizenship that supports democratic choice. The Maastricht Treaty did involve close and hard-fought referendum battles in many European countries. In Canada, the Free Trade Agreement was the subject of a hard-fought federal election in 1988. There is nothing that prevents political leaders, duly elected themselves, from ensuring that the public in their respective countries are invited to vote on critical structural questions. Globalized economic and business networks, broadened by technology's capacity to minimize the issues of geography and nationality, also redefine the geographic relevance of the nation-state's jurisdiction and its reach. Territorial national space is now competing with a more non-territorial networked space.

Political realignment on a global scale has also changed the definitional ground rules. Citizens of the free world, and the nation-states that make it up, have lost the point of that particular definition with the end of the organized and focused "Soviet Threat." The broad advance of the European Union has produced *de facto* citizens of Europe with a host of mobility, investment, voting, and entitlement rights that ensue therefrom. In North America, the North American Free Trade Agreement (NAFTA) provisions on labour mobility mean that in some 60 plus work categories, Americans, Canadians, and Mexicans have mobility privileges as citizens of signatory countries that were far less automatic or accessible in the past. It is sad but true that some of these mobility rights between nations are more easily accessible than similar rights between Canadian provinces.

In some cases, traditional relationships with the nation-state are being replaced with relationships that are more tied to culture or ethnicity, often both individually chosen and collectively validated. Waters (1994) argues that these ethnically or culturally defined citizenships are less open to political compromise. In some cases, supranational bodies have acted, as was the case with NATO in Kosovo, to protect human rights without regard to the particular sovereignty of the allegedly offending state. Others suggest that if the issue of globalized relationships is assessed carefully, what is actually lacking is the supranational institutions that can deliver public goods to citizens, supporting rights and accountabilities that can be truly global (UNRISD 1996, p. 10).

While pessimism about the impact of global pressures on a viable definition of citizenship is always around, there are optimistic scenarios. What Tom Courchene calls the "Global Information Revolution," as he points out in various of his recent writings, empowers citizens to easily access the data that enable them to make more and better-informed choices both as consumers and voters. This empowerment will, he argues, increase their power relative to the nation-state. The challenge of definition, therefore, is one of creating a realistic and contemporary citizenship that reflects what is really going on at the national, supranational, and subnational level, and actually helps people manage their lives and communities of interest in some rational and reasonable way.

While there can be no end of debate on underlying principles of any new definition, it strikes me that to be successful, that definition must:

- accommodate the linguistic and cultural reality by which people may choose to define themselves;

- reflect the different (but not necessarily conflicting) rights and obligations citizens have in the regional, national, and international/supranational jurisdictions of which they are a part;

- underline the points of intersection between region, nation-state, and international/supranational jurisdictions where the citizen has clear interests to be enhanced and protected; and,

- do nothing to limit the individual and democratic rights of citizens to act through duly-elected governments in their collective interest.

Addressing these definitional premises becomes difficult if one views citizenship as a state or as an unchanging statutory status. It becomes much more manageable, however, if one views citizenship as a relationship that, while based on a series of core and statutory foundations, has aspects that are constantly changing. These changes, and the recognition of them in a new and more inclusive definition of citizenship, validate and strengthen the relationships that are encompassed in citizenship. It follows that undue rigidity in the approach to the definition of citizenship is a denial of the dynamism and breadth of relationships citizenship implies — a clear mistake for the nation-state that might confuse rigidity on this issue with strength.

## THE IDEA OF CONCENTRIC CITIZENSHIP

The contemporary citizen is at the same time part of more than one community. She may be, in terms of her own hierarchy of self-definition a Québécoise, a North American knowledge worker, and a resident of Canada. She may be a Scot, a citizen of Europe, and a British subject. To be sure, there can be points of conflict between the jurisdictions of which she is a part, but they are unlikely to be reflected in her day-to-day life. There will be debates about tax points, block transfers, and labour mobility. But these are neither new nor particularly serious at the level of the individual.

A series of concentric circles — with either language and culture, or community and nation at the centre, region or province at the next circumference, and country and supranational framework as the outer circumferences — not only reflects the diversity of the citizenship relationship, but also provides a convenient special context for points of intersection relative to rights and responsibilities. This kind of concentric citizenship makes quite clear what lies at the core of most citizenship relationships. It emphasizes the role of the jurisdictions that are closer to the citizen, like Scotland or Quebec, in the protection of language and culture, as well as their role as a legislative bridge or buffer that interacts with the broader polity (Figures 1 and 2).

Supranational or international agreements on rights, obligations, or new entities that reflect trade or security agreements exist at the outer core, but they can also be accessed by the citizens, and impact upon them, according to the intensity

FIGURE 1: Citizenship and the Jurisdictions of Life

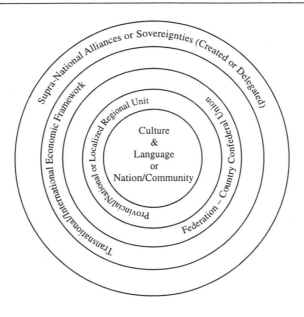

FIGURE 2: Relationships and Linkage Functions

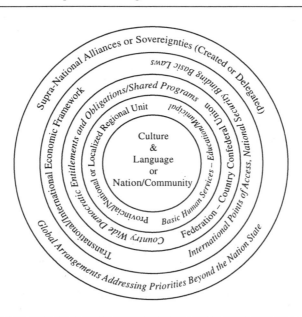

of the issues at the outer locations in the concentric framework. Moreover, as required and made possible by the technologies we now share, citizens can emphasize relationships throughout the concentric range and intersect most directly across those ranges.

The closer the particular circumference of citizenship, the more likely the issues of education, culture, and language will be part of the entitlements and debates. The further out the circumference, the more likely the engagement on economic aspects of the citizen's role. Finally, the circumferences that are furthest away from the citizen are more likely to encompass issues like defence, security, and rules for international trade.

Governments exist at the limit of the various circumferences, while citizens exist at all levels. This speaks to the restrictions on how much governments can do in and of themselves and to the immense power of the citizen to act across the range of levels. Real life does not occur strictly within the defined levels between two jurisdictional circumferences. For many, it exists across many levels at any one time. Moreover, the ebb and flow of issues and networks, and economic, cultural, and social priorities will see some levels in the circumference expand while others narrow at different points of time. Rigid definitions of citizenship can be used to create jagged edges at the circumference; more supple definitions can create smooth and soft membranes or helpful points of exchange. The reality of today's world is that people will move between the levels depending on the issues, opportunities, and technologies that drive their lives.

Governments that seek to make the circumferences between the levels more jagged or impenetrable risk serious political dislocation and disruption quite unnecessarily. Governments that seek to build the framework of cooperation, citizen mobility, and flexibility to accommodate the concentric multi-level reality, will not only strengthen their relationship with the citizen, but actually enhance their own democratic legitimacy.

## CONCLUSION

There is no trade-off between diversity and definition when we reflect on what citizenship has become. One's loyalty to the French language and civilization in Quebec and its preservation does not mean disloyalty to Canada's peacekeeping or military alliances abroad, or even to the central government's approach to trade promotion or monetary policy. One's profound attachment to one's Aboriginal First Nation does not limit one's capacity to serve in the armed forces as was evidenced by the many First Nation peoples who fought and died for Canada in both world wars and Korea. Scottish ancestry and cultural and linguistic passion do not exist in opposition to British security or trade policies. Citizenship is largely viewed as an exclusive right, not only for those who possess it, but for those who seek it as new arrivals in any state or country. To some extent, that is appropriate and unavoidable. But in a world where distance, time, the jurisdiction of the nation-state, and the options faced by many people are changing so rapidly, it would be the ultimate political abdication for a concept as noble and empowering as citizenship to be left in a static context. The democratic, civic, and entitlement foundations of citizenship have always had to co-exist with the responsible, obligatory, and cohesive aspects imbedded in the same relationship.

It is time that the simple territorial aspects of citizenship be broadened to embrace the devolutionary and decentralized realities that can and should counterbalance the global market and supranational context we can no longer ignore. That counterbalance is about self-respect, community, freedom, and social integrity, which is what a dynamic and broad-minded citizenship is supposed to be about.

## REFERENCES

Brown, G. and D. Alexander. 1999. *New Scotland, New Britain*. London: The Smith Institute.

Castles, S. 1997. *Globalisation and the Ambiguities of National Citizenship*. Albany Auckland.

Hiebert, J. 1999. *Wrestling with Rights: Judges, Parliament and the Making of Social Policy*, Choices, Vol. 5, No. 3. Montreal: Institute for Research on Public Policy.

Kymlicka W. and W. Norman. 1994. "Return of the Citizen: A Survey of Recent Work on Citizenship Theory," *Ethics*, 104(Jan.):352-81.

Malleson, J. 1999. *A British Bill of Rights: Incorporating the European Convention on Human Rights*, Choices, Vol. 5, No. 1. Montreal: Institute for Research on Public Policy.

Marshall, T.H. 1950. *Citizenship and Social Class and Other Essays*. Cambridge: Cambridge University Press.

United Nations Research Institute for Social Development (UNRISD). 1996. *Globalisation and Citizenship*. Report for the UNRISD Conference, Geneva, 9-11 December.

Waters, M. 1994. "Globalisation, Multi-culturalism, and Rethinking the Social: Introduction," *Australian and New Zealand Journal of Sociology*, 30(3):229-34.

# 12

# The Dynamics of Decentralization: Canadian Federalism and British Devolution

*Trevor C. Salmon*

## A NEW MESSINESS?

It used to be thought that the meaning of certain concepts was clear; for example, many believed Sir Kenneth Wheare had provided classic definitions of a federal system. It also used to be thought that it was "clear" that Canada was a federal state and the United Kingdom a unitary state. What the original Colloquium and contributions to this book demonstrate is that life is not now so simple, if, in fact, it ever really was.

Federalism in Canada is clearly in a fluid state, there being real debates about the locus of constitutional power and political and pragmatic discussions about the appropriate locus of political decision making. The nature of the federation in Canada is less clear than it was, and, as is forcefully brought out in some of the foregoing contributions, Canada itself is now much more decentralized than it was originally or indeed as compared to other federal systems. In the UK, although absolutely not a federal system, significant changes have taken place with the creation of the Scottish Parliament and Executive, the Welsh Assembly and the Northern Ireland Assembly — each with different legislative and executive powers, and with different relationships with London. Indeed, these situations are still evolving. This raises the question as to whether in the British case there was any rational, logical, or planned basis for developments since 1997. One answer is the Lord Chancellor's comment that there "was no master plan." Kenneth Morgan's contribution suggests that this was important since the subsequent developments were not inexorable. The old verities have been overtaken and there is now a certain "messiness" in seeking to come to definite statements about where constitutional and political power lies.

## Subsidiarity

A central point to emerge is that rather than starting from a constitutional perspective perhaps the real question is what should be done at the regional level? The answer that emerges from the foregoing chapters is whatever can be better done at that level than at any other. Although the word "subsidiarity" does not feature much in this work, in many ways it lies at its core. This is interesting since subsidiarity was written into the Treaty on European Union of 1992 as a deliberate and conscious alternative to the notion of the European Union having a "federal vocation." A problem, of course, with subsidiarity is that although the principle can be identified, it is more difficult to agree or define it in actual policy terms. The specific level which is deemed most appropriate for certain tasks is not always clear and will depend on a series of factors such as the political viewpoint and values of those involved; and these values may not always be reconcilable; for example, there can be tension between choices based on the maximization of economic welfare as against choices based more on identity — key issues in both Canada and Britain. In addition, subsidiarity of itself does not fix a division of powers or competencies; it only provides a principle to do so. What the actual appropriate point of decision is can change over time, domain, and circumstance. The central point of decision in systems based on subsidiarity seems to float depending on circumstance. The appropriate level of decision is not always clear; it can change; and it is a matter of judgement emanating from the values of those making the judgement. Yet there needs to be a guiding principle that can be successfully *applied* in determining what should be done at the regional level.

## Constitutions, Conventions and Practice

A related issue that arises in terms of the new messiness is whether the difference between the written constitutional settlement of Canada and the "conventions" of the United Kingdom are really as clearcut as imagined. The contributions above speak volumes as to how much the Canadian constitutional settlement has had to be revisited, reinterpreted, and re-configured: they do not definitely resolve the question of what is best done at the regional level; on the other hand, the United Kingdom now has the *Scotland Act,* etc., which seek to embed the settlement in law, if not in an absent written constitution. The *Scotland Act* arguably in some senses has more status than normal acts and it was of course somewhat entrenched by the overwhelming support that its principles received in the referendum of September 1997, with 74.3 percent voting "yes" to the establishment of a Scottish Parliament and 63.5 percent voting "yes" for it to have tax-varying powers. Since then in the United Kingdom there have been a series of concordats or memorandums of understanding and supplementary agreements, such as the Concordat on Co-ordination of European Union Policy Issues and the Concordat on Financial Assistance to Industry between the Scottish Executive and the UK government, which have attempted to define the working relationship between the Executive and London, but even here much is left unsaid and potentially unresolved, as Salmon shows.

This leads to another key question: To what extent in both Canada and the UK have administrative arrangements and developments in public policy begun to bypass constitutional debates and formal arrangements? This is raised specifically by Claude Forget in connection with Canadian social policy. Similarly the question emerges as to whether both systems are in practice moving to a collaborative federalism in their intergovernmental relations, even if in the UK the "f-word" must not be used.

## Centralization?

The evolving sense of messiness and the attempt to impose order and clarity upon it — and to seek an intelligent understanding of it — is further demonstrated in the fundamentally different approaches to federalism that emerge. Nearly all the Canadian contributions have focused on decentralization, on the political and economic dynamics of the contemporary situation and their relationship to the formal constitutional position — often to point out the gap that now exists between the two — and on the importance of political motives and economic forces in determining both the nature of and the attitudes to the situation. In Britain there remain many who view federalism as concerned with centralization, with the loss of local control, and with those new centralized authorities acting with overweening power, and almost contempt for the regions. This is the essential message of this edited collection: it is important to understand the reality of dynamic federal systems and not to be captured by myths and misconceptions. The Canadian perspective is that of the centre losing power, not that it is becoming more imperialistic. Also relevant here is the point that as the central federal government seeks to reduce public expenditure, so too the binding community-building nature of federal money is also being reduced. Similarly, as Canadian policy changed on issues such as health provision and social policy, so too did the integrative attraction of federal support, a point made by Harvey Lazar.

## Follow the Money

This train of thought is an echo of the Watergate investigation conducted by Woodward and Bernstein: follow the money. To what extent is there now an era of "fiscal federalism"? Or in the UK context, is it not true that the old adage of politics has a new resonance: real political decisions are about the allocation of values and resources. Invariably these revolve around money: who wins, who loses, and crucially, who pays? As has been evident from other situations, this last question is usually the key to determining policy outcomes and processes. In Canada it appears that taxation and its distribution are becoming the key to understanding the realities of power. In the UK the fact that the Scottish Parliament has limited tax-varying powers could become critical, although the major players have so far issued self-denying ordinances in this regard. However, between 1979 and 1997 there would have been enormous tension between two different approaches to the levels of and nature of public expenditure, and since 1997, as Michael Keating points out, an increasing number of questions have been raised about the Barnett formula which has been the basis of determining overall levels of public expenditure in Scotland as a proportion of overall English expenditure for over 30 years. In the northeast of England complaints are now frequently heard that Scots receive on average £600 per head per annum more than their English counterparts.

## Federation or Devolution?

All of this brings home that the difference between federal and devolved systems is not nearly as great as many may anticipate, although the formal distinctions between a federal system and a devolved system are considerable — not least the issue of entrenched powers and a formal court of appeal. Indeed, decisions by the Canadian Supreme Court have had and are likely to have an important bearing on the future of Canada, not least because of their "raising of the threshold" of secession by ruling that it should not be a unilateral act.

## Regions?

But the "blurring of boundaries," it becomes clear, is further clouded by the need to revisit the issue of the definitions of the region, especially since in many apparently established regions there are developing sub-regions. Here a perception of peripherality and psychological distance appear to be crucial. Both regions and sub-regions have now clearly developed an international/external dimension and have begun to form regional partnerships with each other domestically or with others externally. There is clearly still some argument as to how important these tensions are with some not convinced that these tendencies are as divisive as often portrayed, but others drawing attention to the fact that there are significant trends emerging, for example in trade patterns, with Ontario now conducting over twice as much of its trade outside Canada as inside.

Speaking of regions also raises the question of the visibility of the tiers of government and administration, and of how well individuals are able to locate the real locus of power. Visibility relates directly to the question of identity and the foregoing contributions make abundantly clear just how important this issue is. In Canada it appears in the increasing use of the word "national" rather than "federal" and the question of Quebec versus Canada, or as it may be interestingly put: what is Canada without Quebec — simply the rest of Canada? In the UK the questions are similar: What is the relationship between being Scottish and British? Can one be both? And what is the "rest of Britain" without Scotland, albeit that England makes up 85 percent of the UK? In one sense the question hangs in the air: What is England or the rest of Canada, simply a state of mind or more than that? In both Canada and Britain these are now really pressing issues as is the question as to whether identity is exclusive or not. The questions continue: What is the glue that holds an evolving Canada together and what is it that makes one British?

## Asymmetrical Government

The former clarity about the distribution of power has been muddied by the asymmetries that exist between the real political powers of the individual provinces and the federal government; a situation parallel to the different arrangements between Edinburgh, Cardiff, and Belfast on the one hand and London on the other. The British arrangements are asymmetrical and each scheme is different in both degree and kind. Can this asymmetry survive? How asymmetrical can it become before the stresses caused by them begin to tear the constitutional, political, and administrative settlement arrived at or evolving apart? In both the British and Canadian contexts the question is whether reform stimulates or modifies separatist tendencies. Many argue that the devolution of power or decentralization need not inevitably lead to the break-up of the existing system and that federal systems can survive, but obviously not all agree.

## The Citizens

This leads to the interesting question: For all the changes in Canada and Britain do "ordinary" people, the voters, sense that power is any nearer to them? To cite the Treaty on European Union (Article 1): is there any greater sense that "decisions are taken as openly as possible and as closely as possible to the citizen?" Going back to the psychological point about power made earlier: there is perhaps a feeling that changing the geographical location of power does not always match a change in the actual location of power; other things like money were more important. Increasingly in both Canada and the UK there is evidence of voter alienation or disengagement from traditional politics, and both face important issues relating to the real extent and nature of their democratic values. There are even questions, as Hugh Segal notes, about the very definition of citizenship in this situation. If it is accepted that citizenship is based on relationships rather than having a static basis, then it too needs to be redefined.

This is made even more problematic by the context of globalization and a strong sense that there is an increasing blurring of boundaries, so that the traditional link between politics and economic "space" is breaking down. No solution yet appears in sight as to how this might be resolved. In this context of democracy, Richard Simeon makes the interesting observation that the increasing use of formal intergovernmental agreements may increase the "democratic deficit," since the agreements are almost entirely executive in nature. Others have noted that this is now an ever more pressing issue given the role of the World Trade Organization and the North American Free Trade Agreement, which could have profound consequences for constituent parts of federal systems.

## CONCLUSION

Perhaps the real message of this collection is that the questions that need to be asked are becoming clear but that the answers are not. To cite Scottish law, on many of the foregoing issues the jury's verdict is "not proven." So fluid is the situation in Canada that it is not entirely clear where Canada is going and what it might look like for the next generation. Similarly in Britain there are still legitimate questions as to whether the will of the Scottish people is really "settled," whether people understand devolution and whether those directly involved have the will or wit to ensure that the system works.

It is also necessary to note that on nearly all these questions, no answers can be written on tablets of stone since the answer depends on the political philosophy of the individual, the party or the government providing it. There is no "end of ideology" on these questions, and it is not just minor questions of administrative adjustment. It is about the life-blood of politics: the allocation of values and resources, and increasingly about identity, although there was perhaps a sense, argues Richard Simeon, that in Canada there is not the appetite for these questions that there was just a few years ago. Curiously perhaps, in Britain, it is after devolution has been established that the debate has really begun outside Scotland.

What this collection definitely demonstrates is that politics is about choice. In both Canada and the UK the people, the parties, and the respective governments are still trying to clarify and resolve these choices. As Kenneth Morgan concludes, their answers at the turn of the new century were different and reflected a different world compared with the answers proposed at the end of the nineteenth century.

# Contributors

*Claude E. Forget,* President, C.E.F. Ganish Corporation, Montreal

*Jane Jenson,* Professor, Département de Science Politique, Université de Montréal

*Michael Keating,* Professor of Scottish Politics at the University of Aberdeen and Professor of Regional Studies at the European University Institute in Florence

*Harvey Lazar,* Director of the Institute of Intergovernmental Relations, School of Policy Studies, Queen's University, Kingston

*Nicola McEwen,* Lecturer in Politics at the University of Edinburgh

*Kenneth O. Morgan,* Former Vice-Chancellor of the University of Wales

*Sir George Quigley,* Chairman of Bombardier Aerospace Shorts and of Ulster Bank

*Trevor C. Salmon,* Professor of International Relations at the University of Aberdeen and Professor of the College of Europe

*Hugh Segal,* President, Institute for Research on Public Policy, Montreal

*Richard Simeon,* Professor, Department of Political Science, University of Toronto

*Peter Stoyko,* Doctoral Candidate, Political Science, Carleton University, Ottawa

# Queen's Policy Studies
# Recent Publications

The Queen's Policy Studies Series is dedicated to the exploration of major policy issues that confront governments in Canada and other western nations. McGill-Queen's University Press is the exclusive world representative and distributor of books in the series.

## School of Policy Studies

*Innovation, Institutions and Territory; Regional Innovation Systems in Canada,* J. Adam Holbrook and David A. Wolfe (eds.), 2000    Paper ISBN 0-88911-891-4 Cloth ISBN 0-88911-893-0

*Backbone of the Army: Non-Commissioned Officers in the Future Army,* Douglas L. Bland (ed.), 2000 ISBN 0-88911-889-2

*Precarious Values: Organizations, Politics and Labour Market Policy in Ontario,* Thomas R. Klassen, 2000 Paper ISBN 0-88911-883-3 Cloth ISBN 0-88911-885-X

*The Nonprofit Sector in Canada: Roles and Relationships,* Keith G. Banting (ed.), 2000 Paper ISBN 0-88911-813-2  Cloth ISBN 0-88911-815-9

*Security, Strategy and the Global Economics of Defence Production,* David G. Haglund and S. Neil MacFarlane (eds.), 1999    Paper ISBN 0-88911-875-2 Cloth ISBN 0-88911-877-9

*The Communications Revolution at Work: The Social, Economic and Political Impacts of Technological Change,* Robert Boyce (ed.), 1999    Paper ISBN 0-88911-805-1 Cloth ISBN 0-88911-807-8

*Diplomatic Missions: The Ambassador in Canadian Foreign Policy,* Robert Wolfe (ed.), 1998 Paper ISBN 0-88911-801-9 Cloth ISBN 0-88911-803-5

## Institute of Intergovernmental Relations

*Federalism, Democracy and Labour Market Policy in Canada,* Tom McIntosh (ed.), 2000 ISBN 0-88911-849-3, ISBN 0-88911-845-0 (set).

*Managing the Environmental Union: Intergovernmental Relations and Environmental Policy in Canada,* Patrick C. Fafard and Kathryn Harrison (eds.), 2000    ISBN 0-88911-837-X

*Stretching the Federation: The Art of the State in Canada,* Robert Young (ed.), 1999    ISBN 0-88911-777-2

*Comparing Federal Systems,* 2d ed., Ronald L. Watts, 1999    ISBN 0-88911-835-3

*Canada: The State of the Federation 1999/2000,* vol. 14, *Toward a New Mission Statement for Canadian Fiscal Federalism,* Harvey Lazar (ed.), 2000    Paper ISBN 0-88911-843-4 Cloth ISBN 0-88911-839-6

*Canada: The State of the Federation 1998/99,* vol. 13, *How Canadians Connect,* Harvey Lazar and Tom McIntosh (eds.), 1999    Paper ISBN 0-88911-781-0 Cloth ISBN 0-88911-779-9

*Canada: The State of the Federation 1997,* vol. 12, *Non-Constitutional Renewal,* Harvey Lazar (ed.), 1998 Paper ISBN 0-88911-765-9 Cloth ISBN 0-88911-767-5

## John Deutsch Institute for the Study of Economic Policy

*Room to Manoeuvre? Globalization and Policy Convergence,* Thomas J. Courchene (ed.), Bell Canada Papers no. 6, 1999    Paper ISBN 0-88911-812-4 Cloth ISBN 0-88911-812-4

*Women and Work,* Richard P. Chaykowski and Lisa M. Powell (eds.), 1999 Paper ISBN 0-88911-808-6 Cloth ISBN 0-88911-806-X

*Equalization: Its Contribution to Canada's Economic and Fiscal Progress,* Robin W. Boadway and Paul A.R. Hobson (eds.), Policy Forum Series no. 36, 1998 Paper ISBN 0-88911-780-2 Cloth IBSN 0-88911-804-3

*Fiscal Targets and Economic Growth,* Thomas J. Courchene and Thomas A. Wilson (eds.), Roundtable Series no. 12, 1998    Paper ISBN 0-88911-778-0 Cloth ISBN 0-88911-776-4

**Available from:**
McGill-Queen's University Press
Tel:    1-800-387-0141 (ON and QC excluding Northwestern ON)
         1-800-387-0172 (all other provinces and Northwestern ON)

E-mail: customer.service@ccmailgw.genpub.com